CW01212798

AUSTIN HEALEY

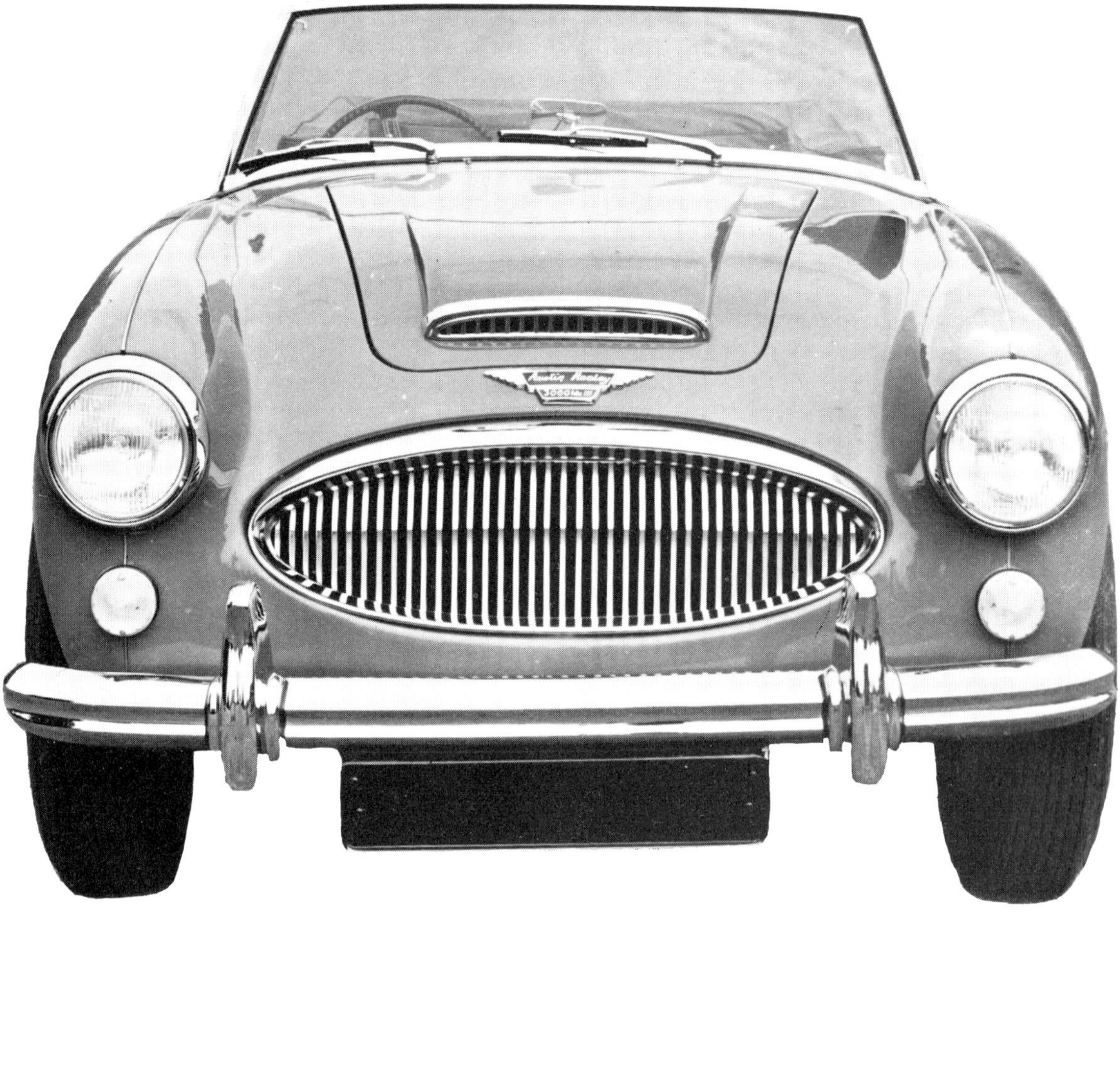

AUSTIN HEALEY

The story of the Big Healeys

GEOFFREY HEALEY

DODD, MEAD & COMPANY
NEW YORK

To Donald and Ivy Healey

First published 1978 in the United States of America
© Geoffrey Healey 1977
ISBN 0–396–07530–4
All rights reserved.
Without written permission from the publisher,
this volume, or any part of it,
may not be reproduced by any means
or in any form.

Printed and bound in Great Britain.

Contents

Acknowledgments *6*
Foreword by Donald Healey *7*
Introduction *9*
Donald Healey and Family *11*
The Origin of the Healey Cars *15*
First of a Line *31*
Improving the 100 *64*
The 100 Six *82*
The 3000 *95*
The Sprite *114*
Those Special Cars *128*
Replacing the 3000 *141*
Competition *147*
Record Breaking *173*
The Clubs *214*
Later Days *224*
Appendices
The Engines *231*
Record of 100 S Sales *244*
Production Figures for the Big Healeys *247*
Specifications of the Big Healeys *248*
Index *250*

Acknowledgments

The author gratefully acknowledges the following for their kind permission to reproduce photographs: *Autocar*, *Autosport*, *Motor*, British Leyland, Edward Eves, Daniel Rubin, Rodolfo Mailander, the *Daily Mail*, Kevin Faughnan, Alan Zafer, John Wright Photography. He would like to point out that it has not been possible to trace the source of all the photographs and wishes to apologise to anyone who is not included in this list for this reason.

Foreword

When Geoff told me he was writing a book about the Austin Healey I was both delighted and somewhat surprised. Geoff is very much one of the back-room boys who did the work and shunned the limelight. He has dug deeply and brought to light many incidents and people previously unmentioned. During the years he has supplied information to a number of writers and we have both been disappointed at the way facts have been distorted. I have always complained about his hoarding of junk, including the servo cylinders off the 1931 Invicta, and now I am delighted to see some of it being put to good use. His account reminds me of the many happy hours and the sheer hard work that went into the Big Healey. The public often remembers the battles of the drivers and forgets what backed up their efforts.

When we went independent after the war, the only grounds on which steel could be obtained was for products that were exported. This drive to export remained with us all the time and our designs for future projects are intended mainly for overseas consumption. I hope that in time revised taxation and and an upturn in the state of the economy will allow some people on this island to enjoy real motoring again. Far too many of my old friends are gone or no longer active in the industry and we are all the poorer for it. The avoidable decline in the British motor industry would not have been permitted by them.

I am always being asked questions about the car by proud owners and am unable to remember the answers. I hope that this book will satisfy their curiosity. Recently I have had the opportunity to meet many more owners at various club meets and their obvious joy in their machines is a source of real pleasure to me. So many of these cars, restored with loving care, are even better than when they left the assembly line. I hope that this book will add to their pleasure and enjoyment.

Donald Healey

Introduction

Over the years I have written a number of technical descriptions and tuning leaflets, and provided information for a number of writers. I have been disappointed with distortions of the facts that have resulted. When Gregory Houston Bowden asked me if I would provide him with material for a book, I had grown weary of the work involved and was feeling pretty bloody minded. I replied that I was not going to help anyone else and that I intended to do the book myself. Far from being offended Gregory said he was delighted and put Christopher Burness of Wilton House Gentry, who was his publisher, in touch with me. It is doubtful that I would have got down to the task without their kindly prodding.

For some months I have been researching the vast amount of material in the possession of the family. I have found many things I had believed to be lost and have enjoyed delving into past triumphs, failures and disasters.

I have worked with my father Donald Healey for the past 27 years pretty well morning, noon and night. Whenever he had an idea – and he is a prolific innovator – all else would go by the board and we would get to work. My mother bore the disruptions to home life with great fortitude, only complaining that engineers were worse than farmers who could only talk about pigs. She warned my wife Margot what life with me would be like and Margot has nobly put up with the same interrupted style of life. She does not even complain about the pile of drawings under the bed, or that the best parts of the house are packed with motoring relics.

Austin Healey: The Story of the Big Healeys

I have attempted to trace the development of the Big Healey, bringing to light the failures that occurred now that I am no longer restrained by commercial involvement. Just over 74,000 Big Healeys were produced between 1952 and the end of 1967 when production ceased, and some 80 per cent were exported. Vastly greater numbers were built of the other small Healey design – the Austin Healey Sprite and the MG Midget. British Leyland continue to produce the MG Midget in sizeable numbers. A large number of Big Healeys still rumble around the world, their proud owners realising that they have a car that will never be superceded.

Much of the enjoyment of producing the Big Healey comes from the very generous appreciation shown by past and present owners. I borrowed Malcolm Eykin's MkIII for some photography and a brief run at the same time that I was testing the latest offering from another manufacturer. The 3000 had lost none of its character and despite its age put the modern device to shame. The Italians have a saying for it: 'Donne e motori, gioie e dolori'. These few words sum it up completely. Motor cars give great pleasure and sorrow in varying degrees. The Austin Healey has, we hope, given a much greater degree of joy to many than most cars.

The designing, the testing, the development and the racing of motor cars fluctuate between success and failure. The bank manager who apparently spends his life sleeping in a cupboard, will provide funds with gay abandon for almost anyone to start a restaurant. The fundamental fact that people must eat to live is the basis of his action. When asked to lend money to some part of the motor car industry, he shudders! He thinks of his mundane saloon that fails whenever he needs it most and whose servicing is a constant drain on his pocket. He quotes from his list of cars that are no more – Argyll, Bugatti, Arroll-Johnson, Ballot, Bean, Ceirano, Clyno, Delage, Gobron-Brillie, Itala, Mors, Richard-Brasier, Scat; he knows his facts, and besides, motor men are nasty rough men, smelling of oil in contrast to that nice property whizz-kid, with that exotic office.

Despite this, most motor men manage to start somehow.

Donald Healey and Family

Donald Mitchell Healey or DMH was born in Perranporth on the north coast of Cornwall on 3rd July 1898. His parents, Fred or JF and Emmie, ran a general store in the village, known as the Red House Shop. Perranporth had been the centre of a number of tin and copper mines, but the mining industry and consequently the village declined in the last quarter of the nineteenth century. JF was to build much of Perranporth between the wars when he was taken for a ride by some up-country property speculators.

There was little future in Cornwall for a young man and JF paid a large premium to secure DMH an apprenticeship with the Sopwith Aviation Company at Kingston-on-Thames near London. Sopwiths made many of the successful First World War fighter aircraft such as the Pup and the Camel, and many talented young men received a very sound grounding in engineering with them. Of the ex-apprentices I knew only Vic Derrington who was a pioneer in 'go faster' parts, including special exhaust manifolds for Austin Healeys.

DMH did not endure to the end of his apprenticeship but like so many young men of the time volunteered for the Royal Flying Corps whilst still under age. He gained his wings as a pilot and served as a night fighter pilot at home and bomber pilot overseas. Engine failures and crashes were frequent hazards of early aviation and after a severe crash he was invalided out of the service. For the rest of the war he worked for the AID – the Aircraft Inspection Department.

After the war, with aid from his father, he built a garage at Perranporth next to the Red House Shop. A pioneer motorist and inventor, JF was most keen on the venture. In addition DMH formed the Perraphone Radio Company and manufactured early wireless sets. He also built an electrical generating plant supplying the garage, shop and house with electricity, and started competing in motoring events, sometimes with his father as navigator. He used cars such as the ABC, a product of the Sopwith Aviation Group, Ariel, Triumph and Riley. He won what might be described as the first RAC Rally in a Triumph Seven, a little sidevalve-engined 4-seater saloon, a car more advanced and expensive than the Austin Seven. (Gordon Parnell, Triumph's chief engineer, was responsible for bringing the Lockheed hydraulic braking system from the USA. He also introduced the Triumph Seven's monobloc engine design from the same source.) In 1929 DMH finished seventh overall in the Monte Carlo Rally in the same car and was the highest placed British entrant. The garage was to become a secondary interest run by a friend, one F. M. Montgomery, as he spent more and more time away on competitive motoring.

I was born in December 1922, followed by two brothers. DMH spent most of the time away from Cornwall, coming home at weekends with a variety of exciting motor cars. We used to go up to a suitable vantage point outside the village from which we could hear and see him arrive. Many great rally experts of the day used to come down to Perranporth with him and they would spend the weekends looking for and trying new trials hills in the area. As boys we spent many a thrilling and breath-taking time with them on their forays in magnificent sports cars.

Blue Hills Mine, between Perranporth and St Agnes, was a famous hill forming part of the London to Land's End Trial, run by the Motor Cycling Club at Easter. On this event a mandatory stop was made at the garage, while JF organised the marshalling and my mother and her friends a very fine tea for the competitors. We boys spent the day watching the competitors assaulting the hill on a really tremendous variety of motor vehicles.

Sir Noel Macklin, Lance's father, gave DMH his first works drive on an Invicta. In 1931 DMH won the Monte Carlo Rally with the $4\frac{1}{2}$-litre Invicta, much of the preparation work and testing having been carried out around Perranporth. DMH also competed with Rileys and Triumphs in many rallies, winning a great number of them.

He joined Riley at Coventry in 1933, living in digs at Barford. In the following year he became chief engineer at Triumph and transported all of us to Warwick. At Triumph he was responsible for the Gloria and Dolomite series of cars and negotiated with Alfa Romeo over their straight-8 design. The straight-8 2-litre supercharged Triumph Dolomite was a magnificent machine, but one which did not stop properly until the Alfa Romeo-type large-diameter drum brakes were replaced by some smaller Lockheed brakes, on the advice of Gordon Parnell. (The rubbing speed of the large brakes had been far too high.) DMH drove the Dolomite in the 1935 Monte Carlo Rally with Lewis Pearce from Newquay, Cornwall, who worked at Triumph. In thick fog they were following another competitor when a strange noise made them believe that the supercharger was about to seize. In fact, the noise was made by an approaching train with which they collided as they entered an unguarded level crossing. Despite severe damage to the front of the car, they were unhurt and spent some time in the local jail until guarantees arrived to pay for the damage – some paintwork at the front of the train.

The Triumph Company failed in the immediate pre-war depression, despite an excellent range of cars and a well-equipped and valuable factory. Like many companies, they were giving too much value for money. The Bank appointed a Receiver and DMH arranged the sale of the company to Thos. Ward. The factory was taken over by H. M. Hobson for the manufacture of their aero-engine carburettors. DMH carried on at the factory for a while and then moved to Humber at Coventry, where he worked on the development of armoured fighting vehicles. The Humber Scout was equipped with the large Snipe sidevalve engine and almost had the road holding of a sports car. During his spare time at Humber, DMH discussed sports cars with A. C. (Sammy) Sampietro and Ben Bowden: these discussions were to lead to the first Healey car.

We boys grew up in the world of fast cars, rally and racing drivers. Holidays used to be spent at Perranporth where drivers of the day such as Humfrey Symons, Tommy Wisdom, Sammy Davis and others were frequent guests. My mother, Ivy, was as enthusiastic as the rest of us in all that my father did. She worked hard and cheerfully all her life, entertaining unexpected guests at odd hours of the day and night. She was always affectionately called Fuss by DMH and later Grannie Fuss by her eight grandchildren. In moments of deep depression and uncertainty she gave us all the courage we needed to carry on. Brought up in a hard school by her widowed mother, her rule was supreme in the home. When DMH had moments of rash spending, she brought him down to earth with her favourite phrase, 'Come on now, cut it out!' Three times she blew herself up with DMH's gas producing generator. She has survived 56 years of marriage and is determined to see a great grandchild and her 60th wedding anniversary.

I served an engineering apprenticeship with Cornercroft in Coventry, at the same time studying at Coventry Technical College. Mr Chisholm effectively instructed us in the workings of heat engines and automobile engineering, but not many of my friends of that day remained in the industry. Somehow with 14 shillings a week pay and parental help most of us managed to run Austin Sevens. Running an Austin Seven and trying to make it hold the road, go faster and stop without spending money is a useful experience. Having obtained my Higher National Certificate, I volunteered for the Royal

Electrical and Mechanical Engineers, REME, and then trained on AFVs.

Early on in my service days I was stationed at Abergavenny. One morning, whilst investigating a series of problems with trucks that REME had overhauled, I met Bill Watson, the Vauxhall factory representative. I told him that I wanted a car and he later came back in a hurry to tell me that he had found a 3-litre Bentley in a barn, and that he could buy it for £28. Bill did the deal and I covered many miles in the machine. I spent most of the latter part of the war in administration in Beirut, with the exalted title of Staff Captain, REME. I had already joined the Bentley Drivers Club and when I was posted to the Middle East their magazine did much to keep me interested and helped pass the time to demob. When I broke the 3-litre back axle, they found me another at little cost. I later bought a $6\frac{1}{2}$-litre for very little from a scrap yard at Didcot. The tax would have cost more than the car, so three of us who had Bentleys stripped it for spares and sold the rest. I later sold Marcus Chambers the half shafts.

After being demobbed, I joined the car division of Armstrong Siddeley at Coventry, to work on the new 3-litre car designed by W. O. Bentley and D. Bastow. Mervyn Cutler and John Densham were my bosses and I learnt much from them. I spent many hours driving the prototypes around the new testing ground of the Motor Industry Research Association at Lindley near Coventry.

Brother Brian, known to the family and friends as Bic, served in the Navy on Woolworth carriers, becoming a car salesman after the war. Brother John served in the RAF and later took over grandfather J. F. Healey's shop and developed the business considerably. My mother still reminds us that she taught us all to drive.

The Origin of the Healey Cars

As the war drew to a close, DMH decided to make his own motor car. He drew up a specification and plan of operation. He was determined to have somewhere near 100 bhp per ton of vehicle weight as he considered this essential to give the performance he wanted. He planned the design with two of his colleagues at Humber – A. C. (Sammy) Sampietro, a brilliant automobile engineer and Ben Bowden, an extremely talented body engineer and stylist.

At the same time, he set about forming a company. After many frustrations he had everything but the name. He tried to obtain the use of a number of defunct car names but in the end had to use his own. He never liked the cumbersome title of the Donald Healey Motor Co. Ltd., but at that time the authorities would not agree to his using the name Healey on its own. Later he was able to do this with Healey Cars Ltd.

The prototype chassis frame was built by Westland Aeroparts of Hereford – its side members were the maximum length that could be accommodated by their largest folder. Designed and drawn up by A. C. Sampietro, the chassis incorporated an expensive trailing link front suspension, which was considered to be the best possible type at that time. The original set-up had a total of 8 inches of wheel movement. The rear suspension used coil springs and the Riley torque tube axle and had only limited wheel movement. DMH had excellent relations with Riley, going back to the time when he had worked for the company in Coventry. He was able to arrange the supply of 2.4-litre Riley units of the pre-war 16-hp design which were later used in the post-war

The 2.4-litre Riley-engined Healey chassis, showing the complex trailing link front suspension. (The Autocar)

The Origin of the Healey Cars

2½-litre Riley. This engine followed the traditional Riley layout. Two camshafts mounted high either side of the cylinder block operated the valves through short pushrods and rocker arms. The two valves at an included angle of 90 degrees were incorporated in a hemispherical head. The inlet ports were siamesed which limited the extent to which the engine could be tuned. DMH had inlet manifolds made to fit two 1¼-inch horizontal SU carburettors. The power output of the 16-hp RAC rated engine was raised from 80 to 100 bhp. Eddie Maher, the engine man at Morris Engines in Coventry, cleaned up the design and improved the layout. The Riley unit powered all the Healey cars with great reliability. Somewhat overweight, expensive to manufacture but efficient, it was to be phased out under the formation of BMC.

Eddie was always a great help to us and to many others in the industry. Sadly, he is no longer alive. He was responsible for all the development work on the Riley engines and many of the Austin Healey and MG units that were to follow. Eddie did not always take kindly to the red tape that strangled the industry in latter days. After the formation of British Leyland I had a phone call from a friend with a large transport business. His operation was threatened by lack of spares for one type of engine that formed the backbone of his fleet. He had tried every avenue without success and phoned me to see if I could help. I spoke to Eddie who responded in a typical manner. He said he had orders to scrap a quantity of similar engines which, although not identical, would provide the parts to keep my friend's trucks operating. 'Tell him to ring me', Eddie said. My friend contacted Eddie and picked up a truck load of engines. Everyone should then have been happy. My friend's trucks were rushing around the country and Morris Engines had been paid considerably more than scrap value for the units. However, overjoyed at his good fortune, he rang up the local dealer and told him to cancel his old order for parts. The dealer was furious and threatened Eddie with a report to the highest authority. Eddie was more than fed up with petty action causing hold-ups like this. He told him that he was not in the least worried about what the dealer would do and that he only hoped the haulier would continue to buy British.

The first Healey chassis was completed in a small workshop which was part of the Benford Ltd. works. Benfords made an excellent range of cement mixers and their chairman, Wally Allan, had been a director of the old Triumph Company with DMH. He readily agreed to lend the small workshop while his office staff helped with the paper work. When on leave from the Middle East, I did some welding so that I could have a run with the first chassis. It was a complete change from the tanks and trucks I had been involved with in Egypt.

After completion and test of the chassis, a large workshop in the Benford complex was made available for the start of the production of Healey cars.

The original factory at Benfords, Warwick. Assembling the original 2.4-litre 'A' type chassis.

Two bodies had been designed and styled for the car by Ben Bowden – a saloon and an open body. Chassis were assembled and tested and driven to either Elliots of Reading, who built the saloon body, or Westland Aeroparts of Hereford who built the roadster open body. Chassis were also supplied to various other body builders, who put some pretty weird bodies on them.

At this time, Great Britain was still subject to rigid controls of materials and resources. The country was impoverished from the war with Germany and Japan and the immense war effort had resulted in considerable shortages of materials. It was necessary to apply to government departments for permits for materials and this was a time-consuming operation, as civil servants rarely appreciate a sense of urgency. Fuel was short and electricity cuts were severe. However, the British still showed that indomitable spirit which had carried them to victory over the forces of evil. Warwick was fortunate in having a truly great Member of Parliament, Anthony Eden, later to become Lord Avon, who did much to help local industry.

Steel was in short supply and the quality extremely poor, and so many parts were made of aluminium alloy forgings – the great use of this material on war planes meant that there was capacity readily available. Many other substitute materials were used simply because they were available. Wood was subject to licence but one source was in ample supply – coffin bottoms. Maybe the planners had taken their usual pessimistic view of life and over-provisioned for death! Coffin bottoms were cut up for some wooden parts.

Ball and roller bearings, of which the front suspension and steering used a great number, were also very hard to come by and caused a bottleneck in production. Attempts to use substitute bronze and plastic bearings were not successful, partly because there was no time to carry out sufficient development work. The tyres were Dunlop 5.75×15 – a new size that later disappeared. The war in the Far East caused an acute shortage of natural rubber and it was to be a long time before tyres suitable for high speed could be made. The early synthetic mixes were unreliable and prone to high-speed failure.

We also found it difficult to get parts accurately machined. During the war, machines had been worked flat out, well beyond the point at which they should have been replaced. Another problem was decorative chrome plate – there had been no need for this during the war and there were very few skilled polishers to do the job. Lucas had at first to supply lamps with painted shells and rims. Luckily Mr J. Fink in Leamington was able to strip and refurbish many components to the desired standard of finish. We had little trouble with his plating.

James Watt, who had been in charge of sales at the old Triumph Company, joined DMH as sales director. A large and lively man, James was to wreak havoc with the early lightweight seats, which were constructed on aircraft light alloy tube frames. James's weight would jam the seat slides and his struggle to push the seat back to its most rearward position would often bend or snap the back off the base. G. R. Wade was another director to render the company most valuable service, supporting DMH on several difficult occasions.

Roger Menadue did much of the assembly and fabrication work. Roger was another exile from Cornwall, who had come up to Warwick years before to work for my father at Triumph. Harry Brandish, who joined the company as works manager, had also been at Triumph with DMH. He had a tremendous knowledge of machining and assembly and was ideal for the job. He was able to ensure that things went right, keeping people at their jobs and designers on the rails. He was one of those people who quietly make the workforce tick and had the knack of bringing home to people the error of their ways. After age and ill health caused him to retire, things were never as well run. Good men who followed him never had a chance, with the growth of a clique determined to run things for their own benefit.

Geoff Price, an ex-Daimler apprentice, joined as tester after he was demobbed from REME. Testing, inspection and final tuning were an essential part of producing a hand-built motor car. He later set up and ran the service department which became busier as the total volume of cars increased. Geoff returned from testing a 2.4-litre roadster prior to despatch in a very despondent mood one day. The local coalman's horse had bolted when passing the stationary Healey and put its front feet on the aluminium bonnet of the car. Geoff was not a great horse lover, having previously been knocked off his motorbike by a runaway horse.

In the spring of 1946, the Riley-engined 2.4-litre Healey saloon was taken to Italy, accompanied by Vic Leverett of the Riley Motor Co. with a 2.4-litre Riley saloon, and Christopher Jennings, editor of *Motor*. Chris had not long returned from war service with REME. He was commanding officer at the REME training centre at Arborfield when I underwent their AFV course as a young second lieutenant. He had produced a number of guides for keeping vehicles safe, including the strong recommendation that vehicles should be parked front first against buildings. This reduced the damage to radiators and engines from straffing. George Harriman issued the same edict at Austin as it

The new factory at the Cape, Warwick. In the foreground, the later 'B' type Healey chassis; left to right: 2.4-litre saloon (Elliot), Duncan-bodied Healey, and another Elliot. Harry Brandish's office was in the far corner. (The Autocar)

also protected the walls from exhaust staining.

On the Como-Milan Autostrada, the Automobile Club of Italy officially timed the car at 106.56 mph over the kilometre. With a weight of 2,350 lb and 100 bhp, acceleration was also good, the standing quarter mile being covered in 17.75 secs. This performance in early 1946 was sensational. The *Motor's* report said: 'No other car has been timed by the *Motor* at so high a speed.'

Assembling 'B' type chassis frames at the Cape. In the foreground, Jack Hawkes. (The Autocar)

I heard the news over in Beirut. With members of the Doom Club, a loose knit club of motoring enthusiasts led by Captain Keith Holdaway, we held a

The Origin of the Healey Cars

monumental celebration, in the midst of which an astonished Timothy Rootes arrived from the Syrian Desert. It was essential to pour the beer into a glass and examine it with the aid of light, as the bottles too often contained pickled mice and cockroaches. The MO and local health officer assured us that the danger of poisoning was not high as the animals crawled into the bottles before the brew was added. The power supply and lighting frequently failed which made inspection difficult, but nevertheless drinking proceeded in the dark with unabated fervour.

The small Benford workshop soon proved too small and so we purchased a site of about two and a half acres. A concrete raft was laid on the somewhat soggy land and an ex-RAF hangar assembled over it, with bricks closing in both ends. This factory, known as the Cape, was where the Nash Healey and Austin Healey cars originated.

The 2.4-litre Healeys were expensive, high quality cars in very limited production. Early in 1948 DMH and I took the roadster on a tour of the United States with a view to selling cars there. We landed in snow in New York and took our driving tests—which we just passed. The American Automobile Association provided us with maps and routes and we set out on tour. We visited Detroit and Chicago and then went south to Texas. We then drove via El Paso to California and Los Angeles. We spent a considerable amount of time in Los Angeles where Ben Lyon arranged for us to visit a film studio. We met a large number of very helpful people, including Oliver Billingsley who was running a motoring magazine called *Road & Track* which was then one year old. Today it is one of the world's top motor magazines, renowned for the quality of its contents. This trip opened our eyes to the potential of the American market and taught us much of what the Americans needed in the way of a sports car. Only a relatively small portion of Healey cars were exported to the USA in the following years but they did establish the name over there.

During this trip—my first to America—I saw the way the hot rodders made Ford V8s go. I came home full of enthusiasm for the idea, determined to build a car of that type. With Ralph Hutt, Dick James, John Saxton, Peter Griffiths and several others, we formed the British Hot Rod Association, meeting at the Queen and Castle at Kenilworth. Luckily, I was able to obtain a lot of scrap Healey parts. I had the discarded prototype chassis frame and many parts off the prototype. The front suspension was an experimental set that had Mintex Halo bushes in place of needle roller and ball bearings. It gave the front suspension about 2° negative camber and a lot of friction damping. The engine was a Canadian-built Bren Carrier unit with the extra number of head studs that the Americans thought so good. I moderately modified it. A rudimentary body with aeroscreen and without hood completed the machine. I covered many miles in this, at times using a petrol/paraffin mixture to eke out the petrol ration. A wartime Bentley friend persuaded me to enter the Nottingham Sports Car Club's Sprint at Rufford. I did one reasonably quick run and on my second really had a go. After a very good start I snatched second gear at peak revs and the gearbox broke with a great grinding sound. However, my first run was good enough for 'Fastest Time of the Day' and a pint pot, and for a first in the unlimited sports car class with a half-pint tankard. Soans, our friendly Ford dealer, provided a new second speed gear but that broke in the middle of Kenilworth ford. Ultimately the Donald Healey Motor Co. needed the back axle and I broke it up. Some friend of Peter Wilkes at Rover bought the engine for a 'special'.

Later that year Mervyn Cutler gave me time off from my job at Armstrong Siddeley to accompany DMH on our first Mille Miglia. We took a 2.4-litre roadster with Westland body that Roger Menadue had prepared with an engine built by Eddie Maher. We carried a sackful of spare Girling dampers, to change en route until we found a reliable set. We drove all the way out to Brescia where Johnny Lurani met us. He was driving a 2.4-litre saloon. Our first problem was trying to keep the car on the road. The Dunlop racing tyres, with their hard compound, lacked all resemblance of grip on the wet Italian roads. Johnny arranged for us to equip the car with a set of Pirellis like the ones he was using. These softer tyres were a great improvement. Johnny also supplied a set of pace notes liberally dotted with warnings of rough roads and dangerous bends.

The car differed little from the standard production model apart from some excellent Lucas driving lamps. We tested it on the local autostrada and fitted a grade harder Lodge plug, as the one recommended passed out at prolonged speed. The car was faster, at about 112 mph, with the hood erected. We covered the first 12 miles of the course in practice and with such advice as we could get from Johnny Lurani were ready for the race.

We started in the dark, following Johnny's instructions to go slowly on the first bit which, he said, was the most dangerous. He was right. We passed several wrecks burning in the dark. As DMH warmed to the job and daylight broke, we proceeded to overtake Italian cars of reputably much greater performance. I did all the refuelling, handing over petrol coupons and pouring in fuel as quickly as possible. We had several dices with other competitors including the great Nuvolari, who would scream past us between having his Ferrari repaired at many of their refuelling points. His car was breaking up: as bits fell off, he tried all the harder to keep going. Near Rome our dynamo failed. I checked out the circuit but it was beyond repair. It later transpired that the armature had failed due to faulty soldering. This was one of only two electrical failures we were to have with Lucas equipment, a pretty good record of reliability. The British Commercial Attaché, Donald Trounson, met us at the Rome control and helped us with the stop – the only time a British government official gave us any help in years of racing. After Rome the brakes began

The Origin of the Healey Cars

to play up; if not used with great care, they would lock up one of the wheels without warning. The road holding on the twisty bits was poor compared with that of the Italian sports cars.

Johnny's pace notes were not as accurate as they should have been. We would slow down to pass over some bad ditch to avoid causing too much damage to the car and speed up again, only to find that we had not identified the correct ditch, which we would then proceed to crunch into at high speed. Several of the roads had not been repaired from war damage. The engine with its failing battery continued to run better than ever as it freed off with the miles. At one stage, DMH turned to me and asked, 'When do we reach Florence?' I consulted the map and said: 'I don't see Florence.' 'What's the next control?' he asked. 'Firenze' I said.

After Florence a large dog ran across the road and we struck it with one corner of the car. We changed the wheel and cut away the damaged wing. Every time we put the lights on the engine missed, so we drove as quickly as possible with only rare use of lights.

We finished ninth overall and fourth in the unlimited Sports Car Class! Johnny Lurani finished thirteenth and won the touring category. Johnny might well have finished in one of the first three places but for the failure of the Panhard rod that located the back axle. He had earlier completed the Targa Florio with the same car, winning the unlimited touring category.

The Italians were most helpful. Count Aymo Maggi, one of the organisers, kindly accommodated the Healey team at his house at Calino, a beautiful base from which to operate. Johnny Lurani looked after me when DMH left with the car to rush back to England. He showed me around several of the small Italian racing body workshops and I then took his car back to England. I soon realised the great effort he had made in finishing the race with it. Without the Panhard rod, the back axle floated sideways until the tyres rubbed the wheel arch and it oversteered in an alarming fashion.

In January 1949 DMH drove a Healey in the Monte Carlo Rally, but had to give up when the third-speed synchro hub jammed. This happened only too often on the early Riley boxes when a build-up of tolerances let the hub travel too far, letting the detent balls and springs escape. The cars also competed regularly in the Alpine Rally. Tommy Wisdom won his class in the 1947 Alpine, gaining a Coupe des Alpes. DMH won his class in the 1948 event, and in 1949 with Ian Appleyard finished second overall as well as winning their class. DMH's close involvement with rallying and racing was naturally to lead to continued construction of cars of his own design, as he knew from personal experience that something vastly superior to the mundane vehicles in general production was both possible and desirable.

In the 1949 Mille Miglia, DMH drove a saloon Healey with Geoff Price, while Tommy Wisdom drove the open car with me. DMH described Geoff as the perfect co-pilot, his only complaint being that Geoff peeled oranges with oily hands between pit stops. The cars were little changed, although at Peter Thornhill's suggestion we added an anti-roll bar to the front suspension. This increased the weight transfer at the front and improved wheel grip, making the car much quicker and easier to drive over the mountain passes. Tommy was a little quicker than DMH and quite a bit harder on the car. Neither driver ever caused me any worry. That year 'Aldy' Aldington was driving a Bristol with Johnny Lurani and for a long time we raced in company. Tommy was determined to beat Aldington whom he referred to as 'Lizard', and I remember the dice well. One long straight had a narrow stone bridge at the end, just wide enough for one car. We roared along the straight side by side at over 110 mph. Tommy said to me, 'Hold on. I'm not giving way – he will.' A little too late for comfort, Lizard eased off and let Tommy through. After that he seemed to lose heart and we left him well behind.

Later that year, DMH again went to the USA. Here he met George Mason, the president of Nash Motors, and an arrangement was made to produce the Nash Healey. Originally this was to have been the open 2.4-litre Healey Silverstone, fitted with the 3.8-litre Nash unit. The chassis of the Silverstone was based on that of the 4-seater roadster and saloon. It was fitted with sporting 2-seater bodywork, with the engine pulled back in the chassis. Nash decided that the Silverstone offered too little in the way of comfort for the American market, and so an all-enveloping body was designed for the chassis. The prototype Nash Healey, a Silverstone fitted with Nash units, would just top 100 mph. It would rush up to 100 and then cease accelerating. We took it to Italy and ran it in the 1950 Mille Miglia. It was good on the mountain passes but on the long straights the small 1100-cc sports cars would overtake the 3.8-litre machine. In addition, it would get hot when kept at maximum for long periods. We tried a multitude of things to make it go. We took the head to the FIAT garage in Como and had $1\frac{1}{2}$ mm milled off the joint face to increase the compression ratio. We opened up the exhaust system, improving the acceleration but raising maximum speed by only a few miles per hour. We ran the race in order to learn what we could do about the car and finished outside the time limit for the class.

Back in England, Armstrong Siddeley put the engine on the bed. It was not giving bad output at about 124 bhp. Aided by Edward Boyle of SU, they cleaned up the carburettors and raised the output to 127 bhp. To get more speed we looked into the problem of wind resistance. We joined up the wings and faired them into the body. We timed the car early one wet Sunday morning on the straight near the radio station at Daventry. It quickly reached 124 mph, which was really 20 mph faster than the separate winged car. That was it for Le Mans 1950.

This was our first entry in the Le Mans 24 hours. Roger and I were the mechanics, while Tom Kenny, the Healey agent in Paris, organised everything over there, including booking a chateau as the base. Our drivers were

The Origin of the Healey Cars

Tony Rolt and Duncan Hamilton. Mort Goodall and Nigel Mann also stayed at the chateau with a 2.4-litre Healey saloon they were running. Our volunteer team consisted of DMH, Roger, Peter Thornhill – an expert on suspension, and Jack Saxton. Our pits were next to those of the Jaguar XK120 team under Lofty England, which with their advanced engines were the potential winners of the race. Our main problem was stopping the Nash Healey, as it had only $11 \times 1\frac{3}{4}$-inch front and $10 \times 1\frac{3}{4}$-inch rear brakes. After practice we carved the back plates about to get more cooling, drilled the drums and fitted impellers. Mintex provided their M20 lining material – easily the best of the day. There was little else we could alter on the car. With its billiard-table surface and long straight, Le Mans is not a terribly tough race on the cars. The sheer length of the race does wear out some of the more fragile engines, but for devices like the slow-revving Nash Healey it is not a problem.

Duncan had one nasty moment in the race. He was slowing for Mulsanne corner at the end of the long straight when a brakeless French Delage struck him up the rear. He limped back to the pits to find that the back axle had been pushed forward, damaging the clutch housing, the flywheel and exhaust system. Roger cut the local telephone cables and used these to wire up the exhaust and body work. Tony and Duncan then carried on at a reduced speed which enabled Sydney Allard and Tom Cole in the Cadillac Allard to beat them into third place. Even so, fourth overall was a pretty good result for a car fitted with an engine which Nash were selling for $100 at the time.

On the way back to Warwick the car was left with the engine idling whilst the team had a quick coffee. When they returned it had stopped and would not start, and attempts at a push start revealed that the crank had broken. The engine was rebuilt with a new crank and new bearing cap and worked as well as ever.

DMH and I drove the 1950, 1951 and 1952 Nash Healeys in the Mille Miglia. In 1952 we drove the saloon 2-seater that Tony Rolt and Duncan Hamilton had driven to sixth place at Le Mans in 1951. In pouring rain we left Brescia at 5.50 am, with 40 gallons of petrol in the huge rear tank. Tommy Wisdom in an Aston Martin left ten minutes later. Leslie Johnson was driving a stripped open Nash Healey with the intrepid W. A. McKenzie, motoring correspondent of the *Daily Telegraph*. Bill wore my army despatch rider's coat as protection against the elements. In appalling conditions we were approaching Rovigo at full speed when DMH attempted to slow the car for a bridge and corner. He shouted to me that something was wrong – the car would neither stop nor steer. He tried all he knew, jabbing the brake pedal and moving the steering wheel. At what seemed the last moment the wheels gripped and he was able to regain some control. We struck the bridge on the exit side where it turned a corner. We had had what seemed ages of warning of the crash and braced ourselves – there were no safety belts or crash helmets in those days. My head struck the windscreen and pushed it out of its Clayton

DMH and the author in a Nash Healey at the start of the 1952 Mille Miglia. Note the escape hatch in the roof.

Wright rubber. Our first thought was to get out before the car caught fire, as there was a nasty hissing noise from under the bonnet. We managed to kick the jammed doors open and escape. Officials of the local motor club then appeared and cleared the wreckage out of the way. We watched Tommy and Leslie pass and soon the road was open. Some enthusiasts drove DMH back to Brescia at breakneck speed while the officials found a decrepit truck to take back the remains of the car. A crowd of spectators lifted the ton weight motorcar onto the truck's flat bed and I then got in it as there was no room in the cab. The truck was an ex-US Army Studebaker 6×4, fitted with a methane gas conversion. It must have fought throughout the whole North African desert and Italian campaigns. The stout-hearted beast carried us very slowly to Brescia, with refuelling stops for *Metano* every 20 miles. At each stop a crowd would gather and the driver would regale them with a tale that grew longer at each telling while the sympathetic Italians gave us wine. Italians love racing cars and I have never known them to rob a wrecked one. At Brescia the car was deposited at the FIAT garage to await shipment to England, as we needed it for Le Mans.

The Origin of the Healey Cars

Leslie and Bill brought the other Nash Healey home in seventh place overall and were the first British car. One incident marred the whole event. Some nasty journalist rang my mother in England. Seeking a sensational story, he asked her how she felt at having her husband and son killed at one go. After that event we did not compete again – our accountants pointed out that an accident like that could wipe out the whole family business.

The production prototype Nash Healey had a low air intake which Nash improved by using a Nash Ambassador grille. The company engaged Pinin Farina as styling consultant for their range of vehicles and decided to give him the job of creating a new Nash Healey. A chassis was driven to Turin where he designed a lower and more glamorous body; in fact, the body was really too low for the comfort of tall drivers. I spent some time in Turin sorting out a lot of the problems with the prototype and also learnt a considerable amount about how Farina built bodies. This was to prove most valuable when the Healey Hundred was designed.

The Nash Healey prototype at Nash Motors, Kenosha. The front has been built up with clay to take the Nash Ambassador grille.

Nash shipped units from Kenosha to Warwick, where we fitted them to the chassis and road tested. (The engines, gearboxes and axles arrived in sets of six in superb wooden cases, which we broke up to build the roof of the stores extensions.) The chassis were then sent to Turin in closed rail trucks for Farina to complete the cars and ship them to the States. Pilfering on the Warwick to Turin journey was a major problem – Lucas wiper motors were obviously very popular somewhere along the route. In all, 506 Nash Healey models were delivered to Nash between December 1950 and August 1954.

In the early days of the Healey Hundred, the design was shown to Nash. At that time they were co-operating with Austin on the NKI (Nash Kelvinator International) project which was later to become the Metropolitan. Austin built some 95,000 Metropolitans for Nash between 1954 and 1962. Nash had a strong engineering team under Meade Moore and they gave us a considerable amount of valuable advice and information which was not available in England at that time. I have a great deal of respect for American automobile engineering knowledge, which is generally more advanced than any where else in the world. Perhaps the car-buying public do not always respect engineering as they should and so often get what they deserve.

The period of Nash Healey production and assistance enabled our company to generate the funds, the knowledge and the team needed to create the Healey Hundred. From struggling to produce wooden-framed coachbuilt bodies, we had now reached the stage where we could design all metal bodies. In addition, we now really understood what the American market required. DMH decided to commit the company to what was to become the Austin Healey project.

First of a Line

The car that was to become the Austin Healey was really conceived late in 1951. The Healey range of cars was well established, the Nash Healeys were being turned out steadily, and there was not a lot to occupy DMH's fertile mind. The cars were expensive and outside the means of most motorists. From his frequent visits across the Atlantic, DMH knew the potential in the American market. He decided that we needed a comparatively low-priced, high-performance sports 2-seater with export potential – the home market was not exactly buoyant and the Jaguar XK120 was giving us a hard time. Bill Lyons had really slipped a crippler on the small sports car market with his high-performance, high-value model.

We discussed what we should do at home most evenings. The future of the Riley units was obscure as the axles were due to go out of production and the engine could follow. It was also fairly expensive. One section of the motoring press was always telling us that the Austin A90 was a very good unit, in a car that did not do it credit. We studied all the reports and decided that perhaps here was something we could utilise. DMH got in touch with Len Lord, the boss of Austin, who said he would be delighted to supply us with units. He arranged for Geoff Cooper of the design department to visit us and discuss our requirements. An ex-Austin apprentice, Geoff knew everything about the units and their availability and he quickly suggested what he considered to be the best unit for us, based on performance, cost and availability. The next day, he sent us all the drawings and specifications we required.

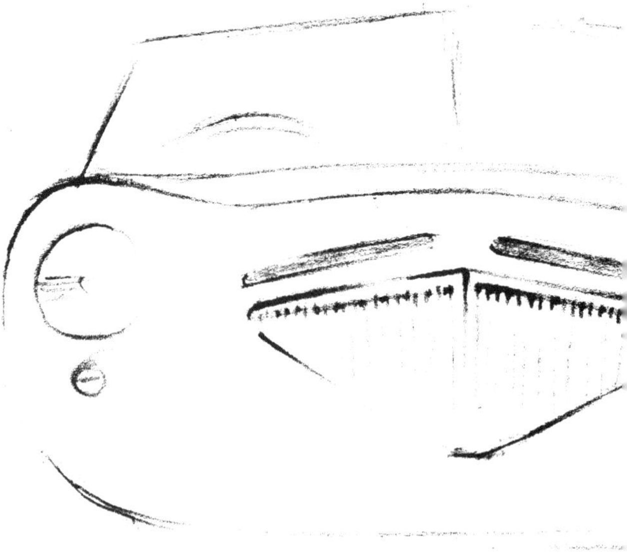

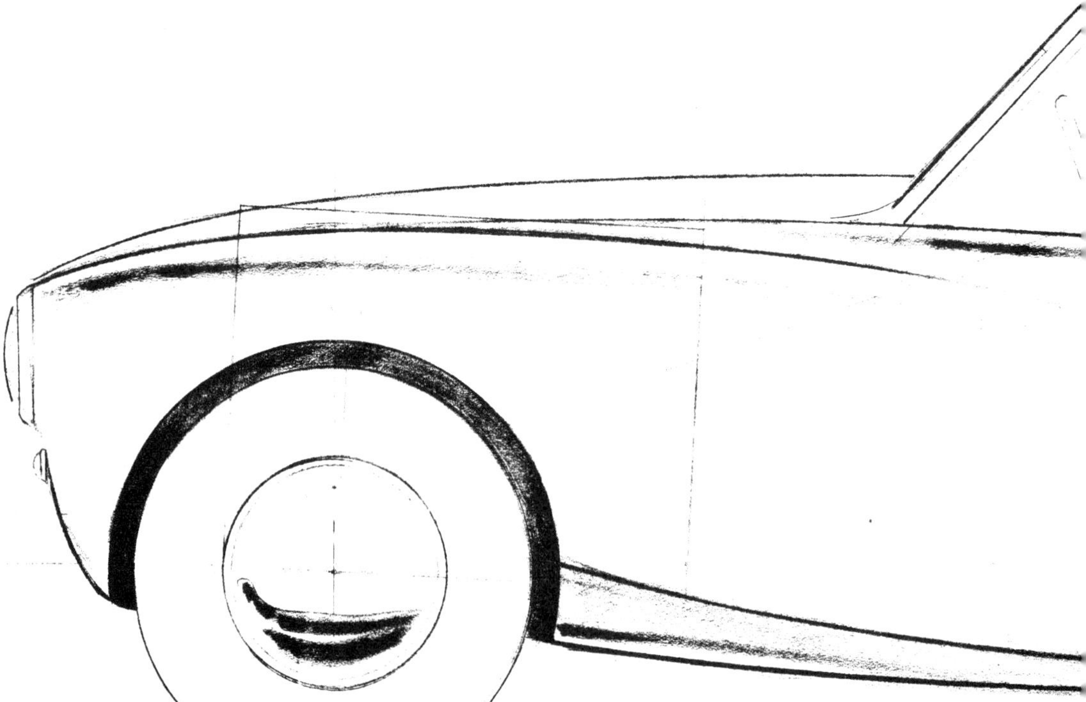

The earliest body scheme for the Healey Hundred. This progressed by stages to the model, a full-size drawing and the prototype built at Tickfords. Even at this early stage, some of the characteristics that survived are already apparent.

Austin Healey: The Story of the Big Healeys

We had only just completed a series of investigations into frame stiffness and ways of increasing it on the Nash Healey, and this was to influence the frame design of the Hundred – or 'J' in our code book. DMH and I worked in the attic at home where we laid out a very simple ladder frame design to accommodate the Austin units. We considered using both the 1500-cc Austin unit and the 2660-cc A90. The A90 was not a lot bigger and gave us the power we needed. The car was kept small to make the best use of output available. All the original design work took place at home in the evenings, as we did not want any knowledge of the fact that we were considering the use of Austin units to leak to our normal supplier, Morris Motors. Morris and Austin had been great rivals in the motor world and it might jeopardise our supply of the 2.4-litre Riley units.

DMH plotted the outlines of the body and designed a method of folding a curved screen, which he was determined to use. I spent many hours stressing the chassis to arrive at the final sizes of the members. It had to have better torsional resistance than our production frames. The method of fitting the body to the chassis was an improvement on that used by Pinin Farina for the Nash Healey chassis. We were both pretty excited at the results of burning the midnight oil. Everything looked right.

The first small-scale model of the Healey Hundred, made from the first scheme. Note that the grille is near to its final form. DMH had the rear wings defined before the start of production.

First of a Line

When we had the basic layout, we took the drawings to the drawing office at Warwick. The two draughtsmen, Barry Bilbie (chassis) and Gerry Coker (body) eagerly got on with prototype drawings. These were happy days for car designers – apart from a minimum headlamp height of 26 inches, there were little artificial restrictions to design. Barrie Bilbie detailed the ladder frame and John Thompson Motor Pressings of Wolverhampton were called in to produce the prototypes. They suggested that the welding system used on the Landrover frame could be utilised with only simple alterations. They agreed to supply two prototype frames quickly for £50 each. As the detail drawings were completed they were sent to Thompsons who started fabricating the part. Thompson's work was always of an exceedingly high standard; of the various frame makers we used, their product was easily the best. In about six weeks the first frame, hand-made to a high degree of accuracy with really beautiful welding, was delivered with a coating of dull red primer.

The Austin components were fitted into the chassis in a small tin shed at the back of the works. Roger Menadue was our experimental engineer and did the work almost single-handed. The brakes were provided by Girling, one of the great suppliers to the industry without whose help many small manufacturers could not have survived. They always produced something better and quicker than any other brake manufacturer, and their installation and after-sales service was and is second to none. Their installation engineer, Ken Light, quickly piped up the brakes and checked out the system. The pipework was simple and beautifully executed, while the Mintex linings provided ample stopping power.

Four rudimentary wings, two seats, a windscreen, horn and rear-view mirror were lashed on to the chassis and it was ready for test – we had always obeyed the principle of making a chassis that could be used on the road with a minimum of addition. DMH and I drove the chassis for about 50 miles. We were delighted. The low-cost Austin units gave superior roadholding and performance and a better ride than the expensive units we had been using on our production cars.

While the design and production of the chassis proceeded, Gerry Coker was designing the body. My father dictated what he wanted and Gerry carried out the design with great rapidity. We had very limited body facilities, so the manufacture of the prototype body was arranged with Tickford of Newport Pagnell (later bought by David Brown to become part of Aston Martin Lagonda). A number of alterations were made as the construction proceeded. DMH disliked the fins on the rear wings and so they were cut off and the wings reshaped.

The chassis was then driven to Tickford and the body was built on it. Once complete, the car was driven back to Warwick. DMH did not like the front end and thought that the grille position looked weak. He called in a local panel beater, Bill Buckingham, who cut out the grille that evening, shaped an

Austin Healey: The Story of the Big Healeys

First of a Line

This drawing by Gerry Coker was developed as a full-scale line drawing, from which Tickfords built the prototype Healey Hundred body. DMH had the bonnet scoop and fins removed when the prototype was partly built.

Three snapshots of the Healey Hundred prototype body under construction at Tickfords, Newport Pagnell. The first shows the original fin on the right-hand rear wing, while the left-hand wing has been modified to form the shape continued ever since. The two bonnet bulges shown in all three photographs were later deleted when SU carbs with shorter dashpots were fitted.

additional piece of aluminium and welded it back. The front end was now right. Tests revealed a weakness in the door area. The door opening moved and we realised that there was insufficient beam strength in the body sill. To overcome this, the depth of the inner sill was increased by welding about $1\frac{1}{2}$ inches of extra steel section over the top. This provided sufficient strength to keep the door opening constant under all loads.

The folding windscreen was a feature dictated by DMH. Gerry Coker executed the design in a most exquisite manner. This attractive feature of the car was later deleted in the 100 Six as certain body engineers blamed it for the rather high incidence of screen cracking. In fact, the later replacement fixed screen had an even worse history of screen cracking. DMH always insisted on laminated screens on Healey cars as he considered that the toughened ones could easily cause accidents.

The hood was made by Mr Dunn of Coventry Hood and Sidescreen. He trimmed the hood while Roger welded up the sills. During this operation Mr Dunn lent over the car, forgetting the presence of a large piece of trim coated with glue, and had the lot stuck to his blue pin-stripe suit. I fear his nice suit was ruined but with the devotion to duty of those days, he smiled and got on with producing that excellent hood.

This glue has an interesting history. The glues or adhesives we used, in common with the whole European industry, failed in the heat of the southern states of the USA. Nash Motors had the glue fail on the first of the Nash Healeys we shipped to them. They sent us a gallon of their American 3M product that had stood up to all their tests. 3Ms in England produced an

First of a Line

identical glue in double short time. Code named EC711, but more commonly called 'wonderglue' by us, this was specified for all trim applications. It had an evil smell and was not popular with the trimmers because of this, and was also extremely difficult to remove from the hands. We were probably the first European manufacturers to produce cars that did not come unglued in hot sunshine. Twenty-five years later some others still fail.

The car was painted in Dockers cellulose: colour – Healey Ice Blue. This was very very similar to a colour introduced by Alvis.

In testing it soon became apparent that the top gear ratio was too low and we could not get a higher back axle ratio. Ian Duncan, who was then at Austin, unearthed a Laycock overdrive unit, which at that time was a good device with little development behind it, and this was quickly adapted. Quite a lot of trouble occurred in the electrical controls – the car had a nasty habit of changing back into direct ratio at high speed. Intensive development work by Laycock and Lucas resulted in a reliable sweet functioning unit that was to play a part in winning rallies and races. After brief acceptance tests the car was registered as a Healey Hundred, registration number KWD 947.

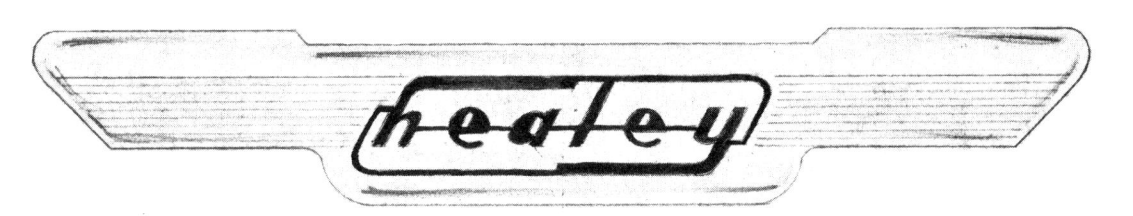

Gerry Coker's original design for a winged badge for the Healey Hundred. This incorporated the Healey motif that had been designed for the first Healey cars by an RAF officer. Gerry later redesigned the badge with the words 'Austin Healey' in Austin script form.

We now had a beautiful sports car ready to go. DMH decided that an official road test was necessary and approached Gregor Grant, who had recently started *Autosport*, a magazine for the enthusiastic motorist. He readily agreed to test the unknown car. The Jabbeke-Aeltre motorway in Belgium was chosen as the venue. Roger and I drove the car to Ostend via the Dover-Ostend ferry while Gregor Grant and John Bolster drove up from the Paris show, meeting us that evening at the Osborne Hotel in Ostend. At dawn the next morning, in heavy drizzle, we made our way to the stretch of motorway, marked and used for record attempts. John and Gregor drove the car over the section to obtain a two-way mean speed of 106.05 mph. They also tested the car over the famed Belgian pavé. The resultant road test appeared in their number at the 1952 International Motor Show at Earls Court, London.

Austin Healey: The Story of the Big Healeys

DMH is never satisfied and he was adamant that there was more to be obtained. So it was back to Warwick where SU Carburettors' expert, Jimmy Harrison, was called in to check the carburettors. Some brief dashes up the main road indicated that the mixture was slightly weak. Richer needles and harder Champion spark plugs were fitted. We decided that the car was now faster and went to Ostende again where the Belgian Automobile Club arranged official timing. Driving the car alone, with the tonneau cover over the passenger seat, DMH recorded 111 mph and various other good figures.

The importance of the press in publicising a new car cannot be over-emphasised. The motoring correspondents of the early fifties were a splendid bunch of men, most of whom had served their country nobly in the war. They were patriots emphasising the good points of British products. The destructive, knocking-the-product style of journalism had not yet raised its ugly head. Our friends were such people as Basil Cardew, Tommy Wisdom,

The prototype Healey Hundred with Healey badge, prior to the Austin takeover. (Autosport)

First of a Line

Courtney Edwards, Bill McKenzie, Pat Mennem, Maurice Smith, Philip Turner, Gregor Grant, John Bolster, Dudley Noble, Harold Hastings, John Bond, Michael Kemp, Bill Paulson, Keith Challen, Max Boyd and Geoffrey Charles. They enjoyed the confidence of the heads of the industry and the respect of the reading public. Contact was direct, without the use of public relations officers. There were no press hand outs prepared by publicity departments–they tried the product and found out for themselves. They took their own photographs and wrote interesting reports in individual style.

On our return from Jabbeke, DMH called Basil Cardew. Basil was in bed with a heavy cold but nevertheless he came out to test the car, heavily muffled in a mighty coat and completely voiceless. Immediately after the test, he once more retired to bed where he compiled a glowing report which was carried prominently in the next morning's *Daily Express*. When he left us we had no idea what he might write as he could only communicate in grunts and sign language.

Then it was back to Warwick and quick preparation for the Motor Show. Dunlop provided knock off 15-inch wire wheels and the gleaming new machine was driven to Earls Court. With a basic price of £850, the car was the star attraction. Len Lord approached DMH and told him: 'I want to make it!' Len Lord and DMH agreed there and then on policy, and overnight the Healey Hundred became the Austin Healey 100, type number BN1. The

DMH, George Harriman, Len Lord and Lord Nuffield with the first car at the Earls Court Motor Show. Overnight, the Healey Hundred became the Austin Healey 100. (Autosport)

The prototype Austin Healey 100 with production type hood. The headlamps were raised on the production cars, increasing the gap above the sidelamps.

badge was changed and the price came down to £750. Thus was born a marque that was to earn Britain millions of dollars.

The basic agreement was that we retained design responsibility – Len Lord said he did not want his people ruining it. Austin would build the car and pay DMH as consultant. They paid a sum of money to cover the work we had to do in producing the drawings for production, and also agreed to contribute to a racing programme. The Donald Healey Motor Co. was given sole rights of supply to US Forces in Great Britain and a proportion of UK cars for retail.

Now the work really started.

The first problem was how to get the body made. Tickfords were low volume specialist coach builders and could not produce anything like the number of cars required. DMH suggested the Jensen brothers and Austin quickly agreed. Tickfords rebuilt the master wooden jig, raising the headlamps slightly (the headlamp height on the first car was below the new legal require-

First of a Line

ments) and delivered it to Jensen. Jensen placed the body tooling with Dowty Boulton Paul, who used a variety of techniques developed during the war on aeroplane production.

It was now early November 1952 and Austin required the first four pre-production cars in the USA by March 1953, in order to introduce the model to the American public. Today vast numbers of over-educated youngsters would take that time to tell you why it could not be done. Fortunately they were kept in their proper place in those days. Barrie Bilbie updated the drawings. The originals were sent to Austin and overstamped with the Austin name and part number and issued to suppliers. The Austin buyers placed orders with all our suppliers, in many cases authorising additional expenditure or tooling to deal with the increased volume. Austin needed three months to clear a space and lay down the assembly line at Longbridge, but in the meantime the first 25 cars would be built at the Cape factory at Warwick. Gerry Coker was busy up-dating the drawings and body details with Jensen while Geoff Cooper organised the supply of 25 sets of components. At the same time the larger brakes of the A90 Atlantic, 11-inch diameter by $1\frac{3}{4}$-inch wide, were specified. The original 10-inch diameter by $1\frac{3}{4}$-inch wide brakes were considered insufficient for all uses. The 11-inch brakes also filled the wire wheels more and looked better.

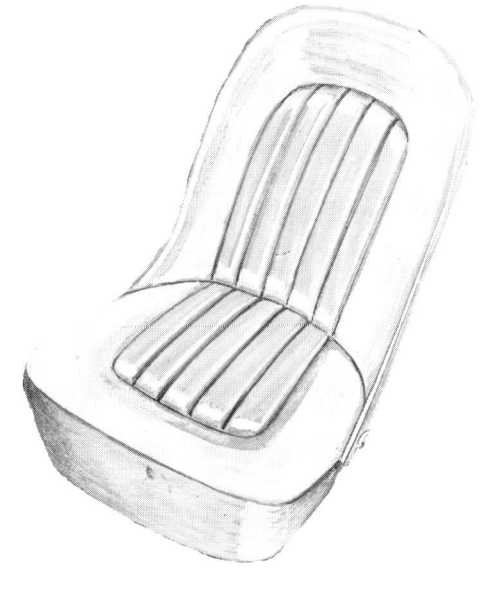

Two of Gerry Coker's trim schemes for the 100. The left-hand scheme was rejected as being too violent. The right-hand scheme was adopted as the basic design.

We also took this opportunity to redesign the steering layout. The original layout used a number of bushes which resulted in a somewhat spongy action. The new layout followed that used by Ferrari on their GP cars and was a vast improvement on that used by Austin. A Burman steering box carried a steering lever with two Engineering Products ball joints. A short fixed-length steering rod ran direct to the lever on the nearest wheel while the centre adjustable track rod connected to an idler lever mounted opposite the steering gear. A second fixed length rod completed the system to the other wheel. When new and when all dimensions were correct, the steering was excellent. However, manufacturing tolerances often resulted in the centre high spot in the steering box not coinciding with the straight-ahead position. The resultant play caused poor straight line running. Wear in the steering joints could reach such levels that the wheel remote from the gear did not really steer the car but trailed. These problems were with the car throughout its life. However, improvements in joint design and close attention to tolerances reduced these faults to minimal proportions in later cars. Today steering deficiencies of this nature would only be accepted by drivers of Japanese cars. Alec Issigonis' introduction of rack and pinion steering to volume-produced cars was a milestone in design and safety.

There was complete co-operation between Austin, Jensen, Healey and various subcontractors. Men worked in each others' factories and accord existed between union and non-union men. All were too busy to worry about irrelevant details. The Austin design office overstamped the Healey drawings, rewrote the parts schedules and updated their drawings of mechanical components. Stan Richardson, their electrical engineer, remounted the wiring loom, saving a lot of copper wire and a small amount of money. This small sum multiplied by the volume produced resulted in a lot of additional profit. Austin toolmakers produced tooling for various suppliers, saving a lot of time. Jensen's engineering team, led by Eric Neale, beavered away on the body assembly line, assembly jigs and small details. The ingenious friction door check was one of Eric's inventions.

The beautifully painted bodies were delivered to Warwick on time and Austin delivered the mechanised units. The assembly at Warwick was not a simple or smooth operation. Geoff Cooper was kept busy bringing us the latest type of components; modifications were produced on the spot and improvements continually adopted. One change of front brake parts resulted in spots of brake fluid dropping on finished bodies. This was rectified almost immediately and the offending mechanic worked even harder. I did some runs around the Warwickshire countryside with Harry Ladd, the technical representative at Austin for Armstrong, the shock-absorber manufacturers, to determine the best settings for ride and handling characteristics.

The first four pre-production cars were shipped across to the USA by Cunard. This great British shipping company ran fast ships from Southamp-

First of a Line

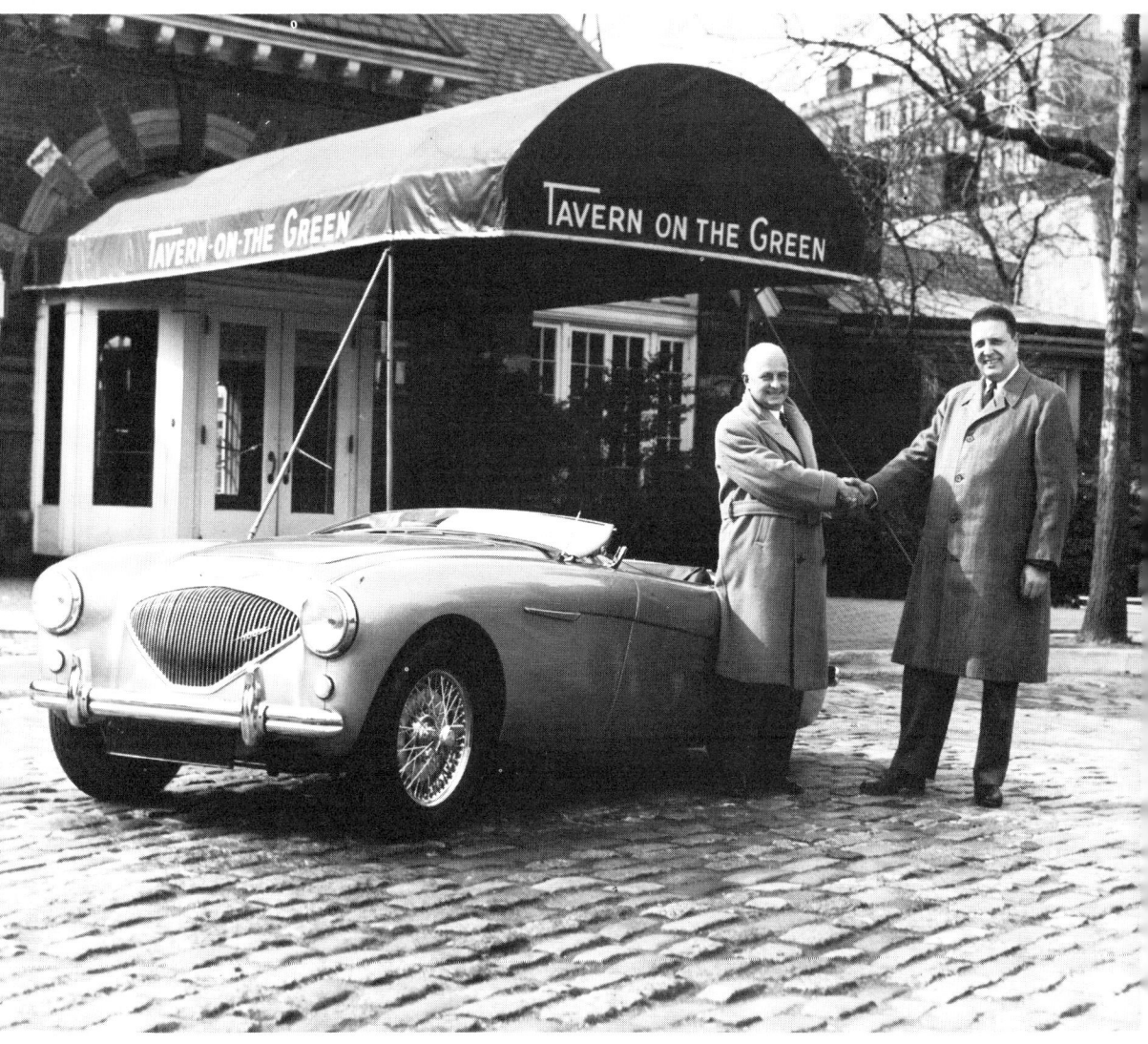

DMH with the first Austin Healey to reach America in 1953.

ton to New York and took great care of their customers' property. The cars arrived on time and looking as good as when they left England. They were received with great enthusiasm by the Americans. At the International Motor Sports Show in New York, the car was named 'International Motor Show Car of 1953', and at the Worlds Fair in Miami, Florida, it gained the 'Grand Premium Award'–a large golden statue. DMH took one of the cars on a tour of the States and gave many television interviews.

DMH in a 100 with Gracie Fields, at the New York Show, 1953.

    Whilst the production of the first 25 cars went ahead at Warwick, the competition vehicles took shape. Known as Special Test cars to avoid any outward show of interest in competition, the bodies were built at Jensen from a specification laid down at Warwick. These cars were to look like production cars but were to be lighter. Wilmot Breeden formed bumpers in highly finished aluminium, saving many pounds, and the bodies were panelled in light-gauge high-strength Birmabright alloy. Austin built four special engines – an assembly of standard production components. The crankshaft of nitrided steel came from their diesel engine. We built a cold air box to feed the larger $1\frac{3}{4}$-inch throat SU H6 carburettors which were fitted to an existing manifold. The gearbox came from the London taxi made by Austin. Auto Transmissions beefed up the pressures in the overdrive and produced a snappy reliable unit.

First of a Line

The Geneva Show was approaching in March and we realised that the only running car available was the first of the Special Test cars. At Austin's suggestion I drove this to Geneva. With its lighter weight, firmer dampers and improved power train, the car was an absolute delight. From the pre-dawn arrival of the night ferry at Dunkirk, I blasted down the road to Geneva. There were no speed limits and very little traffic and I was testing a race car. I found an excellent room in a small Swiss hotel at very low cost and had a good night's sleep. Next day I contacted the Austin staff who expressed horror at my choice of hotel and moved me to theirs. It had more 'stars', a much inferior room and cost a lot more.

We spent the next few days letting various press men and the Swiss distributor try the car. Johnny Lurani, Willy Daetwyler and Robert Braunschweig all took the car out for a run and passed on their comments. The opinions of such experienced men are valuable and were incorporated in my report. I then tried the car up a variety of mountain passes, visiting my fiancée Margot who worked for Thomas Cook in Switzerland. I returned to England via a more southerly route, taking advantage of the snowfree hills to extend the car. In a total of 3,000 miles some minor faults had shown up. The hood leaked, the exhaust mounting rubbers came unbonded, the brakes rumbled and the dampers had lost some effectiveness. My report was circulated and Austin experts instructed the mounting manufacturer in the art of rubber to metal bonding.

Meanwhile at Warwick, the first 25 cars were nearing completion and the remaining three Special Test cars were all but ready. The first competition outing was to be the Mille Miglia in Italy on 1st May 1953.

DMH and I had competed in the 1948 Mille Miglia and for the following four years. After our 1952 crash in the Nash Healey, our accountants had stopped us racing, and so 1953 was to be our first race from the sidelines. Our entry was to consist of three cars: a Nash Healey driven by American John Fitch and Ray Willday, and two Austin Healeys driven by ex-motorcyclist Johnny Lockett with Jock Reid, and ex-Austin racing driver Bert Hadley with Flt. Lt. Bertie Mercer of the RAF. The team drove the 1,000-odd miles to Brescia in northern Italy with additional cars to carry spares. The other British entries included C Type Jaguars driven by Tony Rolt, Leslie Johnson and Stirling Moss, and Aston Martins driven by Tommy Wisdom, Reg Parnell, George Abecassis, Pat Griffiths and Peter Collins. The race was organised by Count Aymo Maggi, Renzo Castagneto and Filippo Tassara, and their competent staff was always helpful and considerate. Count Maggi accommodated a great number of British entrants in his house at Calino. Our team was based at the Villa Mazzotti at Chiari, and Count Binda, whose villa it was, provided us with excellent facilities.

Scrutineering took place in the main square of Brescia, where crowds of Italians generated an intoxicating atmosphere, as loudspeakers blared out

Austin Healey: The Story of the Big Healeys

the latest car and driver to turn up in the piazza. The scrutineers were fair, patient and considerate, completing the formalities with a minimum of trouble. In marked contrast, a French team, who had blatantly abused the regulations, were screaming abuse at the innocent officials, egged on by their womenfolk. After the formalities, our drivers tested the cars for maximum speed on the Brescia–Milan autostrada and also tried out the first difficult miles of the course. To have practised the complete course would have been extremely costly, and in fact the pace notes were updated versions of those Johnny Lurani had given us in 1948.

    The Mille Miglia is run on normal roads covering about 1,000 miles. Cars leave at one minute intervals from 9 pm until about 6.30 am the following morning. In 1953, 488 cars started and 283 were classified as finishers. The difficult first stage from Brescia to Ravenna eliminated 64 cars, including Bert Hadley and Bertie Mercer, and Stirling Moss and Leslie Johnson in their Jaguars. The Austin Healeys had trouble with the throttle linkage. The spring-loaded brass ball joints gave way, locking the throttle wide open or firmly shut. Jock Reid, an excellent racing mechanic, was able to repair and strengthen the Lockett car with wire and the two men perservered with

Johnny Lockett and Jock Reid on the starting ramp for the 1953 Mille Miglia. Note the near standard condition of the car.

An early 100 undergoing tests at the Lindley proving ground, near Nuneaton, driven by Gill Jones with Harry Broom of Austin's development department.

Gerry Coker's original drawing of the two-tone paint scheme on the Austin Healey 100, and, below, the interior styling scheme for the 100 phase 2.

(Opposite) Brian Healey trying an early 100 on Gaydon Airfield.

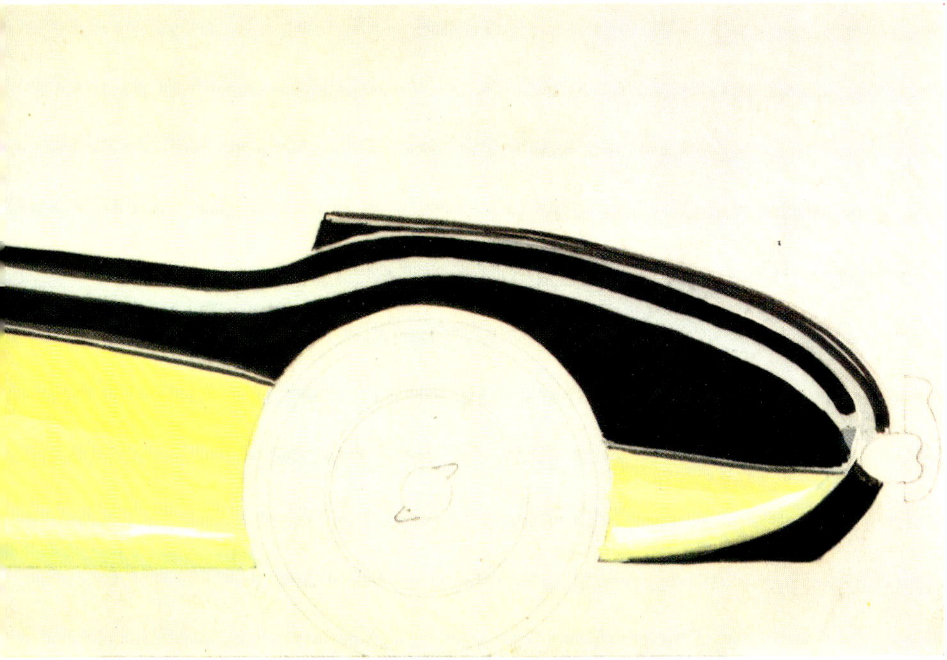

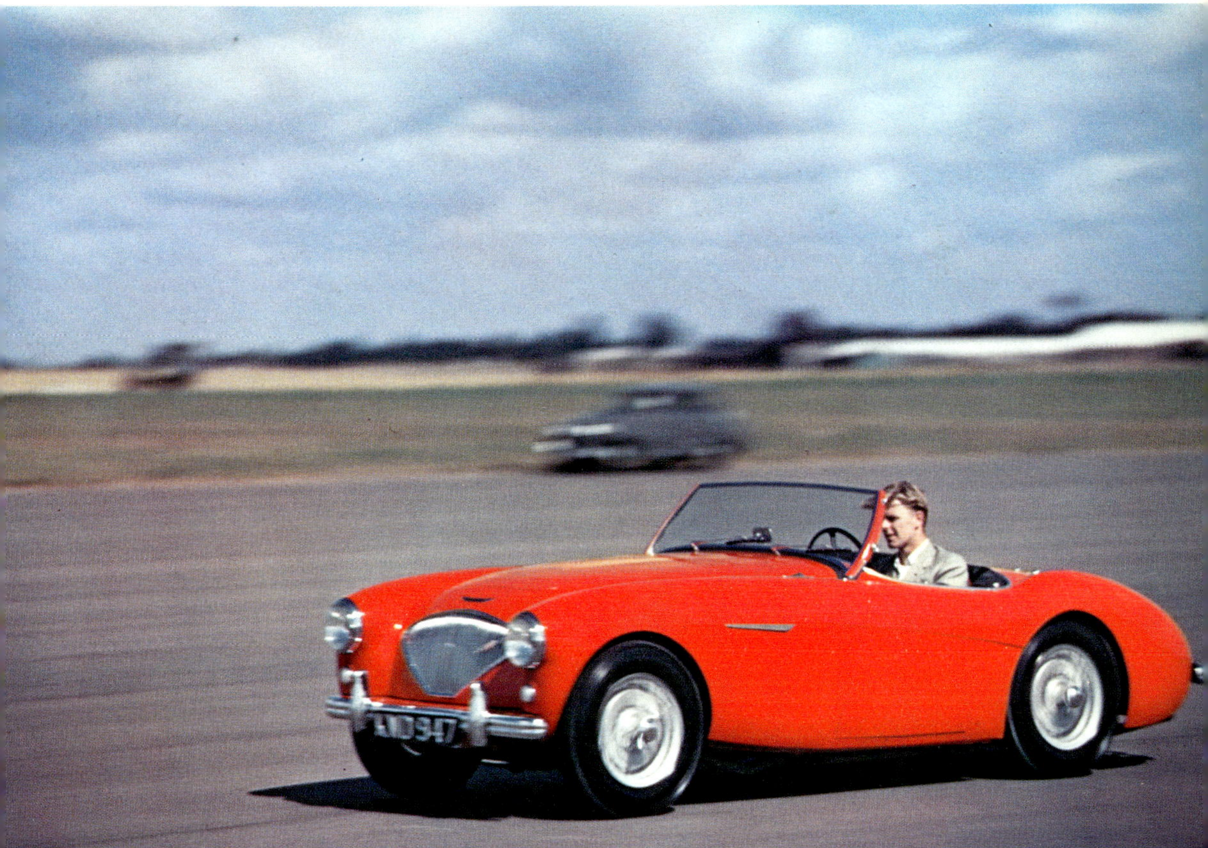

Brian Healey posing in the 100 S prototype, in St Nicholas Park, Warwick. The blue paint on this car had the unlikely name of 'Lobelia'.

First of a Line

it despite its very erratic throttle action. Some 16 miles from the finish, just as they thought they had made it, the clutch plate disintegrated. Giannino Marzotto won the race in a Ferrari. Fangio in an Alfa Romeo came second, Felice Bonetto in a Lancia third, Tom Cole in a Ferrari fourth and Reg Parnell fifth in an Aston Martin. Reg's co pilot, Louis Klementaski, took a wonderful selection of photographs during the race.

The service provided during the race was rudimentary. Mechanics and volunteers armed with spares were located at Ravenna, the first refuelling stop. After dealing with their team they then had a short drive to Bologna where they covered the last refuelling stop. When the roads reopened they would collect their broken-down race cars and return to base.

After the race, the Lockett clutch was stripped and a heated argument ensued with the clutch makers. They were not willing to accept that they had made a faulty clutch plate. However, Peter Aston of Mintex, the brake and clutch lining manufacturers, was able to indicate conclusively where the fault lay. The makers had produced a strong solid centre, but in order to provide cushioning had reduced the number of rivets holding the lining to the steel drive centre. Under rough use the rivets tore free and the lining disintegrated. Peter recommended that the linings should be fitted with many more rivets and be cemented on as well. This process was later followed with little further trouble.

Almost immediately after the Mille Miglia, we started to prepare the cars for the Le Mans 24-hour race.

I have had the misfortune to run cars in some twenty of this dismal event. The heat, the noise, the smell, and the people combine to negate any pleasure that racing cars can give. The sequence of operations leading up to the race is protracted. In February one submits an application, then one completes an entry form, various technical forms and drivers' details. The RAC measure the bore and stroke of the engine and issue a certificate. One applies for the quantity of fuel needed. For 1953, we wanted four entries, two Nash Healeys and two Austin Healeys. A certain amount of lobbying and bribery was necessary to obtain the complete entry, for Le Mans enjoys a tremendous amount of publicity and even a mediocre placement is widely acclaimed. Le Mans was once a great race, when cars were truly representative of production cars and the roads rough and difficult. But by the 1950s, the layout of the circuit with its long straight and billiard-table surface was giving undue advantage to the large-engined cars. In contrast, the Targa Florio and Mille Miglia with their true road surfaces, hills and corners were a comprehensive test of the cars. To win these races, a complete car was necessary.

Three of the Special Test Austin Healeys were prepared for Le Mans– the fourth was being prepared for record breaking runs later in the year. The hoods and windscreens were removed and replaced by an aeroscreen. A mandatory bonnet strap, two Lucas supplementary driving lamps and a

Len Lord about to try a 1953 Le Mans car at Gaydon Airfield, before a race one Sunday morning.

larger fuel tank completed the preparations. The engines had been tested on the bed at Austin and gave 103 bhp at 4,600 rpm. The pistons used were based on the standard casting, machined to give extra clearance and without the split skirt. The higher compression piston to be used in the 'Le Mans Kit' and 100 M was not yet ready or proved.

Bert Hadley, a most competent driver, was promoted to drive one of the Nash Healeys, which with its racing body and 4-litre engine was more likely to gain a high placing. Bert, an old Austin man, accepted reluctantly – the Austin Healey was much easier to drive and less demanding – and was to give his usual polished performance. Two French drivers were selected to drive the second Nash Healey – Pierre Veyron and Yves Giraud Cabantous. The Nash Healey was a good car – it had finished in third place in 1952, behind two exotic Mercedes race cars. At the end of this race, the French had played 'God Save the Queen' for us and refused to play the German national anthem! The drivers selected for the Austin Healeys were Johnny Lockett and Maurice Gatsonides, and Gordon Wilkins and Marcel Bequart.

First of a Line

For some unknown reason, 'Gatso' selected the base – a delapidated French chateau offering primitive accommodation with Napoleonic toilet facilities.

As before, the five cars were driven to Le Mans with some back-up cars and many volunteers, headed by piston expert, Cecil Winby. Restaurant owner Mick Sharp was to provide hot meals throughout the 24 hours. Scrutineering passed with little trouble but Gordon Wilkins, driving one of the Austin Healeys with his lovely wife Joyce, was struck by a drunken Frenchman arriving full bore out of a side road. Joyce suffered severe damage to her mouth. Fortunately Stirling Moss's father, an excellent dentist, was also at Le Mans and he carried out some brilliant repair work. The car was grievously wounded and a major rebuild took place in time for practice. All the race equipment, including engine and transmission, were rebuilt into the spare car. Much extra work was entailed as it was necessary to prove to the scrutineers that the actual car had been rebuilt and that it was not a substitute introduced for the race. This hurried rebuild was to give trouble later, when a vital screw in an inaccessible place came out of the electrical system during the race.

Practice took place on Wednesday and Thursday evening. A combination of French food and Napoleonic sanitation was to strike the team a crippling blow: all the mechanics were laid low with a severe gastric complaint. Our small supply of Dr J. Collis Brown's Chlorodyne helped but was soon exhausted. The mechanics were then fed on animal charcoal on some quack's advice. A few were able to work intermittently and nobly carried the burden of work. A further supply of Collis Brown saved the day and a willing but weakened crew was ready for the race. Fortunately the local eating place was small and the drivers, having more time, ate somewhere else.

Both the Nash Healeys and the Austin Healeys used Girling $11 \times 2\frac{1}{4}$-inch twin trailing shoe brakes and Al fin brake drums. These brakes were good but nothing like the Dunlop disc brakes Jaguar were using. Le Mans is hard on brakes as the cars have to be slowed right down from a long straight at full speed. The rapid heating of comparatively cool brakes used to cause heat checking of the drums. The linings were Mintex M 20, which had good fade resistance allied with good wear. 'Gatso' maintained that the way to save the brakes was to apply them very hard for the shortest possible time.

One incident which occurred before the race illustrates the unscrupulous attitude of some suppliers. At the small garage where we worked on the cars before the race, at Foulletourte near Le Mans, I was surprised to find two French mechanics stripping the Lucas lamps off the Austin Healey, putting them in a van and fitting on their own brand. I asked the mechanics what was happening – they said they had been told that I had agreed. Whilst this went on, a nattily dressed French salesman approached and said: 'Ah! Mr Healey, we are giving you some better lamps for Le Mans.' I told him that we were not having his junk on our cars and that he was to change them back immediately if not sooner! He was most hurt and it took a lot of argument to reverse the position. What annoyed us was that we had spent a lot of time adjusting the lights to give the best results and had to waste time at practice that night getting that fine adjustment the drivers required. We had tried a set of these French lamps previously and had found them to have very poor light distribution, allied with inaccurate filament location in the bulbs.

Race day started early for the team. The cars had to be lined up at 10 am and rechecked by the scrutineers. A long-drawn-out pre-race procedure then unravelled itself until the start at 4 pm. The tactics of the teams varied. Some indulged in short-lived grands prix and others proceeded at a pace considered to give the best finishing positions. The Nash Healey with the French drivers was soon in trouble with low oil pressure. The oil pump was rebuilt and the car left on another lap. To our horror, we saw the mechanic gazing bemused at a steel ball in his hand. 'What's that?' we cried. 'Don't know, it was in the sump' he replied. 'You stupid clot, that's the oil pressure relief valve!' We knew that it was only a matter of minutes before it stopped. Stop it did, with bearing failure, before our signallers could get a message to the driver to pull in at the pits.

One problem at all races is cramped pit space being taken over by people unconcerned with the team. The organisers of Le Mans were in the habit of issuing vast numbers of passes to odd people – National Heroes, VIPs, local bigwigs and to others, one suspects, for cash. It was necessary to be bloody rude to get these people out. Some teams used professional thugs as chuckers out. I used a signalling flag with a sharp pointed end to drive out offenders like cattle when they did not respond to a request in English to leave. It was important to have a clear pit if an unscheduled pit stop was about to occur. On one such occasion, Gordon Wilkins indicated he had a problem with the car and I proceeded to clear the pit. Two Americans I did not recognise had been watching our progress with great interest. When I had cleared all the others I approached these two and abruptly asked them to leave as we needed the room. They immediately left without any dissension. Gordon came in, complaining that the overdrive was changing in and out very rapidly and getting hot. The mechanics had some difficulty in locating the trouble – a loose screw in the junction box feeding the overdrive circuit – and wanted a lot of time. Happily, after the repair, the car returned to normal and Gordon proceeded to lap at the old predetermined speed.

Once things were sorted out, I was accosted by Rod Learoyd, an ex-RAF pilot with a distinguished war record on bombers, who was now working with BMC in America. 'Do you know what you have done?' he demanded. When I said that I did not, he continued: 'You have just slung the two most important men in the US forces out of the pit and possibly jeopardised sales of the car to the USA.' 'What do you mean?' I said. 'Well, one is General Griswold and the other General Curtis Le May.' I was none than a little

First of a Line

Le Mans 1953: an Austin Healey 100 leads a Gordini and a Porsche through the Esses. (Rodolfo Mailander)

horrified, having reached the lowly rank of captain during the war and still being on the reserve, subject to recall. A great leg puller, Rod continued: 'You will probably get court martialled when you get back to England! You had better try and put matters right.' I found the two outside the pit and apologised for being so rude to them. They made light of the whole affair, saying that they fully understood the necessity of clearing the pit at that time. They were more amused at the incident and not in the least offended, putting me completely at ease. Afterwards I was a little more careful about whom I threw out! General Le May was a great sports car enthusiast and did

Austin Healey: The Story of the Big Healeys

much to ease the life of other enthusiasts in the US forces.

Luckily, no press man learnt of the incident, as affairs like this are often blown up to crisis proportions. A woman reporter on an American paper was later to produce a story without foundation that I and the BMC team were anti-American. Once written these things are damaging and no action can effectively undo the impact.

We found that night was the best time of the race. The cars seemed to run better and with the cooler air, the mechanics were able to relax and enjoy some of Mick Sharp's cooking. Mick knew how it should be done but was a little short on practice. The life of the drivers was not made any easier by a stupid ruling that all cars had to have 'type agrée' lamps and yellow duplo bulbs. The resultant loss of illumination was trying for the slower cars and not very enjoyable for the drivers of the very fast Jaguars. Early morning mist or fog was also a hazard. The facilities at the track were primitive prior to the major rebuild after the 1955 accident: mechanics and pit crews snatched a brief rest in deck chairs in the pits. The spare Nash Healey pit was a restful place. Dawn came up with everyone tired and cold. It was to take a long time for the sun to warm one up. By now the field was greatly reduced and many cars were on their last legs. The last hours seemed to drag but at last, at 4 pm on the Sunday, it was all over. The cars finished with:

1st	Tony Rolt/Duncan Hamilton	Jaguar XK120C	2,535 miles
2nd	Moss/Walker	Jaguar	2,512 miles
3rd	Walters/Fitch	Cunningham	2,500 miles
11th	Johnson/Hadley	Nash Healey	2,220 miles
12th	Lockett/Gatsonides	Austin Healey	2,153 miles
14th	Wilkins/Becquart	Austin Healey	2,105 miles

This was a pretty convincing demonstration of the reliability of the Austin Healey at this early stage of its life. Austin dependability had been well and truly demonstrated to some 200,000 spectators. The British contingent were delighted at the excellent showing by British cars.

One must pay tribute to the help given us by many of our suppliers, without whom none of this would have been possible – the ever youthful Ken Light of Girling, Roy Fenner and John Moore of Lockheed and Borg & Beck, and the providers of the good Mintex materials that made the products work even better – Peter Aston, Lionel Clegg and Nigel Parker.

Geoff Packer of Girling was instrumental in getting us to fit their brakes. I can remember him bringing the first set to the Cape one evening, with straight pipes. When I told him that that was no good, he stayed and bent the pipes with his bare hands to fit the chassis. Tony Cross never forgets my making him do the same. These people can do it if you insist. Girling somehow put a little extra into their product which is reflected in the calibre of

First of a Line

their people. George Wood, their installation chief, was not a frequent visitor after I took him for a test run on a Le Mans car fitted with a learned doctor's semi plastic lining. This lining, we were told, would mould its shape to keep pace with brake drum movement and give superb results. After a furious four miles it changed its shape all right, to a handful of rubbery powder.

Jimmy Harrison and Don Law of SU Carburettors struggled to satisfy us, while Stan Glover, George Perry and Ray Wood of Lucas kept us electrically supplied. One of Ray Wood's predecessors, known as 'Speechy', threatened to report DMH for 'Illegal modification of Lucas equipment' when DMH cut 2 inches off an overlong wiper blade in Italy.

For sheer hard work nothing could exceed the efforts of the Dunlop tyre fitters, struggling to change stiff racing covers to keep pace with the cars' appetite for tyres. This was especially true of the incomparable 'Dunlop Mac': his opinion of the first Sebring Race, when Margot asked him how he had enjoyed the trip, was: 'Madam, that's no race, it's a gymkhana!'

Jimmy Hill and Ray Simpson of Castrol, Brian Turle and Keith Ballisat of Shell and Geoff Murdock of Esso rendered superb service in keeping us fuelled and lubricated. Laurie Hands of Champion often succeeded in convincing us that the misfire was not due to his plugs but to the hole in the piston crown. These men and many like them kept things rolling over the years.

In the early days of the Austin Healey we experienced trouble with a well known brand of petrol. Their premium grade obviously had an octane rating much lower than should have been the case with a premium fuel. The 100 would detonate and run on badly after the ignition was cut. I issued an instruction that this fuel was not to be used as it was not suitable. Very shortly afterwards pressure was exerted via Austin and I had to withdraw my instruction note. The star rating system does much to overcome this problem today, but it must be remembered that the good old reliable companies like Esso, BP, Mobil, Texaco, Amoco and Shell produce fuels that are usually superior to other makes of nominally the same rating. Oil recommendations were agreed with Austin and a constant check on their suitability was maintained. Several of the newer continental petrol companies tried hard to get approval but we were not prepared to give this without extensive testing.

By July 1953, some 2,000 Austin Healey 100s had been dispatched from Austin's factory, where production was approaching 100 cars per week. There was a constant feedback of information from distributors, dealers and owners. Complaints were few. The balance of the braking ratio front to rear was altered, and the overdrive governor switch was deleted. This switch brought the overdrive into operation at speeds over 30 mph. Some faulty switches caused the overdrive to cut out at high speeds, which could be very alarming to the driver concerned. Removing the automatic function meant

Louise King, star of 'The Seven Year Itch', with one of the early 100s exported to the USA.

An Austin publicity photo of the 100. In the background, an Austin A40 Somerset, typical of the fifties.

that the driver was in complete command of the unit and could change ratio at any road speed desired. The sidescreens were changed from the one-piece perspex units to framed units with signalling flaps, which made getting into and out of the car much easier.

Back at Warwick, Austin were supplying us with cars for resale. Brian Healey organised a sales department and coverage of the bases of US forces in Britain. Geoff Price ran the service department and worked on the new 100 model, while the engineering department was busy on experimental work and continued preparation of the Special Test cars. We received considerable sums of money under the consultancy agreement with Austin, but spent most of it on development and racing. The small profit made by the sales organisation was eaten up by the service department.

In November 1953, following the Motor Show, Margot and I were married. We took the spare Special Test car to Italy and combined a recce of the Mille Miglia circuit with a honeymoon. The car performed faultlessly, returning 30 mpg average consumption. My fiendish friends in the experimental department had doctored the car. The traditional kipper on the exhaust manifold was quickly found, but a cunningly hidden second one eluded all inspection. Its presence only became apparent when the car was garaged each evening. In the morning the fishy smell would pervade the whole garage although it was not noticeable in the car. The mechanics had to remove a very high fish from under the overdrive where they had hidden it. They also made us a horseshoe in aluminium with the inscription, 'what happened? Geoff got married?' This still hangs up in our kitchen. Married in a thick November fog, we travelled across the Channel overnight on the Twickenham ferry and got on our way as fast as possible. We crossed the Alps 24 hours later and from then on until we recrossed the Alps we motored with the hood down in wonderful Mediterranean winter sunshine. Margot picked the hotels as she was the 'specialist' from Thos. Cook and speaks Italian. Every hotel we stayed in was either under 'seasonal' repairs or just had to have the plumbing fixed. When after all my complaints Margot suggested I chose the next hotel, at Civitavecchia, in the dark, she didn't let on that the railway line ran between the promenade and the beach. So of course, all night long we heard trains

An Austin Healey 100 cornering at speed.
(Robert Mottar)

First of a Line

rushing through the bedroom. Shunting started very early in the morning!

For 1954, we agreed a racing programme with Austin. The 1954 Special Test cars were updated versions of the 1953 cars. Austin were to supply the special Weslake headed engines, which gave around 130 bhp coupled to David Brown 430 close ratio gearboxes, while we agreed to install Dunlop disc brakes. Dunlop supplied Twinpot light alloy calipers with chrome-plated steel discs – a direct result of their aviation experience. Mintex supplied round pads of 875 material. Servo operation of a split hydraulic system was by way of a high pressure Plessey pump driven by skew gears at the back of the gearbox. A tandem mastercylinder originally devised by Girling for BRM provided the control. The sheer power of these early brakes seemed immense. They were ideal for long distance races. Although the hard chrome surface by Metallic Protectives of Warwick wore away and the discs coned, there was little loss of efficiency. Later development of the cast iron disc by Dunlop and Girling was to improve life and reduce coning, which caused taper wear of the pads and increased pedal travel.

The 1954 programme was to have included Sebring, the Mille Miglia and Le Mans. A further record attempt was to follow, with a bid to beat 200 mph. The engineering programme consisted of improving the production car, designing a fixed top coupé and incorporating later type components.

In 1952, Austin had combined with Lord Nuffield's Morris Motors to

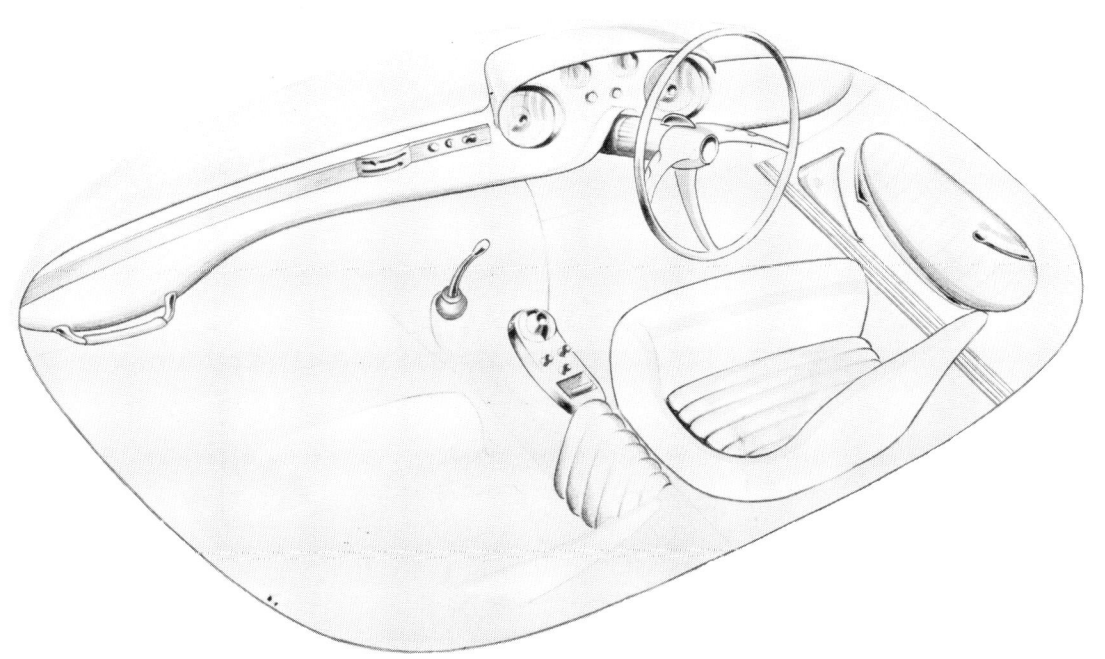

One of Gerry Coker's suggestions for styling the interior and dash panel for phase 2 of the Austin Healey 100. This was never used, as the existing layout was continued with only minor modifications.

form the British Motor Corporation. The feeling had grown that each on its own was not large enough to keep pace with the other giants of the industry. There was a certain amount of rationalisation and several components were to disappear. In some areas, Morris components were better and had a longer future. Morris axles were well engineered and made in a well equipped factory. George Delaselle's C series Morris axle was fitted to the BNI. This was strong enough for 300 hp and no problems were ever known with this unit on any production Healey. It was heavier than the Austin axle and probably reduced the profit margin. It was really too good for the car. $11 \times 2\frac{1}{4}$-inch drums and brakes were fitted to the front of the car and the type number changed to BN2. Morris' four-speed gearbox with cast iron case was fitted later. Designated for more powerful vehicles than the Austin unit, it was a natural replacement. It too was strong and reliable and represented the most important improvement.

Gerry Coker styled a number of beautiful fixed head coupés on the basic 100. Two of these were built at Austin in Dick Gallimore's shop. The first built was chassis no. BN1 142615 and was finished in red with a black top.

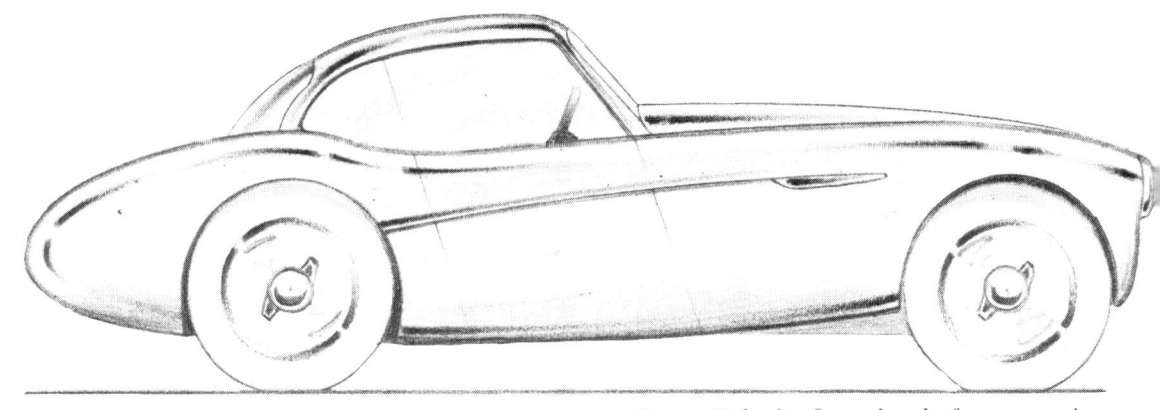

Gerry Coker's first sketch for a coupé top on the 100.

The second was finished in ice blue. The red and black car became DMH's personal car. It later acquired a 100 S engine and disc brakes and was used as a support vehicle at races. Stirling Moss drove DMH on a recce of the Mille Miglia course in it. The one-piece top added considerable rigidity to the chassis and improved the road holding. This car was used in an attempt to develop the 100 S engine as a replacement unit for the 90 bhp 4-cylinder engine.

The Weslake-designed 4-port headed 4-cylinders, later known as the 100 S engine, was always weak in the valve train. This used basic production components and was not up to the job. Harry Weslake reported trouble in this area but it was brushed aside as being due to faulty material. Also there

First of a Line

were so many other things needing attention. The main efforts were concentrated on increasing the power output of the engine. Harry devised an ingenious new cylinder head with carburettors on each side and two ports feeding each valve. Sodium cooled valves were operated by a camshaft specially designed by Austin. This cam form with its high lift, long opening duration and low acceleration was necessary to control the heavier valves. Only six camshafts were produced to this form for the 4-cylinder, but a large number were later to be used in the ultimate competition versions of the 3000. Whilst giving more power, the double entry or cross flow head was structurally weaker than the not unduly strong alloy 4-port head. Harry Weslake was too far ahead: this design could well have provided an answer to many of today's anti-pollution regulations.

The competition side was strengthened by the appointment of Mort Goodall as manager, and Lance Macklin as works driver. Lance was a superb driver. His father, Sir Noel Macklin, had given my father his first works drive for Invicta, with which DMH won the 1931 Monte Carlo Rally. Lance's first major race as part of the Healey team was at Sebring in Florida. With Mort Goodall, Jock Reid and one of the 1954 Special Test cars, he sailed across to New York on board the *Media*. He and Mort Goodall then drove the car down to Sebring, while Jock Reid travelled down with one of Austin's US mechanics. In Sebring, Dunlop Mac attended to tyre service for a number of runners on Dunlop tyres, while another Dunlop mechanic ensured that the disc brakes functioned properly.

The main opposition came from a team of Italian Lancias and some very fast 1500-cc Oscas—a highly developed sports racing car of that era. The Austin Healey, with its Weslake-designed 4-port (100 S) engine, David Brown gear box and Dunlop twin spot brakes, was a potential winner,

The prototype 100 S on the track at Sebring. Lance Macklin and George Huntoon drove the car to third place overall and first in class.

George Huntoon in the prototype 100 S at Sebring, March 1954.

although the 3.3-litre Lancias were slightly quicker.

Lance's co-driver was George Huntoon, an amateur racing driver and resident of Florida. The two men did a fine job keeping up with the leaders. In the closing stages the Austin Healey looked like winning, as its train-like reliability began to tell. However, then a rocker arm broke. Jock Reid struggled to replace the arm and push rod, but a tappet or cam follower had jumped out and could not be put back without considerable delay. The car was made mobile on three cylinders and George and Lance carried on as quickly as possible. Rubirosa on the Lancia was able to overtake the sick car into second place. Moss and Lloyd won with 168 laps on the Osca, followed by Rubirosa and Valenzano with 165 laps on the Lancia. Macklin and Huntoon had to be content with third place and 163 laps. They won the 3-litre class with a margin of 22 laps over a Brooke Stevens Excalibur.

Harry Weslake had warned that something was wrong with the valve gear,

First of a Line

as he had suffered a failure on the test bed on the next engine. But the problem was wrongly diagnosed and time did not permit a change. It was later found that a build-up of tolerances permitted the valve springs to become coil bound and overload the valve gear.

After this we physically checked each valve on full lift with a lever, to make sure that the valve would open an additional 0.040-inch. In addition, we fitted the works engines with a retainer inside the tappet cover that would prevent the tappet jumping out if the valve train failed.

Once we had taken care of this, another failure occurred in the valve gear: a valve stem broke at the collet and dropped in, wrecking the engine on Tommy Wisdom's Mille Miglia car. A further weakness in the valve train was to show up after the engines had covered considerable mileage. Austin had a patented method of ensuring quiet timing chain operation. The space between the teeth of the duplex chain sprocket was increased in depth and a synthetic rubber ring fitted. This rubber ring loaded the inside of the chain and did reduce timing chain noise to a very low level. However the high oil temperature encountered in racing caused the ring to break up and the bits would then find their way into the oil sump pan. Often the gauze filter on the oil pick-up vibrated off and the rubber entered the pump and passed through the oil way and the feed to one of the main bearings. The main bearing oil supply then failed and seized the crankshaft. The rubber would pass the main filter when the engine was started from cold and the bypass valve in the filter opened due to the high pressure. The few engines that failed were quickly rectified and the ring was deleted from production specification: the increase in timing chain noise was just measurable.

Improving the 100

Following the successful outing to Sebring, we decided to produce a limited number of cars at Warwick to an improved specification, designated 100 S (the S referring to Sebring). Austin were much in favour of this development – the sports cars being raced at that time were becoming more distantly related to production cars, and there was a strong demand from dealers, particularly overseas, for such a car. The 100 S evolved from the Special Test cars, incorporating the Weslake-designed 4-port engine, and in fact the prototypes were built out of two of these cars. The first prototype was built in late 1954. The car that Lance Macklin had raced so successfully at Sebring was later updated to full 100 S specification.

The basis was the standard 100 body shell and chassis frame. John Thompson modified the chassis frames, incorporating various strengthening gussets and brackets for the larger DAS 10 rear dampers. The frame was delivered to Jensen, who built the all-aluminium bodies on to it. The aluminium panels were produced on standard tools. Gerry Coker restyled the front end to include a smaller distinctive grille and designed a neat perspex screen. No provision was made for hood or side windows although several owners later fitted the standard 100 equipment.

Austin undertook the supply of mechanical units including the special engine which Morris Motors made in their factory at Courthouse Green. The gearbox came from the BN2 without overdrive. The head was modified from the early type in that the manifold joint face was vertical instead of angled.

The power unit of the 100 S.

Unfortunately the aluminium alloy used was soft. This gave trouble as the head tended to compress under the holding-down studs. The resultant loss of clamping pressure led to considerable gasket trouble. The valve seats were inserted with a taper on the outer diameter, a process used by Nash Motors in America and one which they considered essential. The valve seats could not drop out but it was impossible to replace them without machine shop facilities. Later a harder type commercial alloy was used which eliminated the troubles. Unfortunately the head joint face was not thick enough to allow the heads to be refaced more than once, and this limited the extent to which the compression was raised.

Several unfortunate owners paid good money to have their engines

Brian Healey in the first production 100 S.

improved by dubious tuners. These tuners usually reshaped the Weslake-designed combustion chambers and faced the head to restore the compression ratio. This generally made the engine very rough and prone to detonation. Manufacturers usually produce heads to the best of their ability and experimenting with them can be expensive. BMC issued a lot of extremely useful literature on tuning which provided an excellent guide to owners.

    The brakes chosen were of Dunlop manufacture, with chromium-plated steel discs and calipers with round pads. They were tested alongside Girling units and appeared to be superior technically, having retraction which should have provided more stable pedal travel, longer pad life and less drag. Girling offered a lower cost brake with larger, simpler calipers and thicker discs. The decision to fit Dunlop was taken hurriedly as time was short. Although braking performance was excellent under racing conditions, servicing was difficult and time-consuming. The replacement of pads required the removal of the piston assemblies and refilling and bleeding of the hydraulic system. Peter Wilkes of Rover asked my opinion later on as to which was the best of the three brakes available, and despite my remarks made the same choice we had made. Dunlop continued to improve the brakes throughout the life of the car and the later piston assemblies and cast iron discs were much more satisfactory.

Improving the 100

Twenty-gallon fuel tanks with large, light alloy, quick action caps were fitted. The fuel supply was through $\tfrac{3}{8}$-inch Bundy tubing, twin SU LCS pumps and two $1\tfrac{3}{4}$-inch HD6 carburettors. An oil cooler combined with a filter made by Tecalamit for lorry use was installed at the front.

The production line was set up at Warwick in the converted wartime hangar that formed the heart of the factory at the Cape. Roger Menadue kept a close watch on quality. Jensen delivered all the painted, trimmed and beautifully finished bodies over a very short period. Most bodies were painted white, a blue bottom to the sides giving a distinctive two-tone effect. These colours were chosen because they were similar to the US national racing colours and the USA was the intended destination for most of the cars. The cars were priced at a figure showing a very bare profit – the aim being to get the cars into the hands that would get the best results – but this policy was undermined by Austin America. Deciding the cars were too cheap, they added a considerable mark-up which they used to supplement their racing fund. This fund – and more – was used by them to support private owners. The first six cars were shipped to the USA and allocated by Austin to a number of

Cockpit of the first production 100 S, fitted with a David Brown gearbox from an earlier car.

Six 100 S cars and two Nash Metropolitans being loaded on board Austin transporters for the 1955 Sebring races.

chosen distributors who were actively supporting racing. The two somewhat ageing Special Test cars were refurbished in red and green.

The first race was to be Sebring in March 1955. Stirling Moss and Lance Macklin were to drive the works entry. Lance drove the car from New York to Sebring, collecting several tickets on the way. Sebring, in the middle of Florida, is a resort of mainly elderly people whose main recreation is golf. Harder Hall, where we were based, is the main hotel for the golfing community. The golfers suffered the invasion of the noisy motor racing types with true southern courtesy. One well known Italian ace used to sing in his bath with the taps running. He overdid it one morning and brought the ceiling down on top of the occupants below. The long-suffering manager dealt with this and several other incidents with cool diplomacy. We moved the car

Improving the 100

twice, before ending at a friendly Amoco service station. I always found returning to this place in a grubby condition most uncomfortable, and in later years we were moved to a motel at Avon Park which was much more compatible.

Early practice produced two weaknesses. The clutches were prone to slip and the oil cooler pipes gave trouble. No one had thought to inform Borg and Beck that the cars were intended mainly for competition, and they had specified a clutch which would have been ideal for normal use but was unequal to the stress of competition. Ship and Shore Motors under Ed Bussey scoured the countryside and effectively reduced the local Jaguar clutch stocks to zero.

Austin Healey 100 S cars were in great force that year; in all, seven cars entered the race (the first six production cars and one of our prototypes). Naturally, the Moss/Macklin 100 S was the quickest. The car was well run in and these two drivers were in the top ten. The field included the Briggs Cunningham Jaguar driven by Mike Hawthorn and Phil Walters—which was to win, and the Phil Hill/Carroll Shelby Ferrari which finished a close second. One of the problems of Sebring is the huge entry: 80 varied cars and 160-plus even more varied drivers. The top drivers dislike the additional hazard caused by the presence of some very poor drivers, the worst of whom are those who crawl around, convinced that payment of an entry fee has given them the right to any part of the road at any time they choose. This is a problem with all long-distance races with large entries.

The Florida International 12-Hour Grand Prix of Endurance is organised by Alec Ulmann, ably assisted by race director, Reg Smith. Alec Ulmann leased Sebring airfield for his aircraft business, saw the potential and organised what became one of the world's great sport car classics. With their close involvement with the motor car, the Americans have little difficulty in collecting an extremely efficient and courteous team of officials.

The race started at 10 am on a warm day. The advantage of Dunlop disc

One of the seven 100 Ss that competed at Sebring 1955, passing a Ford Thunderbird. 100 Ss took first, second and third in class, as well as sixth place overall. (Robert Mottar)

Austin Healey: The Story of the Big Healeys

Stirling Moss passing the timers' shack at speed in the 1955 Sebring race: he was placed sixth overall and first in class. (Robert Mottar)

brakes quickly showed, as drum braked cars had to start braking earlier and earlier. The D Type Jaguar was most impressive. Poor Fred Allen had his makeshift flexible oil pipe fail and lost all the engine oil. Jackie Cooper, the

Stirling Moss passing one of the new and potent 550 Porsches at Sebring 1955. (Robert Mottar)

film star, driving the prototype with Roy Jackson-Moore, had a promising run spoiled by a short circuit in the wiring loom. Out of the seven 100 Ss, five completed the gruelling race, Moss and Macklin achieving sixth position overall and first in their class.

Extract from Official Results: Sebring 1955

1	Jaguar D Type	Hawthorn/Walters	182 laps
2	Ferrari	Hill/Shelby	182 laps
3	Maserati	Spear/Johnson	180 laps
4	Maserati	Valenzano/Perdissa	178 laps
5	Ferrari	Taruffi/Schell	177 laps
6	Austin Healey 100 S	Moss/Macklin	176 laps
14	Austin Healey 100 S	Brewster/Rutan	160 laps
17	Austin Healey 100 S	Cook/Rand	156 laps
18	Austin Healey 100	Giubardo/Woolf	154 laps
27	Austin Healey 100	Wellenberg/Wonder	150 laps
32	Austin Healey 100 S	Fergusson/Keith	143 laps
40	Austin Healey 100 S	Cooper/Moore	131 laps

Stirling Moss retiring with a broken front stub axle in the 1955 Nassau trophy. (Daniel Rubin)

Following our successful debut with the two Austin Healeys at Le Mans in 1953, we had entered and started to prepare two for the 1954 event. However, when we took a close look at what type of cars were due to run, we decided to withdraw. In response to queries, we issued a statement to the effect that we ran what were basically standard production cars, that we considered that the regulations permitted cars bearing not the slightest resemblance to production cars to compete, and that racing as such lost its value to the manufacturers and the buying public.

As might have been expected, the French press reacted vehemently, accusing us of not showing fair play and referring to 'Perfidious Albion'. This only convinced us in our belief that we had made a just decision. However, the following year, 1955, saw a further development which we could not have forseen: a number of entries by mediocre drivers of Austin Healeys, which would obviously do nothing but bring discredit to the name.

Somehow Lance Macklin and the powerful French Austin importer AFIVA then engineered it so that the race organisers accepted an entry under Lance's name. Even at this stage, I would rather have ignored the whole thing, but others decided that we must support Lance to the full. MG had entered two MGs to be run by my old friend Marcus Chambers, and it was decided that Marcus should make all the arrangements and that we should co-operate. He booked us in at the dreadful place we used in 1953. We specially prepared one 100 S, NOJ 393, with the high lift long period camshaft and two 2-inch SU HD8 carburettors. Eddie Maher tuned this at Coventry

The author waiting at the head of the works 100 S team for the 1955 Mille Miglia, after scrutineering in Brescia.

to give 140 bhp and did everything possible to ensure that it would last the 24 hours. Lance chose Les Leston as his co-driver. Les was a very good and experienced driver who was well known as a provider of speed equipment and clothing. We had no hope of winning with a basic production car, but had a good chance of a high placing with the train-like reliability of the big Austin 4-cylinder engine. In practice the car was fast and both drivers content with it. Marcus and his team covered timekeeping and tactics while Sammy Davis – one of the great pre-war drivers who had won Le Mans with a Bentley – lent support to the organisation. Sammy owned a 100 and wrote many a word in its praise. He was a mine of information on the Le Mans race. The terrible episode that was to occur was something none of us want to experience again.

Le Mans 1955 quickly developed into a great struggle between Jaguar, managed by Lofty England, and Mercedes under Neubauer. The Jaguar D Types were superb examples of Bill Heynes' engineering and solid Jaguar quality. The output of the Jaguar XK twin cam engines was not high for their capacity but they had an excellent wide band of power and superb staying power. Malcolm Sayer's body design was highly efficient and graceful. Dunlop supplied the disc brakes that did a great deal to help establish British superiority in the sports car world.

In contrast, the Mercedes cars, typical examples of teutonic gimmickry, were flashy and lacked the quality of their British opponents. The Germans incorporated a device to squirt oil into the brakes to reduce a tendency to lock and a movable air brake to assist the slowing-down process. The cars were constructed with a complicated multitube space frame which contrasted with the beautifully simple Jaguar frame design. Jaguar used a normal rear axle located by twin trailing links and an 'A' bracket which was simple, effective, and reliable and gave predictable handling. Mercedes used a swing axle system at the rear, a type of unit most manufacturers have now dropped due to the very poor handling characteristics.

Jaguar quickly showed that their Dunlop disc brakes were vastly superior to the complex drum and air brake combination used by Mercedes. Jaguar had tested their cars on a simulated 24-hour exercise and were justifiably confident that every part and system would perform for the whole race without trouble. Practice sessions and the early hours of the race made it apparent that Jaguar and Mercedes were the only two entrants with a chance of victory.

At the start of Le Mans the cars are lined up in order of cylinder capacity. The Mercedes team's position was in front of the Austin Healey pits. As the flag fell at 4 pm, the drivers raced across the track and leapt into the cars. Fangio, who was driving one of the Mercedes, jumped into his car just below our pits and tried to start it. He tried every one of the many controls without success until the mechanic leant across and showed him the right button to use.

The expected battle for the lead developed between Jaguar and Mercedes, keeping the crowd enthralled. Mercedes had selected Pierre Levegh to drive one of their cars. Levegh was a French national hero after his almost successful single-handed drive in a Talbot against Mercedes in 1952. He might well have beaten the other Mercedes had his crankshaft not broken in the last hours.

I was inside our pits at the time of the accident and did not see what happened. The first I knew was an awful noise. Roger, who had been spotting, leapt down to tell me that Lance had had an accident and it looked bad. I took Lance's wife to the back of the pits so that she wouldn't notice anything. Shortly afterwards an unhurt but shaken Lance arrived in the pit.

The road past the pits at that time was comparatively narrow; in fact, excluding the pit lane, it was barely wide enough for two cars. Over the years the speed of cars had increased considerably but the road had not been widened. Later, when discussing the accident with others who were there, I was able to form an opinion as to what occurred. Lance Macklin was approaching the pit area at about 125 mph when Mike Hawthorn overtook him in a Jaguar and then pulled into his pit. In those days there was no slowing-down lane or chicane to slow the cars before the pits and there had been a

Improving the 100

number of minor accidents in the pit area in previous races. Levegh was about to overtake Lance at a speed of about 155 mph. Having become accustomed to overtaking the Austin Healey at some 60 mph faster on the Mulsanne straight, Mike may have underestimated the speed of the Austin Healey at this point and possibly cut across in front of Lance too abruptly. Lance had to take evasive action which left Levegh little room to pass. Some witnesses thought Levegh moved too far to the left and struck the safety wall before striking the rear of the Austin Healey. The Mercedes broke up in flames and the engine and bits cleared the safety wall to tear through the spectators, killing some 70 of them. Levegh was also killed. Fangio, who had been following him, passed safely through. Lance, Mike and Fangio were all top grade drivers and not likely to make mistakes. Dick Jacobs, a talented MG team driver, was seriously injured in a separate accident.

Mike was badly shaken by the accident, but Lofty rightly ordered him to carry on. This he did, to win yet again for Jaguar. The German team suddenly withdrew their remaining cars at 2 am and the whole team and their vehicles were in Germany before the race ended. I ordered our team to disappear immediately after the accident and get back to England quickly. One did not know what the reaction of the crowd and police might have been to the disaster. I drove the spare 100 S non-stop to the coast and caught the first available boat.

The French investigation under an examining magistrate – Zadoc Kahn – took a long time and I never knew the result. Some speculation involved the apparent violence of the explosion and the ferocity of the fire. It was some 18 months before we got back the remains of the car. The safe construction of the Marston fuel tank we used was convincingly demonstrated. The tank was badly crushed but showed no signs of a leak.

The Le Mans track underwent major alterations. The safety barrier was improved, the road was widened and the pits moved back. Later a chicane was built before the pits to reduce the speed of cars in this area. This certainly makes life a lot safer for pit crews.

My own opinion is that the drivers were not to blame. The speeds of the cars had developed over the years to exceed by a great margin that for which this portion of the track was designed. Anyone trying to come to a conclusive finding so many years later will have a difficult or impossible task, as many of those involved are, sadly, no longer with us. It would have been well nigh impossible for anyone at ground level to have seen the whole sequence of events. The whole affair was a major disaster for us and we stayed away from Le Mans for a long time. The shadow the accident cast over the racing scene was to cause worry in many camps.

In 1956, we sent an Austin Healey team to Sebring once again. We prepared two very special 100 S cars for this race, the most highly developed ever to be raced. The engines were fitted with the long-period camshafts designed for

A 100 S prototype (NOJ 393) and a 1955 works car (OON 439) being tested at Brize Norton Airfield by Lance Macklin and DMH respectively.

the sodium-cooled valves. Twin horizontal Weber carburettors and 4-branch fabricated exhaust manifolds helped to provide 145 bhp at 5,250 rpm. The cars were extensively lightened and very quick indeed. The drivers were Lance Macklin and Archie Scott Brown, and Roy Jackson-Moore and E. Forbes Robinson. In the race, the cars performed well – Macklin and Scott Brown lying in eighth position at the seventh hour. However, both cars were forced to retire well before the end with disintigrated exhaust systems, probably caused by excessive vibration from the 4-cylinder unit. Fangio and Castellotti won in a Ferrari.

Ship and Shore Motors of West Palm Beach had entered another 100 S in this race, one of our older production cars which they had purchased at the end of a long competition life. Driven by George Huntoon and one of their service men, Phil Stiles, it completed the course and finished in eleventh position. After the race, the car was driven the 120 miles back to West Palm Beach. On the way, the gear selector mechanism failed, leaving only top gear usable. Because of some unknown oversight, this was the only gearbox that had not been modified by the use of a new type of selector.

Ship and Shore were justifiably delighted with their result and their efforts over the years at Sebring were much appreciated by the BMC teams. This long-time Austin-supporting distributor was later to lose the British Leyland franchise and sadly then took up the distribution of a Japanese product.

The 100 M appeared as a result of demand for a higher performance car and was introduced in 1955. The engine modifications were in line with those used on the Le Mans race cars in 1953. Two $1\frac{3}{4}$-inch SU HD6 carburettors were fitted to the larger inlet manifolds together with the camshaft as used at Le Mans, giving longer opening periods and greater valve lift.

The carburettors were supplied with air via a cold air box and trunking. The float chambers were pressure balanced with tubes from the lids con-

Improving the 100

nected to the box. A distributor with a different advance curve took care of the ignition.

The high compression pistons were devised one Saturday morning by Cecil Winby and me – Cecil was the British Piston Ring company's piston expert. The piston was created by machining the standard 100 piston casting so as to reduce the size of the bowl in the crown. This also increased the crown thickness which was considered to be beneficial in increasing strength and improving heat dissipation. In those days piston makers were very flexible and able to make changes quickly. These pistons were tested in NOJ 392, one of the ex-Le Mans cars, and were very successful.

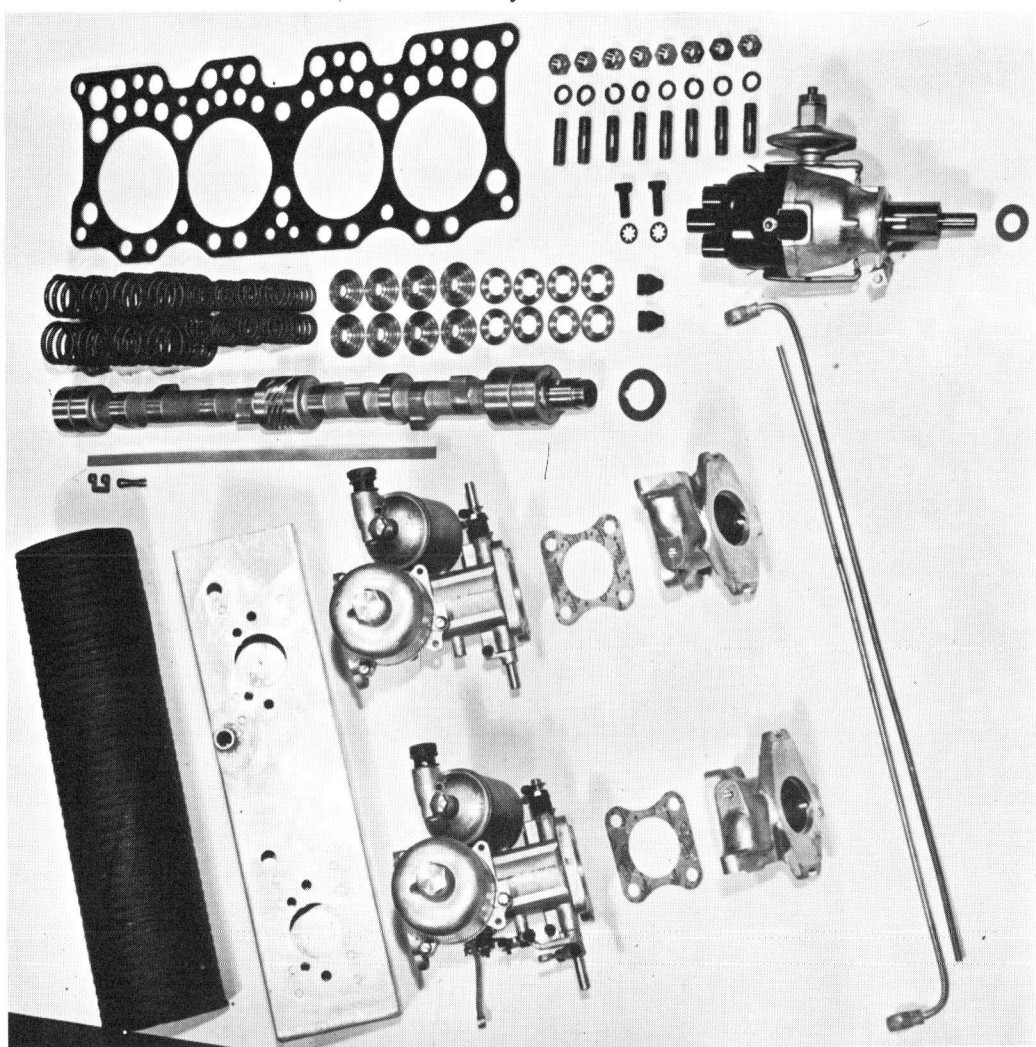

The basic 100 M engine kit. High compression pistons were an optional extra.

A 100 M fitted with a Healey aeroscreen.

Austin had what was known as a 'Butch' test for piston acceptance. All pistons had to be able to stand full power output without seizure or pick-up after less than an hour's running-in period. The engines did not require the careful running-in recommended. Little benefit in engine life came from careful break-in and the engines run by the works were used hard after the briefest of break-in periods. However, the drum brakes could be ruined very quickly if they were not bedded in carefully. Axles would run hot initially but soon wore in to give no trouble at all.

The suspension was stiffened up by the addition of a larger-diameter front anti-roll bar and stiffer damper settings. Armstrong made up valves with heavier leak, bump and rebound settings. To fit these it was necessary to remove the dampers and change the valves on the bench.

Jensen reworked the bonnets to incorporate louvres which reduced the under-bonnet temperature, particularly at lower speeds. A bonnet strap was designed, based on those used on the Le Mans cars, and made by a local Warwick saddler, Frederick Freer, in top-grade harness leather. These were probably the most profitable of all the parts fitted. As a further distinguishing feature, all 100 Ms were finished with a two-tone paint scheme as standard (this had been optional on the 100, at extra cost).

Austin used to deliver transporter loads of Austin Healey 100s to the Cape at Warwick and then pick up the modified cars. Each car was tested twice:

Improving the 100

initially by Austin, and then at Warwick by Geoff Price and his service department, who also carried out the modifications. At Warwick, part of the work included a further road test, often by Geoff Price himself, and a second oil change which ensured that any foreign matter left in during the initial engine build was removed. This double testing and inspection ensured a very high standard. When the 100 M was dropped in 1956, there was much moaning from the service department at the loss of a nice clean job.

The additional costs of transport and reworking were quite high, but it was considered that the relatively small number of vehicles (approximately 1,200) and the extended period over which they were manufactured (2 years) did not warrant interference with the Austin track. Austin marketed the car through its normal sales network. Warranty costs were the same as on the standard cars. These were very low, due to the rugged units, simplicity and ease of service. The special components of the car were also available as engine kits and as chassis and body bits. A large number of these kits was supplied through Austin's normal outlets to people who wanted to up-grade existing cars.

On the road, the tougher suspension and greater power output combined to provide a livelier performance. The car's claimed power output was 110 bhp

Angela Lane, a top model of the fifties, at the Cape with Brian Healey and a 100 M. In the background, a row of 100s awaiting conversion to the 100 M specification.

Keith Boyer's 100 M. This beautifully restored car has been a frequent winner in concourse events. Its highly modified engine makes it a real performer.

at 4,500 rpm, and its top speed with screen folded flat was very close to 120 mph. Fuel consumption was excellent – better than that of the 100 S. Well prepared and well driven 100 Ms were known to give 100 S owners a rough time in competition. The cars were very popular and the limited production has made them much sought-after models. Today, one of the best examples, owned and beautifully restored by Keith Boyer, is a frequent concourse winner.

Specification of 100 M (Changes from standard 100)

100 M	Standard 100
Engine:	
87.3 mm × 111.1 mm: 2,660 cc	
compression ratio: 8.1 to 1	7.5 to 1
camshaft IB2892:	
inlet opens 10° btdc	5° btdc
inlet closes 50° abdc	45° abdc
exhaust opens 45° bbdc	40° bbdc
exhaust closes 15° atdc	10° atdc
lift: 0.435 in	0.390 in
carburettors: 2 × HD6 1¾-in SU	2 × H4 1½-in SU
max bhp: 110 at 4,500 rpm	94 at 4,000 rpm
max torque: 143 lb ft at 2,600 rpm	150 lb ft at 2,000 rpm
Chassis:	
anti-roll bar ½-in diameter	7/16-in diameter
Bodywork:	
louvered bonnet, bonnet strap	plain, without strap
two-tone paint	optional, at extra cost
Performance:	
max speed: 118 mph (screen lowered)	111 mph (screen lowered)
acceleration: 0-60 in 10.0 secs	10.3 secs
standing quarter mile: 17.2 secs	17.5 secs

The 100 Six

Six-cylinder engines were first tried out in the Austin Healey in 1955. The 4-cylinder 2,660-cc units were being dropped from production and BMC needed as much 6-cylinder production as they could get, in order to keep the total volume up and their costs down. The new engine, of 2,639 cc, was supposed to be both lighter and more powerful. We first installed it in a normal 100 car. This first engine, which had run many hours on the test bed, gave 102 bhp at 4,700 rpm and as such represented an improvement. However, it had a terribly rough period around 4,500 rpm, when it felt as if the crankshaft was about to break. Development work by Morris, who had design responsibility for the unit, located the vibration as being due to lack of beam strength in the engine and gearbox assembly. They cured this by fitting a lighter flywheel and a very much thicker steel mounting plate between engine and gearbox.

We decided to increase the wheelbase by 2 inches, as the propeller shaft was too short and fitting and removing the engine proved difficult. This was achieved by reversing the rear spring bracket at the rear of the frame and moving the forward outrigger to the rear. The extra body length was put into the door and the wheelbase finally ended up at $91\frac{23}{32}$ inches. At the same time the pedals had to be moved. The new pendant pedals, and the chassis modification required to clear the engine, reduced the rigidity of the chassis—a situation that was not improved by the 6-cylinder engine mountings being further aft. The road holding of the car was further downgraded by the use

The 100 Six

of stiffer rear springs stipulated by the Austin development department, so that the car could carry the weight of two people in the rear seats without bottoming. DMH had insisted on the 2/4 chummy seating arrangement which was to be of great benefit in widening the market.

The folding screen of the 4-cylinder car had been blamed for the unduly high incidence of windscreen-glass cracking and so a new screen with fixed pillars was designed and fitted. The incidence of glass cracking with this was higher

The engine of the 100 Six, showing the early gallery head which gave poor results.

Cockpit of the 100 Six occasional 4-seater.

at first, but was eventually reduced to satisfactory proportions by the use of improved rubber glazing strips. The brakes were 11-inch diameter with $2\frac{1}{4}$-inch wide drums. These were more than satisfactory for normal use at that time.

Although the development potential of the new engine was obvious, it was only producing 101 bhp at 4,700 rpm and 79 at 3,000. This did not compare too favourably with the 4-cylinder which, at the end of years of development, was giving 94 bhp at 4,200 rpm and 84 at 3,000. Our tests in October 1955 showed the 6-cylinder car to be $3\frac{1}{2}$ mph faster but nearly all its acceleration figures were worse. This period saw some quite bitter arguments between the Austin and Morris sections of BMC over the new engine's uninspiring performance. There were numerous committee and panel meetings which achieved little. We and Austin were pretty blunt in our criticism of the Morris-designed unit and Austin's works manager, Geoffrey Rose, was mainly responsible for making Morris carry out the necessary engine modifications and quelling the outbreak of tribal warfare. Geoffrey, who retired in 1977,

The 100 Six

was an engineer who had the ability to make people see that the merger was a fact and that the two divisions were partners and not rivals. Over the years, he played a vital part in helping us to get better cars.

Production of the new model, designated the 100 Six type no. BN4, was scheduled to start in March 1956. There was inevitably a production gap between the 4- and 6-cylinder models, due to tooling problems, and it was largely due to the efforts of Geoffrey Rose that this was kept to a minimum. Known euphemistically as an occasional 4-seater, the new model had a number of distinctive styling features. The bonnet had a central air intake which was needed to give clearance to the front end of the longer engine. The air intake was a stylist's disguise of necessity and if anything tended to reduce the air flow to the engine compartment. It produced a number of difficulties in pressing and initially a high percentage of scrap due to cracking. The radiator grille was restyled using the horizontal bars from one of Austin's production saloons. This saved some cost over the unique grille of the standard 100. Bumper bars were produced from a stock Austin section and the heating and ventilation system was modernised and improved.

Shortly after the introduction of the 100 Six, George Harriman took the

A page from the catalogue introducing the 100 Six.

The Austin Healey "100 Six" is good to look at in its dual-tone paint finish, the smooth, clean bodylines presenting a delightfully pleasing picture from all points of view.
To suit individual needs, there are numerous items of equipment such as heater, overdrive, and wire wheels which can be fitted at extra cost. But whatever the choice, the four-seater "100 Six" cannot fail to be the centre of attraction and the subject of much favourable comment.

Aluminium framed side screens have one fixed and one sliding perspex panel for ventilation or hand signalling.

Austin Healey

decision to transfer production to MG at Abingdon, as Austin needed the Healey track for a new model. The car now incorporated mainly Morris units and MG, a Morris company, had the capacity and sports-car know-how. At the same time, the question of moving body production from Jensen Motors to Morris's body factory at Coventry was investigated. It was found that without the complete and utter co-operation of Jensen, the body could not be built elsewhere without a big gap in production. Dick Jensen did not take kindly to the idea of the changeover and stuck to his guns, retaining production at his factory. In fact, after the transfer to Abingdon had been organised, Jensen ended up doing more work on the car than before.

MG organised the assembly of the car and assumed complete responsibility for scheduling and purchasing units and components. John Thompson at Wolverhampton made all the chassis and sent these to Jensen at nearby West Bromwich. Jensen built the bodies onto the chassis frames, using many pressings from Dowty Boulton Paul Ltd at Wolverhampton. Paint was supplied by Dockers, ICI and others. Most of the controls were fitted to the bodies by Jensen, including the steering gears which were supplied by Cam Gears of Luton. Jensen fitted all the electrical equipment, supplied by Lucas of Birmingham, and the instruments, supplied by Smiths of Witney. They also made and trimmed the hoods and the car interior. The petrol tanks were made by Radiator's Cowley branch and painted by MG prior to their dispatch to Jensen for installation.

The completed bodies were sent by road to MG at Abingdon. Engines and gearboxes were supplied by Morris Engines at Coventry, and suspension assemblies and axles by BMC's tractor and transmission plant in Birmingham. MG road tested every car and carried out any rectification necessary to maintain the high standard of finish. The Austin sales organisation allocated and issued dispatch instructions. BMC would have liked to reduce the costs of transport of materials: this was fairly high, exacerbated by the dispersed nature of the factories involved.

Tommy Wisdom persuaded the Austin publicity department to back some rally work with the 100 Six. We prepared one car, UOC 741, very much to Tommy's instructions and he drove this with his daughter Ann on the Sestrière Rally in March 1957. They completed the rally but did not feature highly in the results. What was important was that Tommy was able to make a list of suggestions as to what needed to be done to make the car competitive in rallies. Tommy competed with the same car in the Mille Miglia race with Cecil Winby. They won their class and finished 37th out of a field of 365 cars.

We next had it prepared for the Monte Carlo Rally. The car was growing heavier, with two spare wheels and rally equipment. In order to cope with this we fitted heavier front springs and Jack Merrells, a local blacksmith, made and fitted extra leaves to the rear springs. The car could now be driven quickly over rough roads. With high hopes Tommy and his co-pilot, Cyril Smith, a

UOC 741 before modification for rally use by Tommy Wisdom. This ex-Austin publicity 100 Six became the first of the rally cars.

Tommy Wisdom trying UOC 741 round the Warwickshire roads.

Tommy Wisdom at the wheel of UOC 741 with Cecil Winby, at the Ravenna control of the 1957 Mille Miglia. George Phillips of Autosport *took this excellent photograph, capturing Autocar's Harry Mundy on the same assignment. The near standard condition of the 100 Six is typical of the way we raced in those days. (*Autocar*)*

The interior of UOC 741, prior to the 1958 Monte Carlo Rally. Note the simple extras of the day: Lucas dipping mirror, cowls to improve defrosting of the screen, two Huer stop watches, a Halda speed pilot, and extra switches for fog lights.

Tommy's navigator, Cyril Smith, checks chain clearance with mechanic Bill Hewitt. Dunlop snow tyres and studs now make chains obsolete.

world champion sidecar passenger, set forth. The conditions were terrible. Extremely cold weather caused icebound roads, leading to the closure of the route from Paris and eliminating Tommy and the majority of the Paris contingent.

Marcus Chambers, then heading BMC competition, had been perservering with the more mundane BMC vehicles in competition and quickly saw the potential of the car. He rang me and persuaded me to lend him the car for some rallies. We were also able to let him have drawings and specifications of all the special parts and equipment used. Syd Enever redesigned the rear spring to reduce the stress under load and produced the legendary 14-leaf rear spring that was to contribute so much to the success of the 6-cylinders. With the departure of UOC 741 to Abingdon our involvement in rallies was greatly reduced.

We concentrated instead on racing and for 1957 produced three cars based on the six-hour record breaker. Three special 2,639-cc 6-cylinder engines were built by Morris Engines. These incorporated 6 port heads, 3 dual choke

Austin Healey: The Story of the Big Healeys

Weber carburettors, nitride hardened crankshafts and an output of 150 bhp at 5,500 rpm. The entry and organisation at Sebring was handled by Hambro Automotive of New York. Hambro were the Morris importers and with BMC's rationalisation had been given the job of importing all BMC products. Fred Horner, previously with the Austin America organisation, remained in charge of shipping and dealt with the huge quantity of spare wheels and parts sent with the cars in his usual efficient manner. Hambro selected the drivers from American sources. The driver pairings were:

Car No. 25: Major Gil Geitner and Ray Cuomo
Car No. 28: John Bentley and Phil Stiles
Car No. 29: R. Jackson-Moore and Forbes Robinson

Ken Gregory, who later became the company's PRO, was team manager. The cars were fast and should have obtained a good result.

The start of the race was a terrific spectacle as some of the world's greatest drivers were competing: Stirling Moss and Fangio on Maseratis, Mike Hawthorn, Ivor Bueb and Walt Hansgen on 3.8 D-type Jaguars, Peter Collins, De Portago and Maston Gregory on Ferraris, Colin Chapman on a Lotus, Huske Von Hanstein and Ken Miles on Porsches. At the other extreme one P. Frere was pedalling an 845-cc Renault. When one has such a field dicing

100 Six cars were used to parade drivers round the circuit for the benefit of spectators. In the front car, Fangio and Gill Jones of Austin.

The 100 Six

for the lead, a very fast and exciting race is the result.

Ray Cuomo had a frightening experience when he was forced off his line at one of the fast bends. The car struck the kerb and leapt several feet in the air, landing nose-first at 45 degrees. The car was damaged and was driven back to the pits. Temporary repairs were made and the drivers were told to carry on at reduced speed, as to finish was the only possible chance.

The second Austin Healey to be in trouble was No. 28 driven by John Bentley. Shortly afterwards, No. 29 driven by Jackson-Moore also failed. Both cars had broken connecting rods and the crankcase was well and truly vented. The officials asked me why one of the cars had retired and I seriously explained that a bird had gone through the radiator. The official came back later to enquire if I knew what breed of bird it was. I said it must have been a cuckoo. Fortunately the true nature of the failure was never widely known. Gil Gettner and Ray Cuomo proceeded to cover 151 laps and finish in 26th position. Fangio and Behra on a 4,451-cc Maserati finished first with 197 laps. This was the last race for the streamlined 100 Six cars.

The cars were returned to England where Eddie Maher carried out a strip and report on the engines. The engines of both No. 28 and No. 29 had failed rods and it was not difficult to diagnose the cause. Number one rod had failed at the big end, the fracture commencing from the sharp edge left when the rod is counterbored to hold the bolt head. Several other rods cracked in the same place. Both engines had failed after a similar number of working hours. The third had survived only because it had been run at a lower speed. Morris Motors' redesign of the rod was to result in an almost indestructible rod in future 6-cylinder engines.

It was not long before the 'race-proved' 6-port head was fitted to production 100 Six cars. The welcome increase in power of nearly 20 per cent was to result in a much more desirable car. The engine was easily tuneable to produce up to 160 hp. I had always been responsible for homologation of the Austin Healeys and with the assistance of Marcus Chambers I was able to get a very useful range of equipment homologated, which was to increase the race and rally potential of the car.

Routine development work on the 100 Six was concerned with brakes and carburettors. The major area of complaint was heavy fuel consumption. The mixture spread among the cylinders was very wide and unless a rich mixture was used the engine would spit back through the carburettors. This problem was never really eliminated on the 2,639-cc engines. A marked improvement occurred with the 2,912-cc engine, due to the higher gas velocity through the ports.

For the 1958 Sebring race, three 100 Six cars were used. These were based on standard off-the-line cars supplied by MG. Engines were specially built by Morris Engines with two SU HD6 carburettors, the cars being entered in the GT class. We fitted low, full-width perspex windscreens as used in

Europe but the scrutineers disagreed with out interpretation of the regulations, insisting that normal screens be fitted. Some European officials supported our interpretation but the Americans were pleasantly adamant. We complied with their wishes – it was their race and we had never found them anything but reasonable. They also forced several other teams to revert to full windscreens. It was not a matter to get excited about, especially as they were applying the rule with complete impartiality to all nationals in contrast to what happens at some European races.

Hambro were again responsible for organising the 1958 Sebring event. Several drivers from the 1957 team were used, the line-up being: Phil Stiles and Gus Ehrmann; Fred Moor and Col. Bill Kinchloe; Major Gil Geitner, Ray Cuomo and Dr Kunz. Old Austin men like Peter Millard from Austin of Canada attended to general administration. Peter put in a tremendous amount of effort that made life at Sebring very enjoyable. Various BMC distributors attended in force – Fred Royston, a fiery character from Philadelphia, arranged a train to carry friends and dealers to the circuit. He also organised a party before the race which was widely attended by drivers and competing teams and was the social event of the race. Ed Bussey and Frank Wilson of Ship and Shore Motors, BMC distributors in Florida and adjoining States, flew in and after the race gave a party for the team at the Sailfish Club in Palm Beach. The food was the best I have ever had in America, and the sea food probably had not any equal on earth. All the distributors were delighted at the efforts being made at Sebring. If they had any grumbles, they were generally about the number of Austin Healey and MG cars they were limited to for the year. They could see the Japanese infiltrating the gaps left by poor delivery.

The race went smoothly, the only problem being oil on the clutches. The 100 Six gearbox of that era retained the old-fashioned scroll type of seal on the input shaft. Under normal use this type of seal can be very effective but it does not work well when high revolutions are combined with really hard braking. Later cars were fitted with moulded rubber lip seals which worked most effectively and only gave trouble if damaged by some ham-handed assembler.

All three cars completed the course, winning the manufacturer's team prize with their 14th, 17th and 22nd overall positions.

After the race we followed our normal practice of dismantling and inspecting each unit and preparing reports. Stripping out the engines revealed very little evidence of trouble, and the units were then rebuilt with the minimum of replacement parts, to give further excellent service. Any reasonably demanding race would reveal signs of stress in the gearboxes – the layshafts would show excessive wear and the synchromesh cones were usually worn out. Twelve hours at Sebring would produce wear in some areas equivalent to 60,000 miles of normal road use.

There was a constant demand for greater performance from the 100 Six.

The 100 Six

Stuart Mackenzie, sculling champion, uses this 100 Six for transport of himself and his equipment.

This is most readily obtained by increasing the cubic capacity of an engine. The 100 Six was extremely strong and reliable, and as its cylinder bores were well spaced, the capacity of the engine could be increased by using a larger bore of 3.28 inches against the standard 100 Six's 3.125 inches. This increased engine capacity from 2,639 to 2,912 cubic centimetres, making the engine more competitive in the up-to-3-litre class. The increased gas velocity in the inlet ports improved the engine and increased the brake mean effective pressure. The engine also became less critical to ignition setting and mixture adjustment.

Some of the new engine oils caused excessive wear of the camshafts, tappets and oil pump skew gears. These problems stemmed mainly from the introduction of higher levels of detergents. They were not revealed during the oil companies' development work on the new oils: as with all manufactured items, development work – however intense and thorough – often fails to reveal deficiencies that show up later under normal customer use. The higher detergent levels resulted in cleaner engines and longer life, but removed some of the contaminants from the surface of the cams and skew gears which were responsible for their survival. Additives were incorporated in the oils to cope with this situation. Castrol, a conservative company, did not raise the detergent level of their oils as rapidly as some, and as a result Castrol oil did not give any trouble. As one grows older, one tends to become more cautious in making alterations to something that works well.

The 100 Six with the 2,639-cc 6-cylinder engine was in production from March 1956 to March 1959. 6,591 were produced by Austin and 8,391 by Abingdon: out of this total of 14,982, over 90 per cent were exported, the great bulk of these to the USA. Out of a total of 31,000-plus Austin Healeys produced until the end of the 100 Six, 93 per cent were exported. The USA was by far the biggest market, taking 65 per cent of this total production.

Under these circumstances, it is hardly surprising that we gave most consideration to what the USA required. Our relationship with the American distributors and dealers was very close. I had a great number of friends among American and Canadian distributors and owners, and we frequently discussed improvements to the car into the late hours. Many of these men relied mainly on the sale of British sports cars for their living. In contrast, the UK distributors sold a few sports cars as a side line, some even regarding sports cars as a nuisance and only delivering to the persistent enthusiast. It would not be untrue to say that criticism from Britain received very little attention.

The 3000

The Austin Healey 3000 went into production in July 1959. It was not a new model, but a more highly developed version of the 100 Six, the major development being an increase in engine capacity. There had been a constant demand, particularly from the USA, for increased top-gear performance in the 2,639-cc 100 Six. This had always had poor low-speed torque in contrast to the old 4-cylinder, and the easiest way to increase torque is to increase engine capacity.

Eddie Maher, ably assisted by Jack Goffin, Derek Frost, Brian Reece and Bill Clarke, had continued to develop the engine at the Coventry branch of Morris Engines. It was first increased from 2,639 cc to 2,856, and then to 2,912 cc. This size brought it nearer to the 3-litre class limit – it could also be rebored to 2,993 cc. A new cylinder block casting had to be made for the 2,912 cc unit; this was strengthened at the same time. The increase was obtained by using a larger bore and pistons, the stroke remaining unchanged. The ports and valves on the 6-cylinder engines had always been too large for its 2,639-cc capacity and the gas velocity through the large ports too low. The larger capacity increased the gas velocity and enabled a weaker mixture to be used with consequent improvement in fuel consumption. Champion UN12Y plugs were used, which have inbuilt radio interference suppression. These were not the best plugs for the engine – the N9Y gives greater freedom from misfiring, but does cause a measure of television interference.

At this time, the mainstay of MG's production were the Sprites and 6-cylinders we had designed. John Thornley, MG's managing director,

Austin Healey: The Story of the Big Healeys

The Austin Healey 3000 at the 1959 Earls Court Motor Show. Note the illuminated chassis on the plinth: not many cars of this era had separate chassis.

always wanted his lines to be full of sports cars, and the 3000 was to contribute an important portion of the total output. MG's chief engineer, Syd Enever, had a very small team with a large workload. Roy Brocklehurst, Jim O'Neill, Terry Mitchell, Don Hayter, Cecil Cousins, Reg Jackson and Alec Hounslow were to work on the new project with no less enthusiasm than that which they gave to the MG models, at the same time dealing with competition requests and problems. The high quality of the cars produced at Abingdon is a testimony to the devotion and skill of the team. It is no accident that those firms who have been actively concerned with racing produce a better product.

Many features we would like to have incorporated on the 3000 could not be introduced. From an introduction date one works backwards to specification and scheduling, and the time scale on some items is too long. The first Austin Healey 3000s were available as a 2-seater (type No. H-BN7) or an 'occasional' 4-seater (type No. H-BT7). The commencing chassis number was 101. The 2,912-cc engine gave 124 bhp at 4,600 rpm with 167 lb ft of torque at 2,700 rpm. The increase in torque had much to do with the livelier performance.

The 3000

One could engage top gear with engine off, put the throttle to the floor and start the engine without using the clutch. The big six would, apart from a little roughness, accelerate from zero rpm to maximum without any hesitation.

Sebring 1960 was the first race for the new 3000. The BMC team under Marcus Chambers was a pretty formidable assembly: three twin-cam MGAs, three Austin Healey 3000s, two Sprites in the twelve-hour race and one Sprite for Stirling Moss in the three-hour race. We agreed with Marcus Chambers to prepare five 3000s to meet the 1960 GT regulations. The modifications permitted were very limited. Car No. 5 was for Austin's campaign in Canada and car No. 4 was a spare or practice car. The five cars (Nos. H-BN7 6682 to 6686) were delivered from the MG assembly line and rebuilt to specification ST290. The engine changes were as follows:

    The fitting of pistons two grades smaller
    Sports camshaft
    2-inch SU HD8 carburettors
    Polishing cylinder heads
    Competition clutch
    Competition exhaust silencer system
    22290 Lucas dynamo

Publicity shot of the 3000, taken near Abingdon. For some reason, BMC were very keen on horses and often used them as background for their catalogues.

The chassis changes were:
  Fitting Girling 16-3 brakes to front and 12 H to rear
  3.54 axle ratio
  600 × 15 tyres
  25 gallon tanks

All of these parts were homologated and available over the special tuning department's counter.

During the twelve-hour race Jack Sears and Peter Riley circulated with very little difficulty at the agreed pace. Car No. 19 crashed, with Spross at the wheel. At six hours Sears and Riley led Geitner and Breskovich by one lap. Front pads were changed and shortly afterwards Peter Riley came in with the gearbox seized in top. This was changed by the Austin Canada mechanics in well under one hour. For some obscure reason these production boxes were fitted with plain bronze bushes on the lay gear. The other car was also having gearbox trouble and continued at reduced speed to the end. Jack Sears soon had trouble with the second box – the only spare one, which gradually reduced itself to functioning in top gear only. When Peter took the last stint the instructions were to keep going and try to keep out of the way of the faster cars. Peter did a magnificent job, aided by the torque range of the 3-litre engine. He negotiated the slowest corners at under 1,000 rpm and yet dropped less than 25 seconds per lap on his best times. Pit signals were concentrated on keeping Peter alert. His last signal, devised by some wag, was 'Balls out Pete'. Geitner and Breskovich finished 15th and Peter Riley and Jack Sears also qualified. One Sprite won its class. In the three-hour race, Stirling led from the start but was overtaken by a very fast Abarth. A tyre change spoilt any chance of a win and he finished second. Tyre wear was very heavy that year.

The gearbox on the 100 Six and early 3000s was always a source of complaint. One problem was that the change mechanism was an adaptation of steering column change. The Austin Healey side cover had the lever emerging well forward from the left-hand side. The lever was bent backwards to bring the gear change knob to a convenient position and there were complaints about the excessive pressure needed to move it. The position of the knob and its angle was such that the driver's arm attempted to apply force through an unnatural angle. The position as used on the Austin saloon was better and was a great improvement on steering column change. A change to a new gearbox casing with a proper central remote change was under way in 1959. Bill Appleby, chief designer of power units at BMC, knew the problems and tried hard to get the position changed. However, it is very difficult to get senior management to spend money on retooling, especially when from their point of view the problem was to make enough Austin Healeys to satisfy demand. Syd Enever had four levers rebent and distributed for test. This simple modification to the angle at which the knob approached the hand

The 3000

greatly improved the operation. Driver suffering was reduced as skin was no longer rubbed off the hand. For some reason, gear lever knobs were styled for appearance and not for comfort. Nothing really beats a large round ball devoid of any marking or sharp edges. We machined a number of gear lever knobs out of Tufnol, a material made of fabric impregnated with phenolic resin and cured under pressure. The material was strong, machined freely and took a fine finish. It was also pleasant to hold. Whale Brand Round Rod is the best to use for gear knobs.

People also disliked black plastic when applied to steering wheels. We built all the 100 S wheels and a large number for the 3000. These consisted of a high-strength aluminium alloy sheet routed to shape by Cape Engineering

Cover of the 1959 catalogue announcing the 3000.

of Warwick. Coventry Timber Bending supplied the rim in two pieces of $\frac{1}{8}$-inch timber laminated with resin glue and machined to conceal the alloy rim completely. The assembly was riveted and bonded together with an Araldite glue. This wheel would deform under accident forces without breaking whereas some inferior steering wheels broke into jagged splinters of wood and metal.

The first 3000s had two SU $1\frac{3}{4}$-inch HD 6s with automatic choke. The SU device, known as a thermostatic carburettor, is brought into action on a cold engine by a thermostatic switch, located in contact with cooling water near the outlet at the front end of the cylinder head. This switch makes the circuit when coolant temperature is below about 90°F and energises a solenoid on the carburettor. This supplies a rich petrol air mixture through a separate pipe to the inlet manifold. When correctly set, the device provides a rich mixture for starting and by a system using a needle and spring also ensures the correct mixture at idle and various conditions of throttle opening. The cold startability of the device was always good. However, due to some error of specification or supply, the spring controlling the needle was of incorrect strength and the throttle response was erratic when cold. We called SU in and they quickly rectified the settings. However, because of the long time the cars took to travel from assembly line to overseas customers, there was considerable criticism of the device and we decided to change to the more normal type of enrichment control, lowering the jets by means of levers and a pull cable. For some obscure reason SU tended to do a better tuning and setting operation for customers outside the BMC group. In addition to the enrichment device troubles, it was extremely difficult to arrange satisfactory heating of the induction system. With manifolding and hot spots arranged to provide freedom from misfiring, hot starting of the engine became a problem. With the heat transfer reduced to overcome the hot start problem, the engine tended to spit back. It was extremely difficult to install a satisfactory system in the small space available under the bonnet. However, it should not be thought that the carburettor was bad: it was very good but it was not to the standard of perfection we would have liked. Things rarely are.

The introduction of disc brakes added new problems. The previous drum braked models gave lining life in the region of 50,000 miles under conditions prevailing in the USA. The disc brakes, despite many years of development on a variety of cars, showed a high rate of pad wear under conditions of light use. A crash programme of testing and investigation with Girling brought a solution. Splash shields were fitted inboard of the discs with minimum interference to disc cooling and these put pad life up to acceptable levels. BMC Service, a most excellent organisation, provided at that time a spares backing that was without equal anywhere. With the use of a computer they had forecast a very high usage and a 'pad mountain' resulted due to the shield modification cutting pad consumption to low proportions.

The 3000

Production of the 3000 MkI totalled 13,650, comprising 10,825 BT7s and 2,825 BN7s, from July 1959 to May 1961. The improved performance of the 3000 engine kept sales buoyant and the main criticisms of the cars were confined to cockpit heat from the exhaust, lack of ground clearance, and demands for an improved hood.

In May 1961, again largely with the American market in mind, we introduced the 3000 MkII. The American public were conditioned to frequent model changes. American manufacturers usually introduced a new model every year or else included some easily identifiable changes. It was felt that change was necessary to encourage owners to buy a new car. One should always change before demand showed signs of a decline.

There exists a theory that expensive cars have grilles with vertical bars or slats and lower priced cars horizontal ones. For the 3000 MkII, a new and improved grille incorporating formed vertical slats was introduced. The

3000 MkII, showing the new grille. The 3000 is distinctive from any angle but this three-quarter front view is perhaps the most impressive.

Cockpit of the 3000 MkII showing the original metal dash panel carried over from the 100.

styling of air intake on the bonnet was also modified to be compatible. The body shell was virtually unchanged and the car was available as a 2-seater (type No. H-BN7) or an occasional 4-seater (type No. H-BT7). To increase the power output and improve carburation, three SU HS4 carburettors of $1\frac{1}{2}$-inch throttle diameter were fitted with separate inlet manifolds. Maximum power increased to 132 bhp at 4,750 rpm. The use of three carburettors was really for competition purposes. Competition regulations permitted a change of carburettor size but not the number as fitted to the production model. Once the basic principles of the SU carburettor are understood, adjustment and tuning are extremely simple operations well within the capabilities of any competent mechanic. Unfortunately, the world-wide export of Austin Healeys resulted in it being serviced in areas where the necessary skills did not always exist. The more ignorant people are the louder they shout.

The 3000

Between May 1961 and March 1962, 5,450 MkII cars were produced, 5,095 BT7s and 355 BN7s. Both models were then replaced by a third MkII model, H-BJ7. So that this car did not have to go through a series of regulation checks and consequent delays in a variety of countries, it was designated the MkII Convertible.

Owners had been demanding a higher degree of creature comfort, and back in June 1961, one month after the introduction of the first two MkII models, we agreed to tackle this feature at Warwick. The top of the frame under the axle was cut away and lowered by $1\frac{1}{2}$ inches. The top was closed in and the bottom lowered and strengthened at this point. New springs, raising the car by 1 inch, were fitted front and rear. The increased rear axle movement enabled lower rate springs to be used with benefit to ride and handling. Eventually, torque reaction members similar to those used on the early Sprite were added.

A total of 25 items comprised our proposed chassis alterations, many of which were a result of new proposals regarding legal requirements on lamps:

Austin Healey 3000 Face Lift:
Proposed Chassis Alterations

1.	Improved road handling	Healey
2.	Increase rear wheel movement by lowering frame	Healey
3.	New rear springs, lower rate	Healey
4.	Larger rear shock absorbers	Healey
5.	Uprated 'B' series axle? Weight only 10 lb saved	Not available
6.	Increased rear ground clearance $\frac{3}{4}$ inch	Healey
7.	Improved exhaust system	MG
8.	Increased power (150)? 3 off $1\frac{3}{4}$-inch carbs.	Morris Engines
9.	Consider increasing fuel tank	Healey
10.	Brake booster as standard	MG
11.	Consider 16 front calipers and integral stub	MG
12.	Cable throttle	MG
13.	Welding	
14.	Vacuum overdrive switch	MG
15.	Engine with centre gear change	Morris Engines
16.	Shorter steering column	Cancelled
17.	New tank gauge unit bi-metal	See 9
18.	Electric rev counter	MG
19.	Electric temp gauge, instruments' internal illumination	MG
20.	Side jacking	MG
21.	New radiator (if flat bonnet)	cancelled
22.	Revise anti-roll bar links	MG

103

23.	Rack and pinion steering (consider?)	Healey
24.	Widen body 3 inches (consider?)	cancelled
25.	115 lb/inch at wheel front springs?	MG

It was no easy task to fit wind-up windows into the slim shallow doors of the 3000, and several modifications to the body were necessary. In addition, Jensen were tackling eleven modifications to skin panels involved with the new hood and screen. The hood was a vast improvement. Its simple erection and stowage set a standard other manufacturers tried to reach. (Way back in 1949, Tom McCahill of Fawcett Publications had tested and written up the first Nash Healey. He was highly critical of the hood, suggesting that it was the product of a sleazy umbrella maker with the DTs. We were to remember his comments, and tried hard to live down this reputation with the Austin Healeys.) The new and heavier screen highlighted scuttle shake, a problem solved by Sid Enever by fitting a heavy gauge diaphragm at the tunnel bulkhead junction. The screen together with vastly improved weather proofing

The 3000

also increased cockpit temperature. Hot air from the radiator and power unit was flowing through the space between gearbox and tunnel. This was reduced by the use of a rubber seal around the gearbox to engine joint.

We also took this opportunity to retool some body parts. A long production run had resulted in some underbody parts loosing some of their design shape and rigidity, and new tooling was authorised in these areas. We built one car incorporating all the proposed chassis alterations bar the 'B' series axles, side jacking and wider body. The 'B' series axle was not available to suit the car. We fitted the rack from an MG but found that whilst the steering was improved, the high ratio made it unduly heavy. Cam gears were to supply a high efficiency version of the normal steering box that resulted in greatly improved steering, especially after the various limits on steering and chassis parts were reworked to ensure that the high spot in the box was always in the straight-ahead position.

We also decided to revert to a twin carburettor layout, obtaining as small a power loss as possible. A camshaft with increased inlet opening period and

View of the 3000 MkII, highlighting its excellent and easily erected convertible top. The backlight panel could be unzipped to improve ventilation.

reduced exhaust period improved the engine performance, although the power output was still some 4 hp less than the earlier 150-bhp three-carburettor engine. The two-carburettor set-up was less costly and a great deal easier to keep in tune: with development and tuning work this was later to result in the 150-bhp MkIII with two large SUs.

It is not a simple matter to introduce changes to a vehicle that is in production. The alterations first require drawing and specification changes. Supplies need to be controlled in order to phase in the new components at the desired moment. The displaced parts have to be phased out and arrangements made to ensure that there is still an effective parts supply for service purposes. The component or assembly with the longest lead time effectively controls the introduction date of a new model. The total number of changes we had considered would have delayed introduction of the MkII Convertible for an unacceptable period of time. Many items were thus omitted and only came in at Stage Two of the MkI!I. The improvements that could be incorporated in the time available were:

1. Convertible body with wind-up windows
2. Improved steering gear
3. Central change gearbox
4. Higher rate front springs
5. Twin carburettors
6. Improved cockpit heat insulation

Moving the gear shift lever from the left-hand side of the gearbox to the centre, combined with improved heat insulation, was of great benefit to the left-hand-drive export models. The new model, known as the Austin Healey 3000 Sports Convertible, was introduced in March 1962 and was an instant success. The only major complaint, thrown up by rallying and racing events, was a continued lack of ground clearance: because the chassis members passed under the rear axle, the amount by which the car could be raised by resetting the springs was very limited. The retail price increase over the previous MkII, BN7, was only £36, from £829 to £865. In addition, a vacuum brake servo was offered as an optional extra. Everyone has tried to use disc brakes without a servo but they are not really satisfactory, lacking response for check braking.

Jensen had made an extremely effective hard top for the 6-cylinder models prior to the introduction of the Convertible. It was felt that the excellent all-weather protection of the new hood would render a hard top superfluous, but rather surprisingly a demand still existed. Les Ireland designed a new hard top at Warwick. Due to its less flexible construction, a hard top presents a lot of problems, as slight body variations invariably keep creeping in on any new assembly line. These were quite easily taken care of with the convertible

The 3000

Doug Thorpe's scheme for a 3000 coupé. This was modified to use more of the existing panels, without so much alteration to the front.

hood–body assemblies were taken from the production line every so often for hood assembly check and adjustments. The new hard top was designed to be adjustable to these variations by the provision of large rubber sealing members. Originally the tops were moulded and assembled at Warwick, but later on we handed the whole production over to Watsonian Sidecars.

Despite great attention to detail, hard tops invariably leak, and in addition tend to rattle or creak. They did have certain advantages, however. The hood assembly could be removed, increasing interior space and saving weight, and the very large moulded back light provided superior rearward vision. A roll-over bar could also be incorporated to increase occupant protection. BMC's Competition Department were among the first to purchase hard tops, because of these advantages.

In February 1964, the Convertible was replaced by the 3000 MkIII, designated H-BJ8. The major improvement was in engine power. A different camshaft, one of the earlier competition pattern, was fitted together with two 2-inch SU HD8 carburettors. Syd Enever had developed a very efficient exhaust system, essentially consisting of two separate runs for the front three and rear three cylinders. The four silencers gave very low power loss and a degree of silence that would meet future proposed legislation.

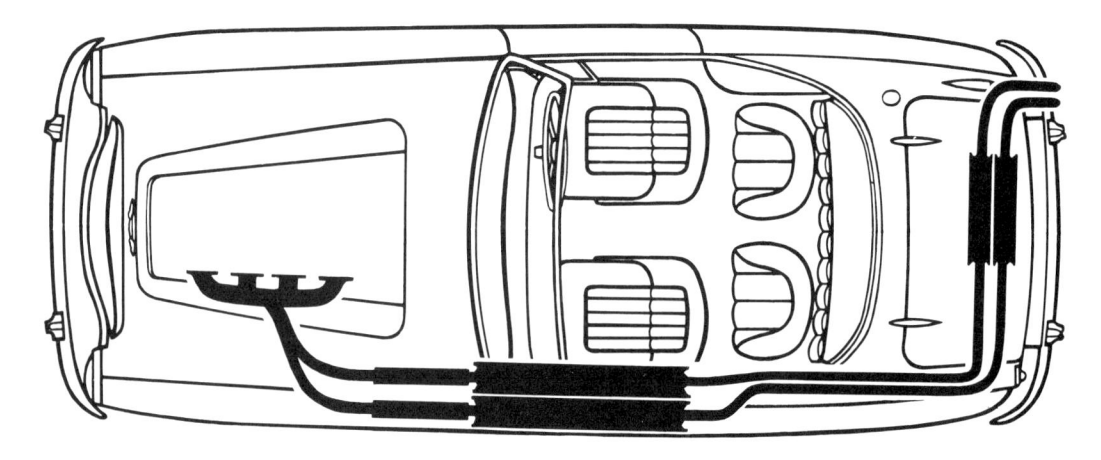

Austin Healey 3000 MK III – NEW EXHAUST SYSTEM

The highly efficient exhaust system of the MkIII gave power without adding to engine stress.

The MkIII differed from the MkII convertible in the following:

1. Increased power from the use of two 2-inch SUs with wilder valve timing and improved exhaust system.
2. Quieter exhaust system with even better heat insulation.
3. Greatly improved dash treatment with wood veneered panels.
4. The mechanical tachometer was replaced by an electronic one.
5. The vacuum servo was now a standard fitment.
6. The basic price was increased by £50, from £865 to £915.

Dick Burzi of Austin carried out the restyling of the interior with suggestions from George Harriman and DMH. Dick was one of the most capable stylists of his time: the way in which he obtained the desired results, at very little increased cost, is an example to others. The old Healey-designed pressed steel panel which had endured for eleven years was replaced by a central console with instruments and glove box in veneered wood panels at either side. Trim quality was increased using ICI Ambla or alternatively real Connolly leather for seating. The back of the rear seat folded down to provide extra luggage space when only two people were carried.

The introduction of the MkIII brought problems. The oil companies had been constantly modifying their products in the search for improved engine life. The high film strength of certain oils resulted in the piston rings not bedding in properly. This caused scuffing of the rings and cylinder bores and could only be avoided by specifying one or two particular makes of oil. The

Power unit of the 3000 MkIII, showing the 2-inch SUs and duplex choke control.

Interior of the 3000 MkIII, showing the extensive use of ICI's Ambla trim material – the nearest approach to leather with no danger of cracking in hot sunshine. Together with the real wood panels, large ashtray and thick carpets, this gave a degree of luxury no longer obtainable in open sports cars.

Americans had an identical problem with their engines. Their cure was to put a small amount of mild abrasive in each cylinder which speeded up the bedding or break-in process. In addition American manufacturers introduced a practice of using an oil of lower film strength for running-in which was changed at the first 500-mile service. Hepworth and Grandage, the piston manufacturers, produced a ring with a taper on the face which bedded in very quickly. The problem was accentuated by the speed limits imposed in

3000 MkIII. The Dunlop white wall tyres featured a very narrow white section which had no effect on their high-speed performance.

the USA. In practice, what we feared would be a major problem, troubled very few owners of the initial cars.

A second and more serious problem arose with the rear hub adaptors used with wire wheels. A very small number failed by shearing at the root of the inner locating cone. Investigation revealed that modifications for ease of production had resulted in an unduly thin section at this point. Failure was generally initiated by impact, followed by high torque application in low gear. A very much stronger adapter was introduced of considerably thicker cross section, and at the same time the threads of the knock-on caps and hub ends were changed from 12 threads per inch to 8. This provided an easy form of recognition. No cases of failure were known with these strengthened hubs.

After 1,390 MkIIIs had been produced, the Stage Two version was quietly introduced. This incorporated those improvements that could not be introduced at the start. These items were:

1. Dropped rear frame.
2. Ground clearance increased by 1 inch.
3. Rear spring rate lowered from 156 to 119 lb per inch.
4. Torque reaction arms on rear axle.
5. Strengthened front and rear splined hubs.
6. Separate parking and direction indicator lamps.
7. Larger Girling type 16 disc brakes in place of type 14.
8. Push-button door handles with slam locks.

3000 MkIII. The Phase 2 version which followed had separate side (parking) and indicator lamps.

The increased ground clearance was most welcome as it reduced the vulnerability of the exhaust system. The increased rear wheel movement

Austin specially finished this 100 Six for the Earls Court Motor Show. All plated parts were plated in gold, and the seats were trimmed in mink. Some metallurgists were alarmed by the gold plating of the wheels, as this could have caused spoke failure.

An enthusiast created this beautiful version of a long-nose 100 Six race car. The drum brakes and one-piece lift-up nose are distinguishing features of this car, which is not one of the works cars.

The Morley brothers, Don and Erle, driving a 3000 rally car to victory in the 1962 Alpine Rally.

John Harris giving the first SR its final test before Le Mans, 1969.

The 3000

The author and family – Margot, Kate and Cecilia (at the wheel), in Malcolm Eykin's 3000.

allied to the softer rear springing improved the already good road holding and ride. The 3000 MkIII was in production for nearly four years, until the end of 1967. Total production was 17,613 units, of which over 90 per cent were exported, by far the greatest market being the USA and Canada. The degree of luxury and comfort in the MkIII has not been equalled in any other sports car to date. It is small wonder that late model 3000s command such high prices today.

The Sprite

As sports cars became ever more sophisticated and expensive, DMH felt that a large section of the buying public was being ignored. He decided that there was a need for a simple, low-cost sports car, and in early 1956 we laid plans for just such a car – the Sprite. This project was developed as the Q model. DMH detailed what he considered the car should do and Gerry Coker did several exterior and interior styling drawings. From these we made our final choice and laid out full-size body lines. At that time, the company was located at the Cape. The factory was centred around the original wartime aircraft hangar, the drawing office occupying an area above the offices at the front end of the hangar and a lean-to extension along one side. Poor ventilation and excessive heat caused problems in the upper office and I had an agreement to provide the design staff with ice cream whenever the temperature exceeded 90°F. Quite a lot of ice cream was consumed!

Barry Bilbie designed the platform chassis and two chassis were built by John Thompson Motor Pressings in about six weeks. Thompson were to make a very large number of these underframes for Sprite and Midget cars. Gerry Coker designed the body and Mr Sprang's pattern-making firm in Birmingham built a wooden body model for about £375. A Midland sheet metal firm built the first two bodies and welded them to the chassis.

The basic mechanical units were A35 units provided via Geoff Cooper of Austin. Full hydraulic brakes were fitted by using Morris Minor brakes on the rear. Originally A35 steering was utilised but we found it difficult to get

The Sprite

The first Sprite prototype with pop-up lamps—a system adopted 20 years later by Porsche.

a suitable installation and therefore fitted the steering rack of the Morris Minor. The engine was modified by cutting and welding the inlet of an MG car with $2 \times 1\frac{1}{4}$-inch semi-downdraft SU carburettors. The AC mechanical pump of the A35 was used to provide the fuel supply.

The electrical system was simple, using a combined headlamp and ignition on/off switch and a direct acting pull cable to the starter switch. The tail lamps came from the Triumph TR series. The original headlamps were operated by cables and rods so that they could be raised for night use or lowered to lie flush with the bonnet. This was hinged to lift up for servicing. The combination of moveable lamps and a lifting bonnet led to expensive complications and there were doubts about the legality of the lamps. These were required to have a minimum height of 26 inches, which creates styling problems on a low car. The rear suspension was original, incorporating quarter elliptic leaf springs and upper radius arms. Originally the upper arm was combined as part of the damping system, but structural failures occurred in use.

The first prototype Sprite, Q1, was completed after the 1956 Motor Show and finished in red with a red and white trim. The results of our first road tests were exciting and DMH immediately contacted George Harriman to explain what we had done. DMH and I then drove the car over to the 'Kremlin', Austin's nickname for the head office at Longbridge. The car was presented for George Harriman's inspection, in the garage under the Kremlin.

Basil Cardew of the Daily Express *drives DMH round the circuit outside Monaco, during Austin's press presentation of the Sprite in 1958.*

He was very interested and immediately saw its sales potential. After discussion it was agreed that Austin would manufacture the car under the project number ADO 13. The name Sprite had to be investigated. It originally belonged to a beautiful little Riley sports car but had been taken over by Daimler for a potential model. This matter was soon resolved. Meetings were held with BMC's body engineers and it was decided that the body would be made by the Pressed Steel Company. They had a gap in their tooling programme looming up and the new model was slotted in. The body engineers disliked some of the heavy gauge metal we used and reduced panels to the thickness used on the A35. Les Ireland, our body engineer, co-operated with Austin in producing detail drawings for production. The original intention was to assemble the A35 line at Austin but this would have meant redesigning so that the engine and gearbox could be fitted from underneath. It became apparent that Austin would face too many problems with the assembly of the car on their line and so it was decided to transfer production to Abingdon where Syd Enever assumed responsibility for the car.

Production started in May 1958 with the chassis number AN5-501. Tommy Wisdom was to describe the early Sprite as Donald's Mobile Hipbath. As we were connected with boats at this time, we incorporated 'self bailing' slots in the floor pan to overcome this criticism. (J. Rix of Austin always maintained that their drawings did not show waterleaks.) Another friend of DMH, Gerry Turner, said of the first Sprite that DMH had designed a sardine tin called the Sprat! Early production was to show up a more serious problem – a weakness in the rear wheel arch region and the hole in the chassis through

116

Count Aymo Maggi, the driving force behind the Mille Miglia races, welcomes DMH and his Sprite to Brescia in 1958.

DMH with an early production Sprite on the Mille Miglia circuit. Note graffiti . . .

. . . Tommy Wisdom at it again, further down the Mille Miglia circuit.

which the gearbox tower entered the cockpit. The rear suspension torque reaction members, due to their combination with the dampers, were feeding unduly concentrated loads into the rear of the chassis. New torque arms with Metalastic bushes at each end replaced the combined unit and normal lever arm, and an Armstrong damper was fitted. Syd Enever's men produced strengthening plates for the weak wheel arch and these were incorporated. Early cars which had already been sold were recalled and the strengthening modification added, which caused a hiccup in production. In all nearly

The XQHS Sprite with Coventry Climax engine, outside the new showroom at the Cape.

50,000 of the original frogeye Sprite were produced until it was replaced by the Mark II in 1961.

The origins and development of the Sprite have been reported elsewhere in a misleading manner. DMH conceived the idea of the car and its market potential. Its design was the product of the Healey team at Warwick, and the original design and prototypes were very close to the production bugeye vehicles. Some have confused the Sprite with an earlier design exercise for a small-engined sports car. This did not then get beyond a few impressions by Gerry Coker. The team were too busy on work on the larger car for it to go further. In 1960 these sketches were dug out and revamped by Les Ireland to become XQHS Experimental Sprite High Speed. This car was built well after the Sprite was in production, as a Super Sprite version on the production understructure with Coventry Climax 1,100-cc single overhead cam engine. Austin discouraged us from proceeding with this project although at that time we had good production space and facilities lying idle at the Cape and were

The Sprite

keen to produce a new model.

The frogeye design of the MkI Sprite was the subject of much ribald criticism and eventually it was decided that we should redesign and eliminate this feature. Austin gave us the job of redesigning the front. We were told to do this and not to talk to Syd about it, but inevitably we discussed it when we met, as we frequently did. We were surprised to learn that Syd had been given a similar brief to design a new rear end. We showed each other what we were doing and possibly a more one-piece design resulted. If both ends had been conceived as part of one design, the result could have been more eyeable. At the same time the plans for the MG Midget version were laid. George Harriman persuaded us to agree to this, the thinking being that the Morris organisation would sell an additional number of vehicles through their outlets to our mutual benefit. The MkII Sprite and the Midget were given the Austin project numbers ADO 41 and ADO 47 respectively. The actual material cost increase of the MkII over the MkI was £12! This so-called 'badge-engineering' undoubtedly did increase the total sales of the car. The problem in those days was selling cars – making increased numbers was not as difficult as it seems to be today. Unfortunately no formal agreement of the procedure was made, and we were to suffer financially when British Leyland dropped the Austin Healey Sprite and continued to produce the MG Midget.

There has always been a strong competitive feeling between the Sprite and the Big Healey boys. At one time a breakaway Sprite group formed a club for

Two early face lifts on the MkI Sprite. They were not considered sufficiently radical for the MkII.

Clay mock-up of the front end that was to become the MkII Sprite and Midget. (Edward Eves)

Sprite owners and some of the big car boys did not consider the Sprite to be a Healey design. Maybe the Sprite name was too good and owners looked on it as being completely independent. A new name – the Spridget – was coined by some wit to become established as part of sports-car nomenclature.

Those who had been loudest in their criticism of the original frogeye or bugeye design were later to sing its praises loudly. The character of this little car began to appeal almost over night and today good examples of the model are much sought after. The Sprite was responsible for introducing many people to the joys of open air sports car motoring. Early Sprites, now referred to as Mark Is, still continue to win their class in sports car racing.

Both the Big Healeys and the Sprite/Midgets are of the same family and share the same parentage. The power units were made and developed in the same Morris Engines factory at Coventry. Eddie Maher, Jack Goffin and Derek Frost did prodigious engine development work in raising the A35 output, first to 43 bhp at 5,200 rpm and ultimately to 110 bhp at 7,000 rpm. The special Le Mans Sprite built at Warwick was to lap Le Mans at over 100 mph, record 150 mph on the straight and win the Motor Trophy as the first British car.

The 1968 special-bodied Sprite under construction, prior to its use at Le Mans.

Alec Poole testing the 1968 Le Mans Sprite at Silverstone. With Roger Enever as co-driver, he was placed fifteenth overall and won the Motor Trophy, at 94.798 mph for 24 hours. The power bulges were necessary to clear the fuel injection system.

Austin Healey: The Story of the Big Healeys

The wooden buck on which panels for the special-bodied Sprite used at Sebring and in the Targa Florio were made.

TFR3, the car built for the third of our Targa Florio forays with Sprites, was my favourite. Devoid of any frills this car had a moderately streamlined light alloy body and a 1,293-cc dry sump engine. Developed for the twisty mountain circuit, it was a delight to drive on the road when fitted with a quiet silencing system. Bernard Foster, the Barford builder, and his partner Doug Green made much of the wooden buck on which the light alloy panels were formed. Builders and carpenters can work to very close limits of accuracy

The 1964 Targa Florio Sprite – the first of a series built especially for this great race. Wisdom and Hopkirk had to retire with a broken half-shaft.

The 1966 Targa Florio Sprite (1965 model with saloon bodywork added). Baker and Aaltonen took it to sixteenth place overall and third in the prototype class.

when given the chance, and the lines on this car were pleasing.

It had more room than most Sprites in the cockpit and the sawn-off raised tail provided good luggage space. One fell into the car and immediately felt at home as the few controls were in exactly the right place. The lovable little thing would cruise effortlessly at 100 mph and return 35 mpg on long runs.

As a reward for his help I let Bernard borrow it to drive down to Cornwall for a weekend's fishing with Trevor Vage and me. Bernard still talks of the fun he had rushing down to Truro. A large man and a really stout friend, Trevor was amazed to find that he could actually get in and drive the car. He could never drive the later Sprite as safety equipment, winding windows and thicker seats consumed the limited cockpit accommodation. Sadly this car was sold and later wrecked in a road race in Italy.

A steel-bodied version of the Targa Florio Sprite. Built with a view to limited production, only this one car was ever made. It was sold to Richard Budd of Leamington.

The special Sprite and a 3000 being prepared for the 1961 Sebring races.

The first Lucas fuel-injected Sprite at Sebring, 1968, with an MG.

Pan Am flew the 1961 Sprites to Sebring, with screens removed. The small size of the car made this economically viable.

It would be futile to pretend that relationships between the various parties involved in producing the Sprite and the Midget were always idyllic. The very nature of the set up, whereby MG built cars to Healey designs, for marketing by Austin and Morris under the British Leyland banner, caused some friction. John Thornley at MG and DMH had some difficulty controlling some of the more ignorant members of their staffs. John Thornley ran a very efficient organisation at Abingdon and saw to it that, regardless of the badge on the bonnet, each model was made to the same degree of excellence. He was to put up a continued battle for the survival of MG as an independent entity. The BMC competition department at Abingdon entered and ran all their cars with equal determination.

Those Special Cars

To sort out the various cars and authenticate them is extremely difficult. It is sometimes possible to trace what a car is when the registration, chassis and engine numbers are known. However, security measures of using confusing numbers, numbers out of sequence, and spurious registration numbers for photographs, probably confused the manufacturer more than the enemy. Certain code numbers and letters do have meaning and these are described below.

The Healey system started with a single letter – A, B, C, etc. J was used for the Healey Hundred. However, variants of the basic model demanded additional letters. We used X to denote experimental, and R for racing models and projects. AHX was used for the early production Austin Healeys completed at Warwick. The 100 S numbering system was arranged so as to confuse observers about the numbers made. The chassis numbers are in blocks of ten with gaps between. The production 100 S records were kept by Brian Healey, who allocated the cars, and a complete list of 100 S models is appended (see page 244). The chassis plate of a 100 S was a valuable item and a number were probably cut off by the unscrupulous and later fixed to ordinary 100 cars to increase their sales value. 100 M cars had no special numbering system, retaining the number of the car before modification. Some 100 engines had the suffix M in the engine number but this did not mean it was 100 M.

The Austin system for Austin Healey cars was as follows:

Those Special Cars

BN1	100
BN2	100 second series
BN3	1 prototype car only
BN4	100 Six
BN5	very basic 100 Six – never introduced
BN6	100 Six – 2-seater
BN7	3000 – 2-seater
BT7	3000 – occasional 4-seater or tourer
BJ7	3000 – convertible
BJ8	3000 MkIII – convertible
HAN5	MkI Sprite
HAN6	MkII Sprite
HAN7	MkIII Sprite
HAN8	MkIV Sprite

A suffix L added to these numbers denoted left-hand drive.

SPL	denoted a special engine or car
XSP	denoted a special engine
XSP 234-2	denoted a special engine built to type 234
ST	sometimes denoted a special test car or more precisely a racing car
TFR	denoted a car built specifically for the Targa Florio Race

Some cylinder heads were polished and specially prepared. Master tuners like Harry Weslake would stamp their identification marks on the head and they could then tell you all about the head, such as its compression ratio, valve material and potential output. Figures on a head sometimes indicated the clearance volume from which the compression ratio could be deduced. Most well known component makers used serial numbers which gave a record of special content.

To avoid confusing the public, special cars usually had different numbers to those used in standard production. For instance, the number HBJ7-63H-73-9 can be broken down as follows: H-BJ7 – based on BJ7; 63 – 1963 race car; H – Warwick-built; 9 – car number 9. However, as special numbers too readily identified cars and engines as being of special or enhanced performance, production-type numbers were sometimes fitted to obscure this fact from scrutineers.

The plate attached by rivets to the engine was not always accepted by race organisers as bearing the authentic engine number, as it was relatively easy to remove or alter it. Some engines were therefore hand-stamped. An RAC stamp next to the engine number usually means that an RAC scrutineer has measured the engine and certified the cubic capacity for some event. Body numbers were usually stamped on plates on the bulkhead.

MG had a love of red paint and the special Austin Healey engines built by them were usually painted this colour. We used to paint sub-standard components yellow, to warn that they should not be used. However, yellow was often used as a code colour and thus some confusion followed.

Many people have assumed that a log book with the manufacturer's name as first owner signifies a works car. Unfortunately, this only means that the company had registered the car prior to delivery to a retail customer. This practice no longer exists.

I have tried to give all the information available. If you cannot identify your own car from this information, I am afraid there is little chance of anyone being able to help you. The fact that some of the composite alpha-numeric systems we used will cause pain to the computer at Swansea (where all UK car registrations now take place) gives some of us pleasure.

We now come to the special cars. Unfortunately not all the cars of this nature can be contained in a work such as this. In the main only the 100 and 3000 series are detailed.

XII was the first Healey Hundred, later changing overnight at the Motor Show to become the first Austin Healey 100. With the chassis number J4001, and engine number 1B136576, it was originally built as a left-hand drive car and registered KWD 947. Its headlamps were below the new height limit: on all cars afterwards they were fitted above 26 inches to the centre. This car was used for tests and early development. It started life on 16-inch pressed steel Austin wheels and 10-inch diameter drums. No accurate record exists of what happened to it.

X220 and X221 were the two 4-cylinder fixed head coupés. ONX 113, painted red and black, started life with a standard 4-cylinder engine number 1B139174 and chassis number BN1 142616. It was used by DMH for many years, ending up with a 100 S engine and disc brakes. A wonderful long-distance touring car, it was finally sold in 1962.

OAC1, the first of the two coupés, started life with a 4-cylinder engine number 1B139123 and chassis number BN1 149458. This car featured an opening rear window operated by a vacuum motor off a New York taxi. The early prototype 6-cylinder engine was fitted for test purposes. This car was sold to Phillip Fotheringham Parker, who had Harry Weslake tune the engine extensively to make it a real flyer. These coupés were built as a possible extension to the model range but were later dropped: it was considered that too many variations would hamper production and the demand for open cars exceeded production.

X224 was a most involved project. DMH purchased a Grand Prix Ferrari

The Grand Prix 2.5-litre Ferrari after being rebuilt at the Cape.

from the Marquis de Portago. Then in a pretty sick state, this Ferrari was reputedly the one with which Trintignant won at Monte Carlo. Peter Collins, at that time a member of the Ferrari team, was a prime mover in this project. He obtained all the technical information and parts to enable the engine to be rebuilt to run on petrol. On a methanol base fuel, the engine supposedly gave over 250 bhp. On a lower compression ratio on petrol it was claimed to give 210 bhp. The engine was rugged, light and reliable, but its power output was well down on claimed figures. It also consumed oil at a very high rate.

One of the long-nosed 100 Six competition cars that had been used at Sebring was cut about, and the Ferrari de Dion rear axle cum gearbox fitted. The mounting points for radius arms were copied from the Ferrari and welded to the chassis. 100 S brakes and hubs were fitted to the ends of the axle. 100 S suspension was used at the front, with MG A rack and pinion steering. The engine was installed with forward mounted oil tanks. It had no provision for a dynamo, and in order to comply with regulations a Lucas 22290 dynamo was fitted in the air intake with a 4-blade propeller. This was supposed to generate at high speed. The battery had to cope with starting only, a magneto providing the ignition. We tried the car late one autumn afternoon on the Silverstone Grand Prix circuit. The road holding and braking were excellent but although very good times were obtained the engine was short of power.

Peter drove this car in Nassau but was plagued with high oil consumption, needing to stop for oil replenishment. On return from Nassau the car was

Austin Healey: The Story of the Big Healeys

fitted with one of the 100 Six competition engines giving 175 bhp. With this engine the performance was much better. Roy Salvadori tried the car on the GP circuit at Silverstone in August 1958, getting down to 1 min 52 sec – some 4 seconds quicker than with the Ferrari engine. Roy drove the car in the Nassau races that year, achieving second place in one race and retiring with oil on the clutch plate in the second. After the race the car was dismantled and scrapped. The Ferrari bits were reassembled in the GP car and this was sold in 1960.

X230–ST 296: this car was used as a face-lift exercise to try a four head-lamp scheme. It was not possible to make a decent looking job of this on the narrow Austin Healey body. It reverted to a normal front and was used to try fitting rack and pinion steering. It was later rebuilt to racing specification and sold.

X300, X301, X303: these numbers related to work done on the 3000 to produce the prototype convertible. One car was the result.

X312 and X313: these were two coupés based on the 3000 chassis. X312 was the more advanced car, incorporating Girling 4-wheel disc brakes and MkIII, Stage Two type rear suspension with torque arms. The engine was a competition type with alloy head high lift camshaft and three 2-inch SU HD6 carburettors. The interior was completely restyled. Peter Wilkes of Rover borrowed it and was critical of the seating, being convinced that more comfortable seats could be fitted without loss of room. Peter had two seats

A special car on show at the 1977 National Day. This Austin Healey consists of an X250 'T' (for tourer) chassis fitted with a front end used as a styling exercise (X230) in grafting on 4 head lamps. The chassis incorporated a De Dion rear axle assembly and was road tested in August 1960. We never liked it.

Those Special Cars

from us and modified them with considerable improvement. This car had the high 3.54 to 1 rear axle and overdrive. The fuel tank was increased to 18 gallons' capacity. Doug Thorpe did the styling and we made a wire framework of the key dimensions. Jensen then built the car onto a 3000 convertible.

The possibility of the car being produced by BMC as a 3000 model was investigated seriously. BMC had Dick Burzi make a second body, X313, with fewer alterations to the 3000 panels and units. However, Jensen's costs for additional tooling to produce the body was considered to be too high. It was also felt that the model would clash with the MG C-GT. The model was designed to be produced as well as the 3000 convertible and not to replace it. The project was dropped and the two cars sold. They are now in the hands of Don Humphries, a keen member of the Austin Healey Club. I will keep Don to his promise to let me try X312 when he has completed the restoration work. In its youth it was a superb car, fast, economical and effortless to drive for long distances.

X220, 221, 312 and 313 were the only coupés produced by the works. Doug Wilson Spratt in conjunction with Jim McManus produced a number of Austin Healey-based coupés called WSMs.

X3 was an exercise carried out in 1953 using a Morris Minor body shell and Austin Healey engine with part of the chassis. This was to see if it was possible to use a low cost production saloon body and make a sports car out of it. No one liked the result and it was sold for scrap. The work load on the design and experimental departments was so high that many projects were abandoned before completion.

X201 known as the P Type multitube chassis, was a project started in 1955. We designed and built a chassis out of 1-inch square section tube with standard 100 front suspension. The rear suspension was a simple de Dion layout, using two cantilever $\frac{1}{4}$ elliptic springs and a single upper radius arm. We built an axle centre, using part of a production axle. The engine and gearbox were discarded 1953 racing units. A rudimentary body was fitted: this resembled a TC MG Midget that had been sat on by an elephant. The ride and handling of this car were excellent but a cost investigation revealed that a properly bodied car of this type of construction would have been much more expensive than the Austin Healey production cars. The car was stripped and the remains sold as scrap. Someone rebuilt the car out of the remains and used it successfully for hill climbing.

A large number of good cars and units were scrapped over the years. The cost of putting these cars into a condition suitable for resale would have exceeded the price that might have been obtained, while to have sold them in their existing state would have created problems with service enquiries.

X170 was an attempt to make a car to carry four people. It again used a de Dion type rear axle. The combination of this rear axle with four seats resulted in an unduly large and expensive car. Austin Healey panels were extended to cloak the car in a body. It was obvious that this was not the way to go with a replacement for the 100 and the project was cancelled. The car was sold to someone on the understanding that it was a one-off and we did not want to know it. I never heard any more about it either.

X207 was the next stage of development from the 100 to 100 Six. Based on the standard 100 car with 90-inch wheelbase, this car was fitted with an early 6-cylinder engine. The body was modified to include two seats for children, to become what we called the 'chummy'. This car was nearly right, but the chassis needed lengthening in order to provide useful seating. However, it did show the possibilities in an occasional 4-seater and led to our decision to make these alterations with the new 100 Six. The car was sold to Peter Wilkes – he came into the factory looking for sports cars and this fitted the bill. Experimental cars like this that were based on a standard body shell were sometimes sold to knowledgeable people like Peter or John Harris, who were capable of maintaining them with a minimum of technical assistance. They also provided considerable amounts of useful feedback in the form of just criticisms and suggestions.

BN5 was to have been very much a base model with single carburettor, 'Windsor' type disc wheels, tubeless tyres and without overdrive. It is sometimes advantageous to be able to advertise a base model at an extremely low price and then only have the expensive luxury model available. The performance in BN5 form was considerably inferior to the BN1 and BN2 models and wisely this model was not put into production. However, one car was built to this specification – BN5 25927, registration number WAC 247. This car was modified to a higher specification and used as a practice car for the Mille Miglia before being sold.

The simple rigid platform frame of the Sprite was an ideal basis for many special bodied and equipped cars. The sheer number of specials produced over its 20-year life is too great to cover in this book. The old design continues today as the MG Midget, and despite its early origin still outperforms the modern exotics with rear engines and wedge lines.

WAEC – a code devised from 'wheel at each corner', was the result of a meeting with Austin. This meeting was devised to rationalise action on a possible replacement for the Sprite-Midget series. The decision taken was that Syd Enever at MG should produce a conventional type sports car with front engine and rear drive, Austin would produce a transverse front engine car

One of the many special Sprites: the Dalton-Colgate Sprite for Le Mans 1960, which used a special Falcon shell. The screen had to be that big to comply with regulations. The car won its class at 85.6 mph for 24 hours. (Edward Eves)

and we would produce a mid-engined car with transverse units. All of these cars were to use hydrolastic suspension. Three cars resulted but none of them went further than the prototype stage. WAEC was not a bad car, but being heavier than the Sprite did not have very good performance. The cockpit was good and roomy but this configuration results in limited luggage space. All three models suffered from the use of hydrolastic suspension. Whilst this suspension system can be developed to give excellent ride and handling, it is difficult to vary or tune it. There are too many possible variations. With a normal spring suspension controlled by dampers it is much easier to achieve the desired result and it is a lot lighter. These three cars never came to anything.

SR was a very special car, built specifically for Le Mans. Over the years, we had been successful at Le Mans. In the mid-1960s we ran special editions of the Sprite for class wins and it was felt that we should make an attempt for a high overall position. The only engine within the BMC range that could possibly do this was the 2-litre twin cam V8 Coventry Climax racing engine. After a career of winning formula one Grand Prix races and the world championship, these engines were now obsolete due to the change to a 3-litre formula. So a plan was formulated to build a Le Mans car for the 1968 race, using one of these engines.

Brian Healey organised the supply of the engine with Lennard Lee and Wally Hassan. Lennard Lee and his firm Coventry Climax have never received full credit for their tremendous efforts with racing engines, which resulted in so many Grand Prix victories and the end of foreign dominance. The 2-litre V8 Coventry Climax engine was a beautiful unit with its light alloy cylinder block and finely engineered components. Two engines remained – one with the later flat plane crankshaft which made the exhaust system simpler. Both engines had had a long and successful career, winning many races. A considerable amount of hard work was put in by Wally Hassan and Harry Spears to rebuild them. Ray Wood, Lucas's competition manager, rebuilt the fuel injection equipment. After a long period of idleness these engines once again gave their rated output of 240 bhp.

The basis of the car was steel monocoque with a suspension system copied from the Ford GT40. The bodywork was of Birmabright aluminium alloy. Two Sprite MkIV cross flow radiators were positioned behind the doors. 15-inch light alloy centre lock wheels carried Dunlop racing tyres and Girling light alloy racing brakes were operated by twin cylinders via an adjustable balance bar. The whole project was produced to a very tight time scale.

The car was very solidly built – in fact it was too heavy and more suitable

SR under construction, showing the Hewland gearbox, Coventry Climax 2-litre V8 engine, Girling light alloy racing caliper, side-mounted Sprite radiator and the monocoque chassis frame.

Clive Baker testing SR at Silverstone, with unpainted Birmabright light alloy body panels.

for a 3- or 5-litre engine. We have always tended to make our cars too strong and too heavy, a feature which brings benefits in normal use but is a handicap in racing. Considerable trouble was experienced due to failure of the joint between the engine and the gearbox. At first it was assumed that the failure was due to a faulty plate but stronger plates also failed. The problem was finally overcome by Wally Hassan, who had additional bosses for bolts welded to the lower side of the oil sump. These constant interruptions to the track development programme did not allow sufficient time for the optimum handling to be achieved. John Harris, an old Healey driver and competitor in GT40s, was not satisfied, but we felt that adjustments to be made during practice at Le Mans would be successful. Fortunately, the race was then postponed from June to September. The delay meant that our entry was just possible.

Our entry for Le Mans consisted of the SR driven by Andrew Hedges, Clive Baker and John Harris, and a 1,293-cc special-bodied Sprite, driven by Roger Enever and Alec Poole. Peter Browning, BMC competitions manager, led our timekeepers with Les Needham. Walter Hassan and Harry Spears of Coventry Climax came to help with the engine and Digger Digby led a formidable team of signallers. Practice was uneventful, only mirror adjustments being necessary. The Sprite lapped in 4 min 53.6 sec, an average speed of 165.15 kph. The SR achieved 4 min 22.1 sec, an average of 185 kph. On the

Rear view of SR, still unpainted.

straight the Sprite was doing 151 mph and the SR 163 mph.

The race started at 3 pm on a track wet with rain. The SR started promisingly but had to stop for a plug change. After 21 laps the clutch release mechanism jammed in the out position. The release sleeve had seized on the gearbox extension and poor Baker was stuck without any drive to the wheels.

Enever and Poole circulated the Sprite with train-like regularity to cover 271 laps at an approximate average speed of 95 mph and consumed 124 gallons of fuel, an average of over 18 mpg. The Sprite won the Motor Trophy for the best performance by a British car. After the race the team enjoyed a lively meal at the Hotel du Croissant. Poor Peter Browning made his speech, at the

SR in the pits at Silverstone. Left to right: John Harris, Jim Cashmore, Barry Bilbie, Brian Healey, GCH and DMH. Note the side air intake to the radiator.

dictates of high authority, to the effect that this would be the last co-operative effort. The proprietor M. L'Hermitte, who was giving up the hotel, provided a farewell drink. During the 20 years we had used his hotel, he never spoke English and I never spoke French, yet we had an excellent understanding.

The SR was rebuilt for Le Mans 1969. Clive Baker and John Harris were the drivers. In practice the car was not pulling anything like its maximum 9,000 rpm on the straight. We checked everything, suspecting that the air flow to the intakes was restricted. Finally in desperation we opened up the gearbox to install a lower top gear ratio. To our surprise we found that Hewland had fitted the wrong ratio. Naturally we carried alternative ratios to those specified but we did not have a spare of the correct ratio. A telephone call got a pair of gears on the plane to Paris, and Brian and Wally collected them while we slept. With the correct ratio all was well. The car lapped in 4 min 13 sec with a maximum of 167 mph. The race started with some very fast laps by the large Porsches with 4.494-litre engines. The SR was lapping swiftly with Baker at the wheel when a tragic accident on one of the early laps blocked the road. In the ensuing traffic jam the engine overheated, causing a leakage at the head joint. Water was entering the bore, and the loss of water forced us to retire the car before further damage was done.

The SR was not finished yet. The next year, 1970, it was rebuilt as XR 37. The body was rebuilt to open form, with advice from Bill Heynes to reduce the drag. A Repco Brabham 3-litre Grand Prix engine was bought from Jack Brabham. This was a very fine adaptation of a basic General Motors alloy V8 design. Its specific output was not high, and on Brabham's advice we used a maximum of 7,500 rpm at which speed it gave 310 bhp. John Harris continued the development work and in the end it handled extremely well. GKN Kent alloys provided some wider wheels. One change that was to give greatly improved handling was the fitting of a new type of GKN plunging drive shaft, which eliminated the stick slip of splines. It was a remarkably efficient piece of equipment. The drivers were our old faithfuls, Andrew Hedges and Roger Enever.

With high hopes we started the race. The weather conditions were appalling. Rain alternated with dry periods, entailing frequent changes of tyres. The Dunlop wet tyres were superb in the wet but would not stand the heat on dry roads. Possibly because of these troublesome conditions, we had great difficulty removing the wheels. Andrew had an unpleasant moment during one of the wet periods. He was unable to come to a complete stop at an accident, and at the same time was struck by another car from behind. The mechanics carried out repairs to the body work but third gear was later to fail. This was replaced in very quick time – a difficult job with a very hot gearbox. At 4 pm we waited for Roger to cross the line on his last lap. Time passed and he finally arrived on foot. The engine had stopped and would not start. The trouble was the failure of a simple wire-wound resistor in the electronic ignition circuit. Undoubtedly vibration had finally been too much for it, and after 23 hours and 50 odd minutes it had expired. It could not have been replaced even if spares were available.

This particular expedition was dogged by ill fortune from the start. On arrival in France, our ferry crushed a number of fishing boats moored to the quayside when docking in Le Havre. We were all delayed – the French customs had a long wait and were in a bloody-minded mood. They checked everything and demanded some extra guarantees, which took some time to obtain from a local shipping agent. This made us late for scrutineering. The officials were also in a difficult mood, demanding that we run the car without the cover over the passenger's seat. We pointed out that their French Matras were allowed through with even greater coverage of the seat, but grudgingly removed it in order to get the car through. We later replaced the cover and ran the race with it.

After the 1970 race, the car less engine was sold to Robert Harrison in Australia. A keen member of the Austin Healey Club, Robert hoped to find a Repco Brabham engine in Australia, where they had been built. However, Repco engines suddenly became popular for use in hill-climb and sprint cars, and the supply dried up. I believe Robert is still trying to complete it.

Replacing the 3000

One is always looking at ways of improving, updating or even replacing a model that is in production. Change occurs for a number of reasons, often obscure to the buying public, and the decision to implement it has to be taken well in advance of the desired change-over point. One is always striving to reduce costs and increase profits and sales. There were fairly frequent changes or modifications to the 3000 each year, and more fundamental measures were under constant consideration by all concerned. There were three car programmes that might have replaced the 3000.

The first proposal was to use a common body for the 3000 and an MG. In 1960 the future of the 6-cylinder Austin Healey was the subject of much discussion between George Harriman, John Thornley and DMH. Jensen had prevented body production being moved to Morris Bodies in Coventry, and thus relations between Jensen and Austin were not too harmonious. The MG B was due to be produced in January 1962 with the 1,622-cc B series engine, and the MkII 3000 was to be introduced in 1961 with three $1\frac{3}{4}$-inch carburettors and the new front grille we had mocked up. There was much to recommend a commonised project – lower unit costs, all production within BMC's factories, fewer spares and increased volume. It had worked with the Sprite and Midget, which were selling in greater volume than a single version could have obtained.

Two prototypes were planned – the ADO 51 Austin Healey and ADO 52 MG. The possibility of pure 'badge engineering', where one car appears as two models, was not considered. There was tremendous marque loyalty for both Austin Healey and MG, of which BMC knew and appreciated the value. For the more discerning type of person who bought sports cars, it was essential that the MG and Healey models should be different in appearance and character, whilst sharing the same main body chassis structure.

The two models were to have versions of the 2,660-cc 4-cylinder AH 100 engine, giving 140 bhp. George Harriman was insistant that three stages of engine tune were settled from the outset with a maximum of 180 bhp. It had been found possible to use a heavy duty diesel camshaft with slightly shorter stroke, giving a nominal capacity of 2.5 litres, and extend the maximum speed of the unit to 6,400 rpm. This engine gave 142 bhp at 5,500 rpm. On paper it was proved that with raised compression ratio and twin choke SU carburettors, 178 bhp could be obtained at 6,200 rpm. This was a very promising sports car unit.

A considerable amount of time was spent scheming the engine into the ADO 23 MG B body unit. The height of the engine was a problem – the bottom end went through the rack and pinion steering and the rocker cover went through the bonnet. By changing the sump, oil pump pick up and crankshaft pulley it was just about possible to clear the steering rack. However, a redesigned bonnet with bulges would be necessary to clear the rocker cover and carburettors. By using a steering box and lever system the revised engine could be lowered sufficiently to enable a bonnet with very slight power bulges to be used. A dry sump lubrication system was investigated as a possible solution to the engine height.

This promising power unit would have been used only in the sports cars as the passenger car requirement was for a 6-cylinder. However, using a common unit for all vehicles would show a significant cost saving and the saloon car engine was not really viable unless a considerable number were also used in sports cars.

To add to the confusion the 6-cylinder Australian 6 was brought into the running. This engine was a 6-cylinder version of the 1622 A series 4-cylinder. Its 3-inch bore and $3\frac{1}{2}$-inch stroke gave it a capacity of 2,433 cc and on a compression ratio of 8.3 to 1 it gave 115 bhp at 5,200 rpm. It was about 106 lb lighter than the 2,912 cc C series unit then in production, and with three SU carburettors and steering box and levers it could be fitted with minimal bulges on the bonnet. The MG B had been designed for a 4-cylinder engine which was fitted as far back as possible in the chassis. The 6-cylinder unit extended 8 inches forward of the front wheel centre line with adverse effect on the weight distribution. This engine was to grow in size and weight until it was as heavy as the 3000 unit yet without its durability and power output.

The original concept of ADO 51 and 52 as a common MG-Austin Healey sports car had a good deal of merit, but the final version was a great disappointment to all concerned. After a somewhat confused origin in 1960, it was eventually announced, as the MG C, in 1967. 56 per cent of the new 6-cylinder engine's weight, with its seven main bearings, was centred on the front wheels. Handling was poor, with very strong understeering characteristics. Despite using the same bore and stroke as the Healey 3000 engine, the maximum power was down and the low speed torque very poor. In fact, the performance of the new engine was but a shadow of that of its predecessor. The car was available as an open 2-seater and as a closed GT car. Its appearance was uninspiring—externally, it was distinguishable from the MG B by larger 15-inch wheels and an awful bulge in the bonnet. It bore no resemblance to the 3000 either in looks or in performance. BMC made great efforts to make a successful competition car out of it, using 3-litre engines with all-alloy cylinder blocks to reduce front-end weight and light alloy bodies to reduce total weight. It was dropped in 1971, after some 9,000 units had been produced.

BMC tried very hard to persuade DMH to agree to his name being used on ADO 51. A number of attempts were made to upgrade the car to a form that was acceptable, but all left one with the feeling that the one-piece classic design of the MG B had been butchered to produce a mediocre sports car. The expensive tooling of the MG B body/chassis assembly (in contrast to the low-cost tooling of the Austin Healey) inhibited any fundamental alterations or improvements. I spent a lot of time with Syd Enever on the project, and though he did everything possible to make a success out of it, I felt that he realised that it was not the way to go. Perhaps if DMH had agreed to his name going on the car, extra development funds might have been made available and it might ultimately have been a success. As things turned out, however, DMH was undoubtedly right to refuse to have his name connected with this unsuccessful vehicle.

Another design to be offered as a replacement for the 3000 was the Austin project XC512. According to which faction one was in, this car was referred to as 'The Thing', 'The Monster' or 'Fireball XL5'. In the mind of its creators, this was to have been the sports car to end all sports cars. The frame featured a very large central tunnel to provide a high degree of torsional rigidity joining two structures carrying the suspension units. The suspension units incorporated the hydrolastic elements developed for the Austin 1800. The front suspension units of conventional top and bottom wishbone type links were carried on heavy rigid platforms bolted to the chassis. At the rear, suspension was also hydrolastic, the wheel being carried on a trailing arm pivoting on an axis at right angles to the chassis centre line. This resulted in the wheel camber angle varying exactly with vehicle roll.

The power unit was the Rolls-Royce 4-litre engine used in the Princess 'R'. These engines with aluminium alloy cylinder block and head used overhead inlet valves and side exhaust valves. The FB engine gave a maximum of over 170 bhp in the form used for the Princess 'R'. To obtain this power, Rolls used a camshaft of wilder characteristics than they liked which resulted in a somewhat lumpy idle and poor low-speed acceleration. The gearbox was a Borg Warner automatic which with its hydraulic torque converter consumed quite a lot of power.

The car had a very wide body of distinctive appearance, with a deep, wide and sharply raked screen. Due to the wide tunnel the seats were set well apart. The body style showed the influence of a project built and displayed by Pinin Farina at the Earls Court Motor Show. This had been built on an Austin Healey 3000 chassis as the result of a design competition won by three students.

Fireball XL5 proceeded to grow under very tight security. DMH and I were shown the thing when it was first completed and being tried. Much of the tooling for production had already been completed or sanctioned and there was not much that anyone could do about it. The thing was a monster, consuming vast amounts of skilled labour, time and money.

DMH and I were struck completely dumb. We could not believe that anyone could conceive that such a device could be seriously proposed as a sports car. It completely missed meeting any requirement that would have made it sell successfully. But the originators seriously believed that they knew better and could produce a better sports car than those who had spent a lifetime with sports cars. The stupendous waste of money – that could so well have been used to produce a common MG-Healey vehicle – was horrifying. Whatever we had said would obviously be ignored.

Disenchantment struck when a well known motoring journalist tried the car on a track. He soon convinced the perpetrators of the Monster that its road holding and handling were diabolical.

This dismal project was to consume yet more money as attempts were made to improve matters by altering the rear suspension to a semi-trailing design that reduced the angles adopted by the wheels on roll. The difficulty was that much of the body structure was already tooled. With its weight and high frontal area, the car's performance was mediocre and to overcome this, Rolls-Royce were requested to produce more power from the engine. Beyond a certain point, with an inlet over exhaust type engine, it is not practical to produce more power. Raising the compression ratio restricts the breathing. The engine was extremely good at its designed output, but to get the additional power demanded called for a new cylinder head. Jack Phillips at Rolls-Royce built a twin overhead valve cylinder head for it. He was amazed at the ease with which he was able to obtain the necessary horsepower: the lower end of the unit was very strong and could readily cope with 300 bhp. In this case it was more than sufficient for the Monster.

Somehow, in the end, common sense prevailed and XC512 disappeared quietly in an ooze of silence and security, having in its short life consumed over a million pounds sterling.

To us, being used to the principle that you make something as quickly and cheaply as possible, and produce a testable representation of the design before committing any tooling, the procedure on XL5 seemed totally wrong.

Whilst Fireball XL5 proceeded at Longbridge, we hatched up another plan. We would fit the Rolls-Royce engine in a 3000 and at the same time would alter the 3000 to enable it to pass all American safety regulations. We obtained an engine from Austin and a body assembly from MG. We took a version of the 3000 axle used on the Princess 'R' which gave an increase in track of almost exactly 6 inches. The idea was to widen the body by 6 inches. This is not an original procedure. My old boss at Armstrong Siddeley, Mervyn Cutler, had done this some years previously and Len Lord did exactly the opposite when he had the prototype Cambridge cut in half and made narrower. In this case, the resultant model was a highly successful one for Austin in terms of long production run and profit. The prototype was built in 1966. We cut the whole assembly in half along the centre line and the two halves were then accurately aligned at 6 inches apart and rigidly fixed. The chassis was re-worked to take the Rolls-Royce engine. The steel understructure had simple 6-inch-wide pieces added while the bonnet, scuttle and boot lid had the pieces welded in and polished smooth. The aperture in the front shroud was reduced to take the normal grille. Two sections were added to the windscreen which was 'glazed' in perspex to save time. The hood also underwent the widening process. The 3000 steering column was cut down and fitted with two universal joints and an AC Delco safety column. It was not possible to use the normal engine-driven fan, so two Smiths electric units were installed.

The Rolls engine was lighter than the iron 3000 unit and with normal 3000 springs and dampers the resultant ride and handling was a great improvement. The car cornered with a minimum of roll and had high directional stability. Even with the power loss in the automatic transmission, the performance was most impressive. As might be expected, the Rolls engine produced a degree of smoothness and silky power unknown in previous sports cars. We took the device to Austin where it was viewed and tried by the top brass at the Kremlin. The reaction was most favourable and instructions were issued for the project to proceed with all possible speed. Syd Enever was to have overall responsibility for the project under the code number ADO24.

Syd quickly and clearly defined the areas of responsibility. We were to arrange the chassis redesign and the collection of material and assembly.

Jensen were to be responsible for the body. Several brief and purposeful meetings were held to finalise the procedure and in February 1967 Austin gave instructions for six pre-production models to be built – two with 4-speed Jaguar gearboxes, two more with additional overdrives, and two with automatic transmission. We were to be reimbursed at the rate of labour at cost plus 150 per cent for overheads and 10 per cent for profit.

Syd's careful planning and clear instructions ensured that the project proceeded very smoothly and rapidly. Thompsons delivered modified frames to Jensen, who delivered finished body assemblies to us. Rolls-Royce were responsible for modifying the engines to meet the USA emission requirements and supplying engines with flywheels for the gearbox versions. Jack Phillips gave me a lesson on how to design the clutch housing that joined engine to gearbox so as to retain the smoothness of the power unit. It is a pity one or two other manufacturers don't take his advice. We had patterns and castings made locally and the whole assembly was to go together quickly and accurately. Due to an ambiguity in the safety regulations, or a misunderstanding, the attractive veneered wood fascia panel of the 3000 was dropped and replaced by one of unattractive appearance.

Two cars were completed, one with Jaguar gearbox and one with gearbox and overdrive. The axles incorporated special hubs of larger size to take Jaguar-pattern wire wheels made by Dunlop. Triple-eared hub caps of chrome plated bronze were provided by the Manganese Bronze and Brass Company. These cars then underwent test and development work. The elimination of the losses in torque converter and automatic transmission produced a much livelier performance. Top gear acceleration figures were better than the 3000 while maximum speed, due to increased frontal area and power, remained the same at 125 mph. The speed at which the radio could be heard in comfort was much increased, and the enlarged interior and boot room most useful.

When the first two cars were nearing completion, at the end of April 1967, Austin reduced the number of pre-production vehicles from six to two. The target date for production of the car had been January 1968, to follow on from the 3000 MkIII which would then be out of production. Shortly afterwards, when everything was proceeding swiftly and smoothly, the whole project was suddenly cancelled and the two cars sold. Just why Austin decided to kill the model will probably never be known. It is probable that the expense of a new model at that time strained the overall budget. Possibly Jaguar spoke out against it, fearing the impact on their sector of the market, possibly the engine commitment was no longer a problem, or possibly the sheer work load on the various departments was intolerable. With the death of the ADO24 project, all hope of a successor to the 3000 ceased.

Competition

After the BMC merger, a regular series of competition committee meetings was inaugurated, with John Thornley presiding, to try to make sense of the various demands from the different publicity departments concerned. The programme for the year was usually agreed late in the preceding year. Previously, the Healey side had covered racing, rallying and record breaking, but gradually the preparation of rally cars was taken over by the BMC competition department, leaving Warwick to concentrate on racing. This produced better results in both fields – the particular objectives for each event were clearly delineated and cars were built to obtain specific results. This also made a good deal of practical sense. Vehicle specifications for rallying and racing differ considerably. The rally car is developed to carry two people, two spare wheels and extra equipment, whilst the race car is built to be as light as regulations and time permit.

The competition manager's life is not a happy one. If he is very successful the advertising budget becomes exhausted and his efforts much less valuable. Some publicity men are so successful in building up the image of a car that senior management become convinced that their product is so good that it does not need the backing of a competition programme. Success can often be more dangerous than failure. The wiser ones find a career in a different field.

The Austin Healey was soon to establish a dominating position in European rallies. The rugged strength of the chassis frame, allied to the reliable units, made the cars excellent long-distance machines. At Abingdon, Marcus Chambers had developed a formidable rally organisation, lacking only a suitable car to achieve real success. In 1958 he took the first step towards establishing a long line of rally successes when he took over the ex-Tommy Wisdom 100 Six, UOC 741. He entered the car in the Tulip Rally, with Jack Sears and Peter Garnier of the *Autocar* as drivers. Together they put up a terrific performance, highlighted by very fast times on hill climbs and circuits. Victory eluded them when the distributor drive failed. The 6-cylinder distributor drive was taken by skew gears from the camshaft and it also drove the mechanical tachometer through skew gears. It was a rather bitty arrangement with too many parts for reliability.

This exciting performance gave Marcus the lever to obtain more support for his efforts. He then entered a team of five cars for the 1958 Alpine in July. John Gott, veteran of many rallies and a great rally planner, led the team. The team pairings were John Gott and Chris Tooley, Jack Sears and Sam Moore, Bill Shepherd and John Williamson, Pat Moss and Ann Wisdom, and Nancy Mitchell and Gill Wilton-Clark. The full potential of the cars was not to be realised, owing to mechanical troubles. A blocked breather pipe caused an excess of oil to get into the clutch of the Moss/Wisdom car and they lost what would have been a certain Coupe des Alpes. They did, however, win the Coupe des Dames. On later rally cars a duplicate breather was added. This improved crankcase ventilation and lowered the pressure in it. The rear crankshaft oil sealing was by means of a thrower and drain tube which could not cope with more than a small amount of pressure in the crankcase. It was an inexpensive arrangement and normally performed adequately throughout the life of the car.

Shepherd and Williamson finished in seventh position overall, collecting a Coupe des Alpes as one of only seven crews to achieve a penalty-free run. Only John Gott was to fail to finish. This car, which had been leading the team, sheared a rear hub extension on the timed climb of Mont Ventoux. I received a monumental blowing up, as this car was the old Tommy Wisdom rally car and the blame was passed on to me. However, I was able to show that this was a standard component which had done the 1957 Sestrière Rally and the 1958 Monte Carlo and Tulip rallies. After the heat subsided, Syd investigated the situation.

The 100 Six used a hub extension designed by one of the BMC factories to fit wire wheels. Due to a series of changes, mainly to ease production, the section at the root of the inner cone could be too thin. Modification can create a gradual weakening of a component until continual increase of power and harder useage results in failure. There was some pretty frantic work on this part, to ensure that such a failure did not occur again. The final design of rear hub extension BTC406/7 was increased in strength by about twelve times.

Competition

The hard life this car had led, and its age, made its retirement from the front line of competition sensible. It was sold to Peter Smith, who continued to campaign it with success.

The Liège-Rome-Liège or Marathon de la Route is best described as a high speed blind over 3,000 miles of some of the roughest roads and toughest passes in Europe. This is covered in four days of non-stop motoring. Rules are simplified without handicapping and with results in overall positions, as in a motor race. It had generally been dominated by foreign cars. Abingdon prepared four 100 Sixes for the 1958 event. Three were entered for the manufacturer's team prize and with John Gott and Ray Brookes in an MG A made up the British entry for the Club Team Prize. Pat Moss and Ann Wisdom put up an astounding performance to finish fourth overall and first in the unlimited GT category. Gerry Burgess and Sam Croft-Pearson finished tenth, and Nancy Mitchell and Anne Hall fifteenth. This gave them the manufacturer's team prize. John Gott and Ray Brookes finished to complete the victory with the club prize for the British team.

To start off 1959, Jack Sears and Peter Garnier again contested the Tulip Rally to win the Grand Touring category, beating Ferrari, Aston Martin and Mercedes. This year also saw the introduction of the 3000 with its 2,912-cc engine. The additional engine capacity with increased power and torque provided a welcome improvement – the 100 Six with its 2,639-cc engine had always been at a disadvantage in the 3-litre class.

A team of three of the new HBN7 3000s was prepared at Abingdon for the 1959 Alpine. The drivers were to be John Gott and Chris Tooley, Jack Sears and Sam Moore, and Bill Shepherd and John Williamson. Tommy Wisdom and Jack Hay were to drive a Sprite specially prepared to Tommy's instructions at Warwick. The busy rally drivers made a 'recce' of the rally stages and were unanimous in the opinion that the time set by the organisers was impossible for the GT category. In contrast, the time allowed for the touring cars or saloons was considered to be too easy.

The rally was to be in four stages. The first stage started at Marseilles, followed secondary roads over the Cols d'Allos, Cayolle, Vars, Izoard and Montgenevre into Italy, via Biella and Monza to Bolzano in the Dolomites and ended at Cortina d'Ampezzo. There were two tests in this stage – a speed test over the Col d'Allos on a road reaching 2,250 meters above sea level, and three timed laps of the famous Monza circuit. Stage two took the competitors into Austria, on narrow roads with pretty poor surfaces which were an added handicap to the faster cars. The route crossed the Brenner Pass and returned to Italy, completing the second stage at Merano. From Merano the third stage took in the Stelvio and Gavia passes. The Stelvio, with a maximum altitude of 2,758 metres, the scene of many hill climb events, is always popular with the big car drivers because of its superb engineering. In contrast, the Gavia Pass which follows is a minor route and very poorly surfaced. Europe's oldest pass, the Grand St Bernard, completed the section to end at St Gervais in France. The final stage of 750 miles to Cannes was to take the field of tired crews and tired cars over ten more Alpine passes. The final test was Mont Ventoux – often used as a speed hill climb and part of the Monte Carlo Rally course. At 2,000 metres, drivers, cars and support crews suffered the effects of a rarified atmosphere. It was always difficult to close special sections effectively to ordinary traffic. In an earlier Alpine Rally, Tommy Wisdom accompanied by his wife Bill had a very nasty accident when a tourist who had been picknicking in the mountains came down the road to meet him head on. Tommy and Bill ended up in some hospital from which DMH rescued them. Medical assistance on rallies can never compare with closed circuit racing and is a constant nightmare for competitors.

The best laid plans often go awry, and this was to be the case with the 1959 Alpine. Jack Sears dropped out when the fan cut the radiator in pieces, and Bill Shepherd cracked the sump and lost his oil. John Gott and Chris Tooley, sole survivors of the three car team, finished second in their class, despite losing considerable time trying to repair a damaged radiator. The 3000s had shown great speed on all the tests, leaving the opposition far behind.

In the following Liège-Rome-Liège, Peter Riley and Rupert Jones won their class. Pat Moss and Ann Wisdom – the most successful women's team of all time – beat many of the all-male teams on a very large number of events. In the 1959 German Rally they made fastest time on every test but one, to finish in second position. Don and Erle Morley finished fourth in the RAC Rally on their first drive with the Austin Healey team. The results were somewhat confused by conditions and protests. The 3000 was performing well but revealing a weakness in the gearbox.

1960 brought further successes. Pat Moss and Ann Wisdom continued to outperform the men drivers, the high point being their convincing win in the Liège-Rome-Liège Rally where 3000s filled the first three places in the class. Pat and Ann also won a Coupe des Alpes and the Coupe des Dames in the Alpine Rally, being placed second overall. John Gott narrowly missed obtaining a Coupe des Alpes. The 3000 dominated special stages but was not obtaining the number of outright victories it deserved. Sometimes the system of marking weighed heavily against the Healey. The standards set for Grand Touring cars were far too high in relation to those applying to Touring cars. The Scandinavian drivers, used to driving on rough roads, snow and ice in their home countries, figured regularly in top positions on some pretty ordinary cars.

In 1961 the Healey drivers continued to do battle. The Morley brothers won the Alpine Rally outright and finished fourteenth in the Tulip. Peter Riley came third in the Acropolis Rally. Stuart Turner now replaced Marcus Chambers as competition manager. Marcus had born the brunt of the hard

After the 1960 Alpine Rally, Pat Moss and Ann Wisdom display the collection of individual and team trophies won by the three Austin Healey 3000s.

The 1962 Alpine Rally: Don and Erle Morley on the way to their second consecutive victory in this tough event.

In the competition department at Abingdon, Peter Browning (left), Stuart Turner and Timo Makinen with two 3000s for the 1964 Spa-Sofia-Liège.

work over the department's early days and had established the Healey as a rally winner. Stuart made a number of changes, including the later introduction of some Scandinavian drivers. Pat Moss finished second in the RAC Rally to Eric Carlsson, one of the great Swedish drivers, whom she later married. Her co-driver Ann Wisdom later married Peter Riley.

    The Morley brothers repeated their 1961 Alpine success by winning the rally outright in 1962. The red Healeys with their white hard tops were an impressive spectacle in full cry up an Alpine pass. The great strength of the cars permitted them to be driven at great speed over rough surfaced and dirt roads. The combination of Laycock overdrive and 4-speed gearbox, giving

The works team for the Spa-Sofia-Liège Rally, 1964: Timo Makinen and Don Barrow; Rauno Aaltonen and Henry Liddon (who won the race outright); and Tony Ambrose and Paddy Hopkirk. In those days, these six men were the best.

a usable total of six speeds, was a great contribution enabling the driver to keep the car 'on the cam' and have plenty of power available at all times.

Paddy Hopkirk, a very energetic Ulsterman, came into the team and was to become one of a select band of drivers capable of holding their own with the Scandinavians. He gained yet another second place for the Healey in the RAC Rally in 1962, with Pat Moss third. In 1963 Paddy finished sixth in the Liège and won the Austrian Alpine Trial in 1964. DMH had won the pre-war edition of this race event on an Invicta. Paddy also won the Monte Carlo Rally in a Mini, beating the two Finns, Timo Makinen and Rauno Aaltonen. In 1964, Aaltonen won the last Spa-Sofia-Liège with the Healey.

Paddy Hopkirk and Henry Liddon on the way to sixth place overall in the 1963 Liège-Rome-Liège Rally.

Timo Makinen in action. This is the fastest way to rally through a forest!

Under Stuart Turner the competition department started selecting 'horses for courses' and began to rely less on the Healey. It was important to obtain successes with the Mini as this was being produced in large numbers. The Healey production was limited, partly by the ability of Jensen Motors to sustain output at a weekly rate of 150, and the future of the car was shrouded with uncertainties.

During 1965 the Commission Sportive Internationale, the international body controlling motor sport, introduced changes in the regulations for cars taking part in races and rallies. These revised regulations were to exclude the Austin Healey from many international rallies. Changes of formulae and regulations are one of the hazards of competition motoring. However the 3000 was entered in a number of events and the Morley brothers won their

Don and Erle Morley climbing one of the tough mountain passes in the 1965 Alpine Rally. They achieved second overall position.

Timo Makinen setting the pace for second overall position in the 1964 RAC Rally. Co-drivers like Don Barrow had to have nerves of steel and a singular ability to concentrate upon their duties.

Competition

class in the Tulip Rally, the Geneva Rally and the Alpine. The times set for GT cars in the Alpine prevented any of these cars winning a Coupe des Alpes.

The highlight of the 1965 season was the performance of Timo Makinen with Paul Easter as co-driver in the RAC Rally. In 1964 Timo had finished second. In 1965 he led for the greater part of the rally. Extremely slippery ice on a Welsh hill enabled his team mate Rauno Aaltonen to overtake him on a Mini and win. BMC were naturally pleased with first and second positions, but all concerned with competition were sad that Timo had not won on the 3000 after one of his best performances. The Mini was of course the Giant Killer of all times. Timo's car, EJB 806C, later found the best possible home with Ted Worswick.

Over the years we had competed in various of the Targa Florio races in Sicily. The first time was in 1948 when Johnny Lurani and Serafini ran a Healey saloon. Tommy Wisdom and Bernard Cahier raced a Sprite in the 1959 event. Both cars finished well up in the results. In 1965 I learned by accident that Castrol were to make a film of the race. I immediately rang up Stuart Turner who was naturally interested in any additional publicity. A team consisting of Paul Hawkins and Timo Makinen on a 3000, Andrew Hedges and Paddy Hopkirk on an MG Midget, and Rauno Aaltonen and Clive Baker on a Sprite were entered. Abingdon's mechanics drove the cars to the race where various members of the team converged from a variety of starting

Timo Makinen on the 1965 RAC Rally, with over 300 watts of Lucas lamps in use. Light and sound helped to warn spectators of the cars' rapid approach.

points, Aaltonen coming from Finland, Timo from Holland after the Tulip Rally, and Paddy from Luxembourg. Margot came to do the interpreting. We organised accommodation in the Hotel Lido at Trabia, roughly half-way between Palermo and the start of the race.

The Targa Florio was started in 1906 and was run over normal roads in a mountainous region. The 44.7-mile circuit starts and finishes at Cerda. Climbing from 273 metres to 600 metres at Bivio Caltavuturo, it then winds down to Scillato at 250 metres to climb up to 570 metres at Bivio Polizzi. It continues to wind up and down to Campo Felice at 50 metres, which is followed by 6 kilometers of straight, the fastest piece of the course. The road finally climbs slightly to the start/finish. Its 44.7 miles includes interminable bends of varying shape and camber. Each one seems to be different. A mistake at any corner can result in striking a solid bank or a series of granite posts, or going over the edge and down a rocky hill slope. The countryside is pretty barren but beautiful. It is a difficult course to learn because of the numerous bends. The road surface is repaired before the practice starts but pot holes soon develop. Sicily in spring can produce almost any type of weather and because of the length of the course this can vary from start to finish.

For unofficial practising and learning the course, competitors usually hire Fiats from Hertz. These clapped-out cars must be sold very cheaply later. In 1965 we took round an additional 3000 for practice. Timo drove one of the Castrol photographers round in this to record an excellent impression of the course. The race is hard on the cars and drivers. The 1965 race was won by the local schoolteacher, Nino Vaccarella at 68.27 mph, which gives some idea of the difficulty of the course.

Tyre wear was a real problem with the 3000. In order to cover three laps and combine a fuel stop with a tyre change, the car had to be driven at well below its best speed. Timo and Paul were understandably disappointed at not being able to go flat out. The Sprite was naturally the fastest, having been developed for this race. However, well planned races seldom go to schedule. The cars started at half-minute intervals, with the smaller slower cars in the lead. On the fifth lap, Paul had an ignition failure and ran back to the pits for a rotor arm, only to be told that the spare was in the door pocket. With some typical Australian expressions, Paul toiled up the hill, fitted the new rotor and continued. However, valuable time had been lost—more than enough to give class victory to a Ferrari GTO. The Sprite came in after a very rapid four laps for refuelling. The front disc brakes jammed on, due to the heat generated on the many bends, and John Harris and I took 13 minutes to get the pistons back and the pads free. The brakes did not function properly for the rest of the race. The slower Midget had a trouble free run. The best lap by the Sprite was 43 min 42 sec, by the 3000, 44 min 45 sec and by the Midget 44 min 26 sec. By coincidence, each car ended with second place in its class.

The Hotel Lido where we were based consisted of a restaurant and a row

Timo Makinen in the 1965 Targa Florio. With co-driver Paul Hawkins, he came second in class. On roads like these, a very long drop awaited the reckless or the unlucky.

of small concrete rooms on the edge of the beach. Early morning swimming was the order of the day. We occupied the whole place and worked on the cars in the dusty forecourt. We spent one evening with Dereck Blunsden, a friend from Cornwall, who was working in the sulphur mines. He was a great help at the various races until he returned home. The Mafia is a part of life in Sicily. They are not known to trouble tourists and I learned that they provide more effective insurance against theft at lower cost than the insurance companies. One of the Porsche entrants made some rude remarks about the Mafia during scrutineering and got some harsh treatment for his pains. Unfortunately this also affected the rest of us – the scrutineers immediately closed up and worked to rule. This meant that we had to find bumpers for the MG B, which we had removed in the UK. Paul Hawkins passed a touring MG B parked on the course somewhere, which had an Australian flag on it. He stopped and left this message on the windscreen: 'Report to Stuart Turner, Hotel Lido Trabia, immediately, Paul Hawkins'. Two young Aussies drove up later full of excitement. We soon stripped their car of all the necessary bits and gave them two passes for the race, asking them to call in at the factory at Abingdon on their return to England. They were absolutely thrilled to have bits of their car running in the race, and of course wanted the original bits back at the end.

In a later race, poor Baker was to collect a spectator on the bonnet of the Sprite when the unfortunate fellow tried to run across the road. With his vision obscured, Baker hit a granite post on the outside of the bend and put the Sprite out of the race. The man's friends, fearing police action, removed him into the mountains. The police arrested Baker – we believe for his own protection – and later returned him by helicopter to the pits – a free man, without a stain on his character! Another year, Baker broke a half shaft in the mountains yet lost little time on the lap, claiming to have carried out the repair singlehanded. Later we met the two young English enthusiasts who were fortunately at the scene and did most of the work.

It is sad that many people will never know the spectacle of this last of the great road races. Despite an almost unblemished record, with very few serious accidents in well over fifty races, new safety regulations caused it to disappear. The difficulty of the Piccolo Circuito delle Madonie and the low average speed of the cars were a great safety factor. The enthusiast visiting Sicily today should drive round this circuit, where at various times the greatest drivers spanning sixty years of racing have done their best.

Stuart Turner left BMC in 1967 to join Castrol who, although a relatively small oil company, provided service and support to the majority of successful teams. Peter Browning took over the reigns of the Competition Department until it was disbanded under British Leyland reorganisation. (Stuart later took over Ford's competition activities and many of the rally drivers naturally followed him. Ford then proceeded to dominate the rally scene as they did Grand Prix racing, with the Keith Duckworth-designed 3-litre V8.)

For the 1967 RAC Rally, the portents appeared to be right – a 3000 could run in the class for Group 6 sports cars, and it would be a likely winner. All the works rally 3000s had by then been sold, but Peter Browning owned one of the 1964 cars which he had re-registered with his personal number, PWB 57. Rauno Aaltonen was very keen on the project. Although the 3000 had never won the RAC, it had been runner-up no less than four times and had finished seven of these great events.

Competition mechanic Nobby Hall (Luigi) proceeded to convert PWB 57 into the ultimate in rally-winning 3000s. The passenger side of the car was cut away so that the exhaust system ran above the floor ending in front of the rear wheels. This took care of the one weakness the Healey had as a rally car – ground clearance. The engine was based on the aluminium alloy block, bored 'forty thou' oversize to 2,968cc. Three twin choke 45 DCOE 13 Weber carburettors with magnesium alloy manifolds controlled the mixture to the light alloy head. With the careful assembly lavished on it, the engine output

The 200-hp engine of the 1967 RAC car, with its 3 Weber carbs.

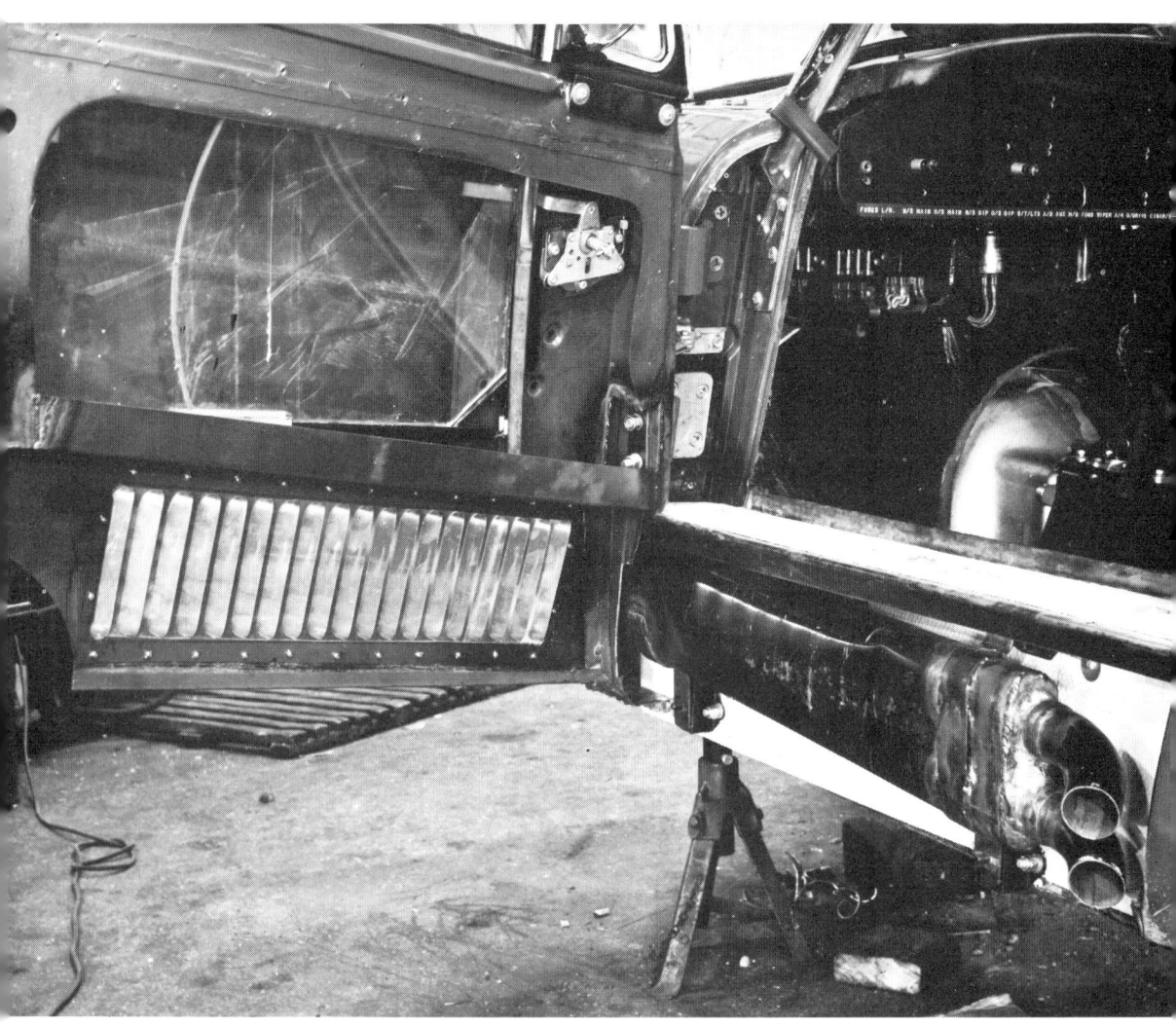

The 1967 RAC car under construction. The raised exhaust system, occupying part of the door aperture, increased ground clearance considerably – and also helped to keep the navigator awake! Many owners would have appreciated this modification.

probably exceeded 200 bhp. A Borg and Beck diaphragm spring clutch coupled the engine to the close-ratio straight-cut gearbox. An overdrive with boosted pressures, controlled by a switch in the gear lever knob, operated only on top gear. The 3000 C series rear axle was fitted with 4.3 to 1 ratio and Girling disc brakes and was sprung on 14 leaf rear springs. Pretty extensive undershielding protected the under belly and 15-inch Minilite magnesium

Competition

The last competition 3000 – the 1964 rally car after it had been rebuilt for the 1967 RAC Rally. The rally was cancelled due to an outbreak of foot and mouth disease.

alloy wheels were fitted to the standard 3000 splined hubs. Dunlop produced some special radial ply weather master tyres of 185 section that gave fantastic grip under rally conditions. Flared wheel arches and a Healey fibreglass hardtop with roll-over bar completed the bodywork. Special seating and rally equipment brought the weight up to 2,700lb.

The ultimate rally car was tested and pronounced ready to go. But a cloud hung over the country: foot and mouth disease had spread from continental Europe to attack our cattle. Right up to the last moment it was hoped that it would be safe to run the rally, but reluctantly it had to be cancelled in the

Austin Healey: The Story of the Big Healeys

public interest. Peter, Nobby, Rauno and the many thousand Healey supporters were disconsolate that the machine should have been denied the opportunity to win the rally – given any luck at all, it most surely would have.

Peter, sadly, disposed of PWB 57. It was not really suitable for normal use with its appetite of 8–15 miles per gallon of five star petrol and limited accommodation. Thus the last of a great line of rally vehicles had to make way for the less inspiring cars that were to follow.

The 6-cylinder cars were also to establish an excellent record in the world of track racing. It was apparent early on that the British market could never absorb the output of British manufacturers and this led BMC to concentrate on overseas events. Promotion of the Austin Healey in particular was always geared to increasing sales in the USA, and of the American races the Sebring event was chosen as having most impact on the market. Occasionally, circumstances forced us to compete in track events in Britain, but in the main this was left to private owners.

Sebring 1963 was a memorable race. The BMC entry consisted of:

No. 34 Austin Healey 3000	Paddy Hopkirk and Don Morley
No. 33 Austin Healey 3000	Bob Olthoff and Ronnie Bucknum
No. 69 Austin Healey Sprite	John Colgate and Clive Baker
No. 47 MG B	Jim Parkinson and Jack Flaherty
No. 49 MG B	Denise McCluggage and Cristabel Carlisle

Clive Baker with one of the works Sebring 3000s, 54 FAC, at Nassau, 1963.

Competition

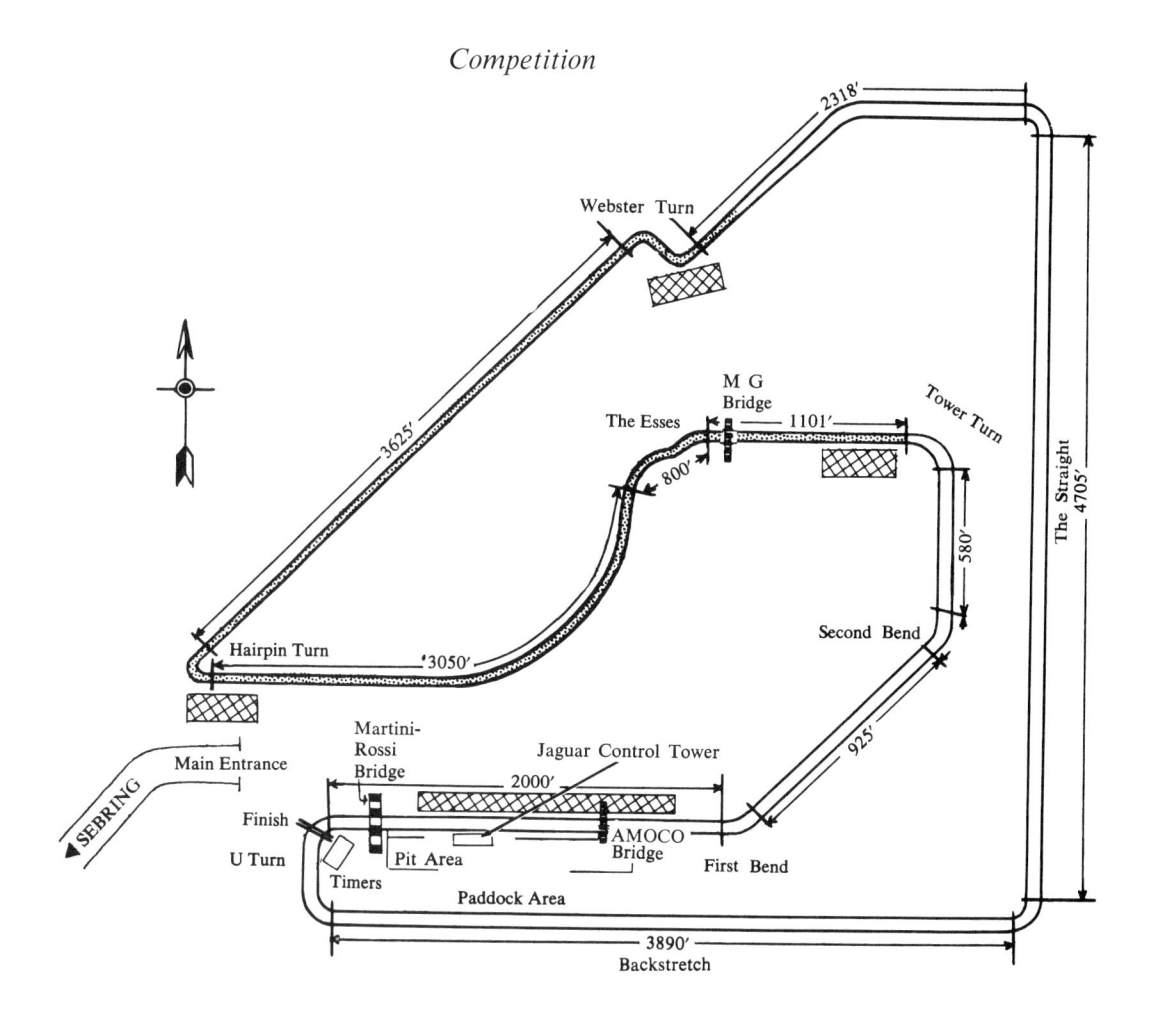

The clever layout of the Sebring race track, Florida, built on the old Hendryk's Field wartime B17 bomber base. The first FIA 12-hour Grand Prix of Endurance was held here in 1952. Sebring is one of the longest (5.2 miles) circuits based on an airfield. Aircraft use the wide runway (the backstretch) during the race.

At that time, Triumph were the main competition for sports car sales in the American market. No less than five Triumphs were competing, together with two Morgans with the same 2,138-cc 4-cylinder Triumph engine that Ted Grinham had designed for the Vanguard, nearly 20 years before. From a production saloon and Ferguson tractor engine it had developed into a very fine sports car power unit. The field was large, including two 5-litre Chaparrals, six 4.7-litre Shelby AC Cobras, six 5.3-litre Corvette Stingrays, eleven

Ferraris, five Porsches, four 3.8-litre Jaguars, four 1.3-litre Arbarth Simcas, two 1.2-litre Lotus cars, two 1.6-litre TVRs, a Volvo, a René Bonnet, an Israeli Sabra and a 1,098-cc Austin Mini Cooper.

The BMC team under Stuart Turner were a pretty effective band of people. Denise McCluggage and Cristabel Carlisle were the top women drivers of the day and could be relied on to do well. Jim Parkinson was a sports car dealer for BMC in Burbank, California and Jack Flaherty worked for Kjell Qvale at BMCD. Extremely competent on the track, this pair were good amusing companions when relaxing. Paddy Hopkirk and Don Morley were better known as rally drivers but were also extremely good on the track. Paddy had the ability and determination to jump in a car at the start of a long race and put in very fast opening lap times as he worked his way through the heavy early traffiic – one sign of a truly great driver. John Colgate and Clive Baker were also a well matched pair of proven endurance race ability. The pairing of Bob Olthoff and Ronnie Bucknum could have appeared unusual to some. A South African, Bob had come to England and worked his way up in the racing world, at the same time scraping a living in the MG factory. Ronnie Bucknum had worked his way up through the American sports car racing scene.

We were shocked one morning to read a report in an American national paper that BMC was anti-American and that I was almost public enemy number one. This story by a woman reporter inferred, entirely without foundation, that Ronnie Bucknum was being held back to run as second to Bob. This female had visited our base at the motel and talked to some of the team. It almost appeared to be an attempt to split up the team, besides being very damaging. Rod Learoyd and the PR people decided that the best course was to ignore the whole thing entirely.

Another complication arose. An unknown competitor had made an entry with an Austin Healey Sprite. It appeared that this individual had some political axe to grind which could have caused trouble on race day. The organisers asked me if I knew anything about his claim to have competed at Brands Hatch and other European circuits. I was able to find out that he had competed in Europe, but that his sole claim to fame was his regular disappearance off the track at the first bend. He solved the organisers' dilemma by crashing the car on the way to the track. He then hounded the team for spares and assistance. We were not in the habit of carrying spare chassis frames and would not have helped even if we had all the parts available. It often happened that private owners got an entry for a race and then tried cajoling or blackmailing the factory team into rebuilding their wreck.

In the race, Paddy and Don on car 34 were plagued with oil surge on corners and underbraking. The oil pressure would drop to zero for a long period. This was a problem that occurred occasionally with the modified large capacity oil sumps. The baffling of the sumps had to be enough to avoid

Sebring 1963: DMH between Ronnie Bucknum (left) and Bob Olthoff, who finished in twelfth place overall in the 12-hour Grand Prix of Endurance.

impeding the flow to the oil pick up, and the holes and space small enough to restrict the flow away from the pump. It was not possible to effect a cure and the two drove in such a way that oil pressure drop was kept to a minimum. The slower lap times resulted in their covering only 166 laps against the 187 of the other Healey.

Poor Clive and John Colgate had the Sprite engine fail after 11 hours and 4 minutes. The year before, John and his co-driver Steve McQueen had had the centre main bearing cap break after 4 hours 40 minutes. This time the strengthened cap had remained intact but it had taken the centre web of the crankcase away with it. It was not until the strengthened caps had been fitted into crankcases with very thick central webs that the engines were to

Austin Healey: The Story of the Big Healeys

prove to be really reliable long-distance cars.

The two MG Bs suffered engine failure early on in the race although they had led the Triumphs comfortably for the first three hours.

Bob Olthoff and Ronnie Bucknum finished twelfth overall, beating five Ferraris, two Jaguars, all the Corvettes and five Cobras in the process. Carroll Shelby's 4.7-litre Cobras were true sports cars and held second place for some time. Some of the best lap times are interesting:

Ferrari	3 min 12 sec
Cobra	3 min 20 sec
Chaparral	3 min 14 sec
Corvette	3 min 31 sec
Olthoff/Bucknum 3000	3 min 36 sec
Hopkirk/Morley 3000	3 min 39 sec
Triumph	3 min 57 sec
MG B	3 min 47 sec
Porsche	3 min 35 sec
Colgate/Baker Sprite	3 min 50 sec

Bob and Ronnie put up an excellent performance and one could not detect any difference in their lap times. BMC were delighted with the Healey result but bitterly disappointed with the MG B performance. The B had shown that despite giving away 348 cc in engine capacity to the Triumph it was by far the quicker car.

Dick Jeffrey and his team from Dunlop provided wonderful service throughout the race for a major portion of the field. Sebring has an abrasive surface and the high ambient temperature helped to produce a rapid rate of tyre wear. Girling under Tony Cross were also kept busy rendering their usual competent service to most of the leading cars. Girling brakes were far ahead of the opposition at that time.

The 1964 Sebring race should have been an even better event for the 3000. Paddy Hopkirk was as usual very well up at the start. Unfortunately, he collected a puncture on the first lap and had to drive a long way on a flat tyre. A new tyre and wheel were fitted and he proceeded to give a demonstration of high speed reliability, working his way past 30 cars in three hours to hand over to Grant Clark. Clark managed four laps before he overturned the 3000, seriously damaging it. Clark had been selected by the Canadian operation and was not an appropriate pairing. He lacked Paddy's skill and had no hope of keeping up the scorching pace set by his co-driver. With the 3000 giving 197 bhp at 5,750 rpm, and with its excellent road holding and ability to do the race with three pit stops, the chance of a high place was a distinct probability–if only we had been given one of many other capable Healey drivers. The rugged 3000 engine and units were so reliable that any trouble in

Peter Browning keeps the Sebring lap charts and timing, while GCH takes it easy.

this department was not conceivable.

    1965 was a year with some interesting races. Stuart Turner masterminded the whole operation, producing crisp, concise instructions for all, including drivers, mechanics and assistants. The first race was the Sebring 12-hour race and the BMC entry consisted of:

Austin Healey 3000 H-BJ8	Paul Hawkins and Warwick Banks
Sprite	Paddy Hopkirk and Timo Makinen
Sprite	Rauno Aaltonen and Clive Baker
MG B	Merl Brennan and Frank Morrell
MG B	Brad Picard and Al Pease
MG Midget	Andrew Hedges and Roger Mac

At Sebring, Rauno Aaltonen, Stuart Turner, GCH and Clive Baker worry over the fine print in the regulations. Stuart's knowledge of what race organisers intended played a large part in many successful forays.

Roger Menadue and Tommy Wellman were the mechanics and Peter Browning was in control of timekeeping. BMC supplied the remainder of helpers from their Canadian and USA operations. The team left London airport at 1 pm on Sunday 21st March, arriving at New York with just enough time to catch the flight to West Palm Beach. At West Palm Beach we picked up cars and drove the 140 miles to Avon Park, our base, arriving at midnight. Quite a long hard day when you add the six-hour time difference.

The next week would be spent preparing the cars, fitting the latest components, testing and practising. The race started at 10 am on the Saturday. The field of 70 cars ranged from 7-litre Corvettes, 5.3-litre Chaparrals, 4.7-litre Ford GT 40s and eight 4.7-litre Cobras, down to a 1.1-litre René Bonnet. The early laps were spectacular with the large cars thundering around. Our entries were running to a planned speed, calculated to produce class wins. In the afternoon a tremendous thunderstorm struck the circuit. The pit lane was 8 inches deep in water with spare tyres and wheels floating away. The excellent Lucas equipment performed without fault. The Sprites leaked, of course, and the drivers were sitting in water. At one time only four cars, including the Baker/Aaltonen Sprite, were lapping at over 60 mph.

Competition

Of the fastest fifteen cars, six were MG or Austin Healey, the Sprites being third and fourth fastest. In the last hours of the race, when Warwick Banks was due to take over from Paul Hawkins, Warwick dropped a bombshell – his stomach upset had reached such proportions that he felt unable to drive. We were faced with a problem, as one driver could not drive for more than four consecutive hours without a break. An uncomfortable Warwick was talked into driving three laps. Paul's comments, when informed of the situation, are not repeatable, but he willingly completed the rest of the race. Stuart Turner and BMC were justifiably pleased with the results: first in class for the 3000, with all six cars finishing well up in the results.

Throughout the Austin Healey production I was responsible for compiling and submitting the FIA homologations forms to the RAC. Every effort was made to cover all the items required for rallying and racing. A lot of effort went into ensuring that sufficient numbers of a part had been made to warrant its inclusion. We worked on a very limited competition budget. We managed to stretch this by using the competition department's drivers and local mechanics. Most of the money went on the preparation of the cars and this often had to stop short of the best possible, because of shortage of funds. Generally, at the end of a season, the cars were sold to private owners who proceeded to campaign in them with success.

The 3000 was very popular with private owners. For many the car was to

John Gott using his ex-works rally 3000 to great effect in a club race.

Austin Healey: The Story of the Big Healeys

prove a stepping stone into the big time, leading to contracts with the top teams. Many owners, like John Harris, bought old and somewhat bent 3000s or 100 Sixes and converted them to competition form by making their own manifolds or obtaining worn and discarded competition parts. Others bought competition vehicles that had been retired because of old age or obsolescence. Men like John Gott, Clive Baker, Ted Worswick, David Dixon, John Chatham, to name but a few of many, campaigned these cars with great success in club, national and international events. Spares were limited and difficult to obtain, because of the relatively few competition cars that were built and their long active life. After the end of 3000 production, many owners continued development, taking advantage of advances in tyre design to fit wider tyres and wheels and keep the cars competitive, to the embarassment of drivers of the newer more powerful E Type Jaguars.

High oil consumption was a problem which was cured by fitting an additional breather pipe to the engine and blocking up the oil spray holes in the top of the rockers. Valve gear lubrication was more than amply supplied by oil passing through the rocker bushes. Blocking these holes has a dramatic effect on consumption on old engines.

The highly loaded cam followers pitted badly. This could be reduced by impregnating the surface of new followers with molybdenum disulphide paste. The spray compounds from Du Pont now available are ideal for this purpose.

Cylinder bore life was good and normally in excess of 100,000 miles. Main bearing caps sometimes broke when standard materials were used but SG iron caps eliminated this trouble. Flywheels were sometimes fitted with eight bolts instead of the four used on production. The belated development of diaphragm spring clutches by Borg & Beck at Leamington, part of the Automotive Products Group, was most welcome. Their $9\frac{1}{2}$-inch diaphragm spring clutch proved very reliable and sweet in action.

I now regret that I was not able to keep one of the Big Healeys. Being deeply involved, I always had to run the latest offering, to keep up to date and show the flag. Meanwhile, the sales department somehow always managed to dispose of the old and faithful steed, to boost their own profits. Other cars may excel the 3000 in cornering power or performance, but nothing since has had that magic – something that distinguishes the truly great machine. Now fetching their true value, they are too expensive to buy!

Record Breaking

Record breaking was undertaken as a publicity exercise. One always looks for ways of obtaining good publicity and to some extent the value of racing and rallying had been lowered by certain manufacturers' practice of advertising victories in the most insignificant classes and events. Record breaking had not really revived following World War Two and a lot of valuable records were open to us. Captain George Eyston, a director of Castrol and three times holder of the land speed record, suggested to DMH that record breaking would be a good way to publicise the new Austin Healey in the USA. Castrol had always supported record breaking, both as a publicity exercise and for patriotic motives.

Austin readily agreed to a small budget being made available for 1953 to publicise the new Austin Healey 100. George Eyston organised all the facilities for the attempts at the Bonneville Salt Flats, Utah, USA. The plan was to take the American stock car records with cars drawn from dealers' stocks in the USA. In addition we would build one Special Test car to capture National and International records up to 24-hours' duration. Our experience of record breaking was limited to earlier runs on the Belgian and Italian motorways and a run at the Montlhèry track in France. In a number of conversations, George briefed us on the difficulties and intricacies of running for a long time at Bonneville. Without his guidance we could not have mounted a successful operation. The timing of the attempts was dictated by the period when evaporation and lack of rain produced a satisfactory surface

DMH shows the 1953 high-speed endurance car to George Harriman and Len Lord, on Gaydon Airfield near Warwick.

on the Salt Flats. This usually occurred in August and September and would coincide with quantity supplies of the new car arriving in the US dealers' showrooms.

George Eyston laid down the general plan of when and what records would be attempted and set up the whole operation at Bonneville. I organised the specification and build of the Special Test car, spares and equipment, provisioning and shipping from England. Austin developed the engine based on Harry Weslake's 4-port head that was later used in the 100 S.

The spares, the Special Test Car, DMH, Roger Menadue, George Perry of Lucas and I sailed from Southampton on one of the great Cunard liners. Arriving in New York in a heat wave, we were met by Fred Horner who arranged the despatch of car and spares to Bonneville some 2,000 miles across America. Fred sent us to some of his friends, who supplied us with clothing more suited to the occasion at most reasonable prices. He organised our travel from New York to Salt Lake City on the train, which gave us the chance to become used to the American scene and see something of the fabulous

(Opposite):
1953: the power curve for the hurriedly produced Weslake 4-port head unit. Note the good fuel consumption figures.

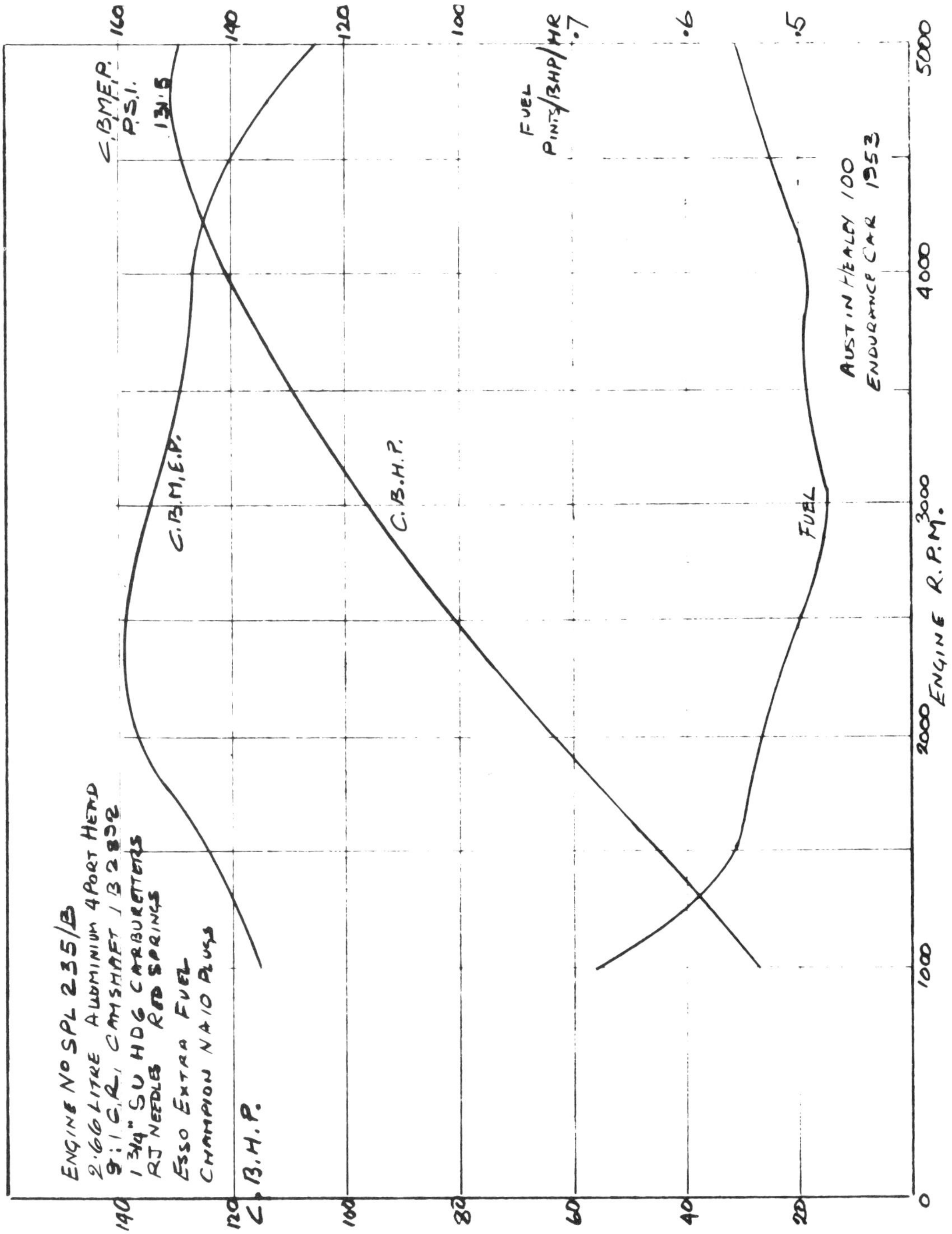
ENGINE NO SPL 235/B
2.66 LITRE ALUMINIUM 4 PORT HEAD
9:1 C.R., CAMSHAFT
1 3/4" SU HDG CARBURETTERS
RJ NEEDLES RED SPRINGS
ESSO EXTRA FUEL
CHAMPION NA10 PLUGS
C.B.H.P.
C.B.M.E.P.
P.S.I.
131.5
FUEL
PINTS/BHP/HR
C.B.H.P.
C.B.M.E.P.
FUEL
AUSTIN HEALEY 100
ENDURANCE CAR 1953
ENGINE R.P.M.
0
1000
2000
3000
4000
5000
140
120
100
80
60
40
20
160
140
120
100
.7
.6
.5

countryside. We arrived in Salt Lake City in the evening and met up with the mechanics from the Austin America operation, mainly ex-apprentices, highly skilled, loyal and hard working. We drove a variety of cars along the US Highway that crosses the Salt Lake desert to Bonneville on the western edge of the Salt Flats. The Austin mechanics taught us a great deal about what was needed in servicing a car in America. They were able to suggest improvements from the American viewpoint, which we later incorporated.

George Eyston had not wasted any time setting up the organisation. We lived at the Clarence McLeod's Motel at Wendover, some 11 miles from Bonneville. This was a very compact unit with air conditioning and an excellent restaurant. Someone should explain to British planners how one of these places operates: good cooking, a variety of drinks, reasonable prices, absolute cleanliness and civil efficient service are in marked contrast to the usual British copy. One fault was that of tea, which was made using water from an urn controlled to 185°F. We soon found a way of overcoming the regulator and producing boiling water.

The Special Test car to attack the national and international class records and the two stock cars to attack American national stock car records had already arrived. The stock cars were under the control of the American Automobile Association, who had provided two officials to select two Austin Healeys at random out of a dealer's stock. The Austin mechanics, Phil Harris and Gordon Whitby, then drove the cars to Wendover with officials alongside. The AAA lay down strict rules as to what may be changed and the maximum running-in mileage permitted. The officials were fair, co-operative and sticklers for the regulations.

The Bonneville Salt Flats are a vast area of comparatively flat salt, formed in the bed of a lake. Evaporation of the water leaves a solid salt residue. At the edge of the Flats, extraction of salt and phosphates is carried out by a mining company. To the west lies a ridge of hills, their flanks cut horizontally at odd intervals. These cuts were made ages ago by the lake crust, as it fell to its present level. The lake surface is not usable at all times: rain raises the water table, changing the salt from a hard crust to a mush and finally to liquid. The surface is likely to be at its best sometime between August and September, when the lowering of the water table and the high rate of evaporation leaves it rough but level. The Utah State Highway Department drags a length of railway line over a selected area, leaving a smooth surface with a tolerably high coefficient of friction. The grip between tyre and road is good until wheel locking or skidding takes place, when the friction drops sharply.

The mornings are usually superb in Utah. The 4,228-foot altitude and clear atmosphere combine to produce an exhilerating start to the day. In contrast, as the day gets hotter – and it can become very hot – the humidity rises and tends to induce lethargy. The rising sun and temperature can also produce very strong winds – the air is usually most still just before dawn.

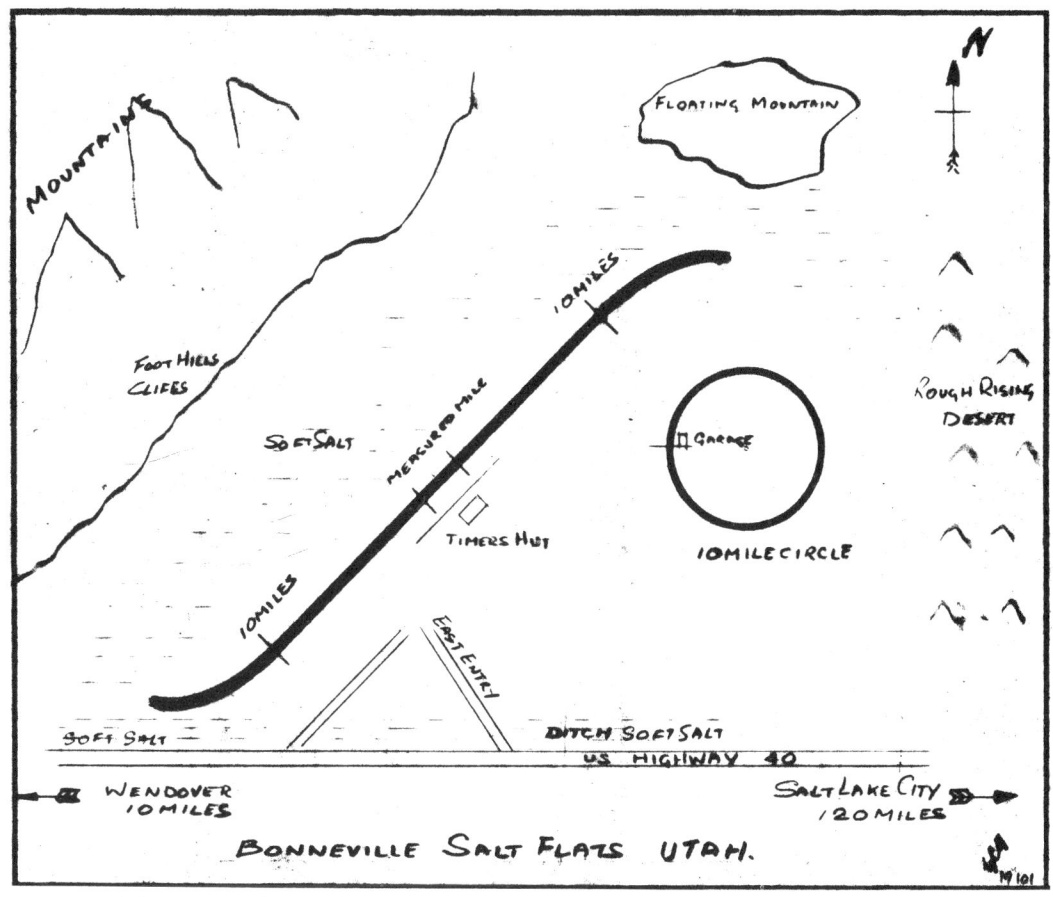

Layout of the prepared straightaway and 10-mile circle on Bonneville Salt Flats, which was used for so many record attempts.

The area selected for our record breaking attempts had been divided into a circle of 10 miles' circumference and a straight of about 15 miles. The usable length of the straight was determined by the quality of the surface at either end – any car that was driven too far off the test area would simply sink through the crust. The circle and the straight had been surveyed and marked with black oil and conical rubber markers, the straight being marked off in 10, 5, 2 and 1 mile and kilometre distances. With the aid of the local authority, George Eyston had constructed a large wooden garage, open at both ends, which was to be used as our refuelling and service point during the endurance records on the 10-mile circle. A 50-gallon oil drum was mounted at roof height on a wooden tower, and a flexible 3-inch hose and nozzle with valve led inside the garage. The gravity feed was to be filled by means of a hand pump from a mass of 50-gallon drums. The AAA's timing equipment was housed inside a red wooden shack on wheels. It used light beams and electric eye cells to control the timing mechanism.

In an attempt to prevent a heavy build-up of salt, the underside of all three cars, particularly the wheel arches, was liberally coated with a dark brown lanolin-based grease. This would break off cleanly when a heavy weight of salt accumulated. We readied the stock cars by removing the hood and fitting an aeroscreen, covering the passenger seat with the tonneau cover. The aircleaners were removed and a cold air box fitted, and the 4.125 to 1 axle centre was changed to the optional 3.667 to 1 ratio.

The Special Test car had been prepared in England and required little attention apart from the anti-salt grease treatment. The engine was the forerunner of the 100 S unit. Harry Weslake of Rye, Sussex, one of England's greatest tuning experts, had designed a 4-port light alloy head for the engine, both of which were built by Austin. The compression ratio was 9.4 to 1 and it gave 135 bhp at sea level. At the 4,228-foot altitude of the Salt Flats, the less dense air would reduce the power output but also the wind resistance of the vehicle. The carburettors were 2-inch SU H8 units fed by dual high capacity pumps. The brakes were of Dunlop design using very small calipers. The Dunlop 16-inch diameter light alloy wheels, with 5-pin drive and centre-lock nuts, carried 5.50 and 6.00 special racing tyres. A large alloy fuel tank of 40 gallons took up most of the boot space. The power train consisted of the taxi box, Laycock overdrive and 2.93 to 1 rear axle ratio. This gave a cruising speed of over 135 mph at 4,000 rpm.

The first time we tried out the cars on the Flats, the stock cars lapped the 10-mile circle at a maximum of about 111 mph and the Special Test car at 140 mph. One of the stock cars lost performance. The engine had a noisy piston which an engine strip revealed to be scored. Austin and the piston manufacturers decided that complete absence of piston tap on a sports car was not essential and all future production cars were produced with greater piston clearance. The battery in the Special Test car was getting over-heated and so George Perry obtained some fibreglass from one of the Hot Rod boys and moulded an effective heat shield.

Before dawn on 12th September 1953, the cars were taken out to the straightaway. The road tyres were replaced with the special tyres, inflated to 50 lb per square inch. Conditions were good – it was cool and the wind blew lightly from the west. DMH made two runs with the stock car and inevitably, as is often the case, the timing equipment did not function properly. We decided that the trouble was caused by the position of the front bumper and fixed a metal plate to the front of the car, to cut the timing beam consistently. This worked. On the next two runs all of the US National Stock Car records were broken, at distances of up to 10 miles at over 109 mph. The Special Test car running for International Records and US National Records in Class D (2 to 3 litres) also broke a number of records at high speeds.

George Eyston (in the cockpit) and Roy Jackson-Moore during night testing at Bonneville. 1953.

The team then retired to the sidelines while the National Hot Rod Association took over the straight. A vast assortment of home-built specials then proceeded to put up some amazing performances. The cars varied from Model A Ford-based saloons to beautiful streamlined devices. The highlights were a run by the Shadoff Chrysler driven by Malcolm Hooper at 235.87 mph, and a Fuller diesel driven by the maker, a truck owner, at 169.32. The Shadoff was a beautiful little streamlined car fitted with a Chrysler Hemi engine. The Fuller was somewhat less advanced, being powered by a General Motors diesel with two stages of supercharging. The ducting work was built in fibreglass which had difficulty in coping with the boost pressure – the duct usually burst at maximum speed. Fuller laid on more and more fibreglass and resin which cured rapidly in the heat. Eventually it was strong enough and he took a number of well earned records. The Hot Rodders were a very likeable bunch of people. We spent many hours discussing the problems associated with motor cars and they willingly lent us material and gave us valuable help.

A number of their machines were running on nitro and the blow-ups of over-stressed production-car engines were spectacular. Iskendarian, a camshaft specialist, supplied nearly all the camshafts used. This man was probably the world's greatest expert on camshafts for power and was later to supply many shafts for Austin Healey and other British cars raced in the USA. This dedication and specialisation was typical of American expertise that was later to put a man on the moon.

A German motorcycle team were there attacking a number of records for small-capacity bikes. Their teutonic thoroughness was in marked contrast to the Americans. They provided light relief, however, by cornering a skunk and attempting to capture it. The little beast defended itself in the only way it knew and squirted them with its defensive fluid. The Germans stank for a long time afterwards and were given a lot of *lebensraum*!

Next the long-distance attempts were started. The drivers were a mixture from both sides of the Atlantic. In addition to George Eyston and DMH, there was Bill Spear, actor Jackie Cooper, Roy Jackson-Moore, Mort Morris Goodall, and John Gordon Benett. The stock car was run until it had covered 5,000 kilometres at an average speed of 103.94 mph. The list of records broken was now growing to enormous proportions, totalling something over 50.

Next the Special Test car was brought out and run round the 10-mile circle. It proceeded to shatter a number of international records at an average speed of 122.95 mph over 3,000 kilometres. Just a little later, when it was being driven by John Gordon Benett, it suddenly expired. Poor John thought he had done it. This was not so. Some unknown production engineer had altered the connecting rod design for ease of machining and a rod had broken at a sharp corner where the bolt fitted. (These were standard rods, highly polished and balanced.) This is almost the traditional form of rod failure – an identical

*Refuelling the 1953 endurance car in the
'garage' on the salt flats.*

failure all but eliminated the first 6-cylinder team at Sebring later on. Deteriorating weather conditions were given as the reason for abandoning the attempt. An innocuous storm was built into monstrous proportions. Only a very small percentage of the world's population knew the truth. Roger and I later removed the engine from the car at night, and after removing useful parts and the offending rods, buried the remains on some waste ground in Warwick. The secret was well kept. Restorers of Austin Healeys should look out for early rods with a sharp notch and hole for the snug and replace these with the later pattern.

Some trouble occurred with the tyres on the Special Test car when the tread splice showed signs of separating. The splice is the joint in the tread rubber and it is difficult to ensure a perfect bond. Lyle Hysert of Dunlop solved the problem by examining each tyre and determining the direction in which it had to rotate in order to keep the splice closed. Each tyre was then marked and fitted to the car in the appropriate position.

The fuel used was Esso Extra. Esso have an enviable record for quality and consistency. Not all companies have the knowledge or take the care necessary to produce and market good fuel: the myth that all fuel comes out of a hole in the ground and is similar, should be ignored.

Castrol R 40 was the oil used. R is a vegetable base oil obtained from castor oil which performs better than most mineral oils under high loadings. Its drawbacks are high price, a tendency to cause gum and corrosion and its high viscosity at lower temperatures. Extreme care must be taken to avoid mixing mineral oil with it or it will gum and ruin the engine.

A weary crew returned to base to celebrate. The celebration took place at the Stateline Hotel in the all-singing and dancing state of Nevada, but a short walk away from our Motel in the dry state of Utah. The meal consisted of prawns from Florida, steaks from Kansas and baked potatoes from Idaho. American potatoes are bigger, better and cost a fraction of what we pay in Europe. We swam in a local water hole despite the abundance of rattlesnakes and generally unwound.

The success of competition results in relation to sales depends on timing and the efforts of the public relations staff. This time everything was right. The Austin Healey was reaching America in good numbers. The Austin PR people obtained excellent world wide coverage and Austin made good use of the car at the Earls Court Motor Show. One unnecessary aspect of the follow-up operation was that the sales allocators in New York were using the Austin Healey to sell another Austin model that was sticking. The dealers were naturally clamouring for Austin Healeys which sold rapidly without being discounted. The allocators were promising dealers one Austin Healey if they took three of the other Austin model. This type of operation prevented the full potential of the model being realised and resulted in a lowering of the penetration of English sports cars in the US market. DMH was wild, but was only able to obtain a modification of the policy.

Austin Healey 100
Summary of Record Results: Bonneville Salt Flats, Utah, USA

9th September 1953: 14-mile straightaway course
Driver: Donald Healey
For American Certificate of Performance: Non-Stock Car
Flying Start:

	sec	mph
1 km	15.69	142.55
1 mile	25.24	142.64

12th September 1953: 14-mile straightaway course
Driver: Donald Healey
National Class 'Unlimited' &
National Class 'D'–Stock Car
American Stock Car Class 'D' &
American Stock Car 'Unlimited'–
Open Car Division
Standing Start:

	min	sec	mph
1 km		34.68	64.51
1 mile		48.53	74.19
5 km	1	59.78	93.38
5 mile	3	1.92	98.94
10 km	3	42.36	100.60
10 mile	5	47.64	103.55

American Stock Car Class 'D' &
American Stock Car 'Unlimited'–
Open Car Division
Flying Start:

	min	sec	mph
1 km		20.48	109.24
1 mile		32.96	109.22
5 km	1	42.25	109.39
5 mile	2	44.77	109.24
10 km	3	24.90	109.17
10 mile	5	30.92	108.79

14th September 1953: 9.9972-mile
circular course
Drivers: Healey, Eyston, Benett, Spear
National and International Class
'D'–Non-Stock Car
Standing Start:

	hr	min	sec	mph
1,000 km	4	53	33.25	127.00
1,000 mile	8	9	9.55	122.66
2,000 km	10	5	35.54	123.35
2,000 mile	16	15	23.25	123.03
3,000 km	15	9	42.69	122.95
6 hours	742.50 miles			123.75
12 hours	1,474.96 miles			122.91

15th and 16th September 1953:
10.0013-mile circular course
Drivers: Healey, Cooper,
Jackson-Moore, Benett, Eyston
National and International Class
'D'–Stock Car
Standing Start:

	hr	min	sec	mph
3,000 mile	28	47	39.53	104.19
4,000 km	23	49	51.95	104.30
5,000 km	29	53	34.09	103.93
24 hours		2,503.18 miles		104.30

15th and 16th September: 10.0013-mile circular course
Drivers: Healey, Cooper, Jackson-Moore, Benett, Eyston
For American Certificate of Performance: Stock Car
Flying Start:
30 hours   3117.9923 miles   103.93 mph

15th and 16th September 1953:
Drivers: Healey, Cooper, Jackson-Moore, Benett, Eyston
American Stock Car – 'Unlimited'
American Stock Car – Class 'D'
Open Car Division

Flying Start:

	hr	min	sec	mph		hr	min	sec	mph
25 km		8	55.44	104.44	500 mile	4	46	50.41	104.59
25 mile		14	18.91	104.78	1,000 km	5	56	2.78	104.71
50 km		17	45.42	104.98	1,000 mile	9	34	43.72	104.40
50 mile		28	33.25	105.06	2,000 km	11	52	54.14	104.59
100 km		35	24.71	105.28	2,000 mile	19	8	28.55	104.49
100 mile		57	1.63	105.21	3,000 km	17	49	14.67	104.60
200 km	1	10	53.09	105.19	3,000 mile	28	47	17.98	104.21
200 mile	1	54	5.14	105.18	4,000 km	23	49	34.13	104.32
300 km	1	46	20.73	105.17	5,000 km	29	53	26.48	103.94
300 mile	2	51	2.05	105.24	1 hour		105.1849 miles		105.18
400 km	2	21	47.10	105.18	6 hours		628.3579 miles		104.73
400 mile	3	49	40.14	104.50	12 hours		1,255.1497 miles		104.60
500 km	2	57	11.91	105.20	24 hours		2,503.6210 miles		104.32

All performances certified by the Contest Board of the American Automobile Association.

The 1953 efforts were successful but we could have done better if the connecting rod on the Special Test car had not failed. For 1954 a new series of runs at Bonneville was planned, with the aim of doing 200 mph with a specially streamlined car based on the 100 and improving the distance records up to 24 hours. From the 1953 runs we had learnt a tremendous amount about what was needed for a successful record operation in the USA. We knew what materials could be obtained locally and were able to provide better spares cover.

The 1953 Special Test car was fitted with the improved 100 S type engine now developing 142 bhp at 4,700 rpm, some 10 bhp more than the 1953 unit, and it had far better connecting rods. It was to be used to raise the speeds of the 3-litre International Records up to 24 hours.

DMH was keen to exceed 200 mph with an Austin Healey, as he considered this to have great publicity value. All of the Austin Healey record cars were based on the standard production 100 chassis frame and centre body section. George Eyston favoured the use of a fin on the high speed car although aerodynamicists maintained that a properly streamlined vehicle did not need it. I have little doubt that the fin improved stability and it did make the car

GCH testing the 1954 streamliner at 150 mph, on the 9,000-foot runway at Gaydon Airfield near Warwick.

more visible on the vast salt flats. Gerry Coker, DMH and George Eyston worked on the 200-mph car. The basis of this design was the 100 bodyshell with the nose and tail cut off at the wheel centre line. Gerry styled the car and produced a scale model which was tested in Armstrong Whitworth's wind tunnel at Whitley, now the site of Chrysler UK's Engineering Headquarters. Armstrong Whitworth suggested a variety of alterations needed to reach 200 mph and they predicted the required hp which was later used in Austin calculations. A body was provided by Jensen which was sent for modification to Lionel Rawson, who ran a small body shop at Slough. He had constructed the very advanced Sportsmobile bodies. Lionel faithfully reproduced Gerry's lines in light alloy and engineered the necessary understructure.

Austin undertook the development of the engine in Doc John Weaving's

The Shorrock supercharger, driven by Laycock couplings from the nose of the crankshaft, on the 1954 streamliner. (Robert Mottar)

research department in the East Works at Longbridge. Bill Leyland, a tuner of the old Austin, practical sort, was responsible for the build and test of the power unit. The 4-port Weslake-type engine was fitted with a cast iron head of lower compression ratio. A Shorrock supercharger was directly driven off the front of the crankshaft by two Layrub couplings. A very large SU carburettor provided the mixture. The manifolding was fabricated from steel and four short vertical exhaust stacks completed the unit. Bill had considerable trouble getting the power required and finally ended up with wire gauze in the inlet manifold to correct a distribution fault. With 9.6 lb of boost, and fuel compiled of $66\frac{2}{3}$ per cent methanol, $33\frac{1}{3}$ per cent benzole plus 11 cc of castor oil per gallon, it gave 224 bhp at 4,500 rpm. When adjusted to the altitude at Bonne-

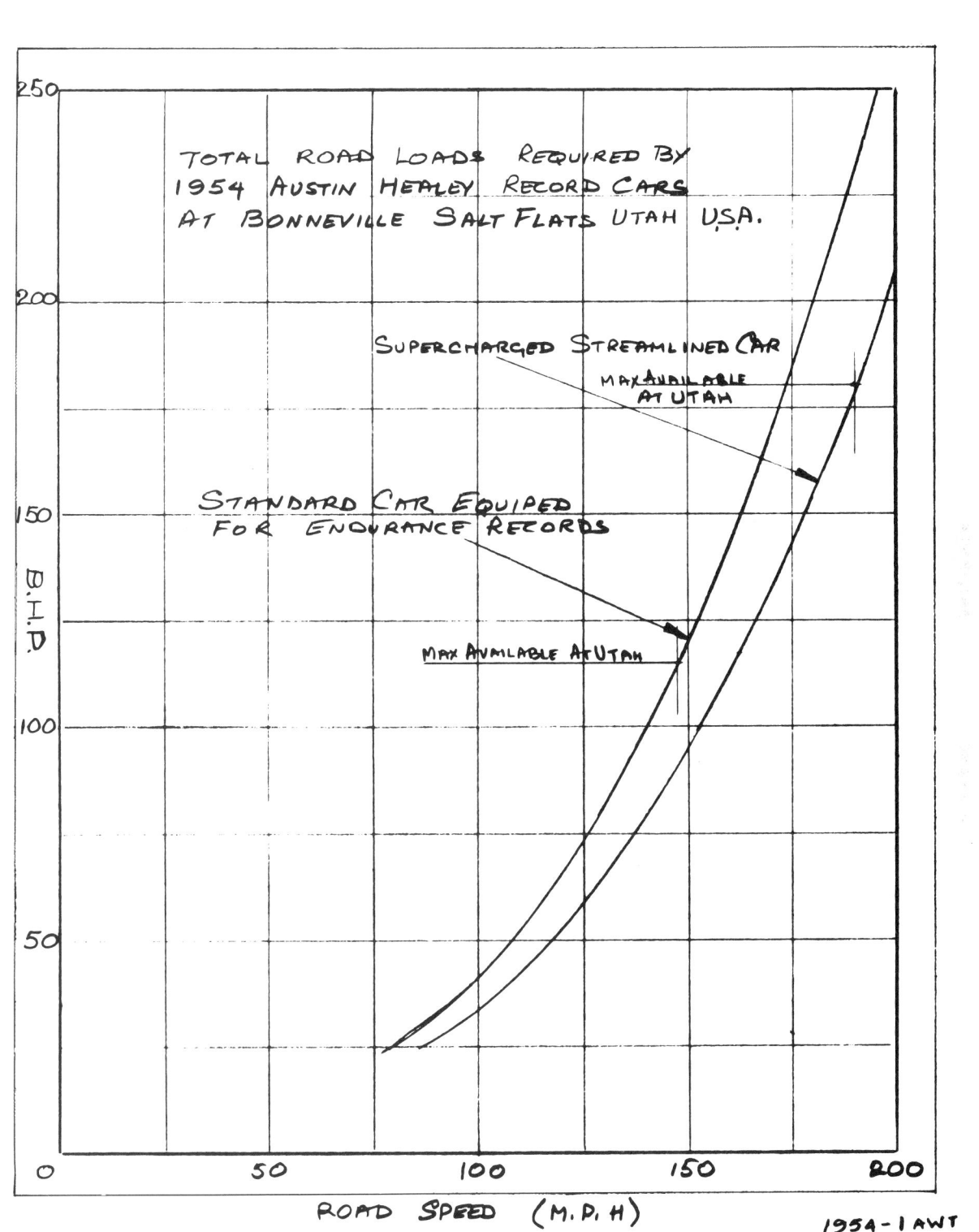

Comparison of the wind and road resistance of the 1954 standard and streamlined record cars. The actual results at Bonneville corresponded very closely with these wind-tunnel figures.

ville, the power was calculated to be 183 bhp. Doc Weaving tested the body in the Austin wind tunnel and predicted a speed of 192 mph, with a possible 2 to 3 mph bonus if climatic conditions were favourable. The maximum day temperature at Bonneville is in the region of 105° F, falling to the low 40s at night. Mean atmospheric pressure is only 12.53 psi, resulting in reduced air drag and reduced engine output, although tyre resistance remains the same.

John Wyer of Aston Martin provided a 5-speed David Brown gearbox for the sum of £150. Some years later he repurchased the box from us for the same sum for use in one of the Le Mans Aston Martins. The back axle used was the earlier spiral bevel Austin Healey pattern with 15-tooth pinion and 37-tooth ring gear, giving a ratio of 2.467. With the 0.825 overdrive ratio, 200 mph was equivalent to 4,734 rpm.

At the same time Austin were preparing the endurance engine. This used another cast iron head with a compression ratio of 9.4 to 1. Two 2-inch SU's provided the air fuel mixture. This engine gave 141 bhp at sea level (115 at Bonneville). Doc Weaving estimated the speed to be 147 mph and that it would be capable of running at 140 mph continuously.

Bonneville 1954. George Eyston, Roger Menadue and GCH waiting for the wind to drop before starting high-speed runs. (Robert Mottar)

Record Breaking

Our base for the 1954 attempts was, once again, the Clarence McLeod's Motel in Wendover. When we arrived, the Austin American-based mechanics had already offloaded the cars and spares and were ready for work. The streamliner for the 200-mph attempt looked quite beautiful in its new environment. George Eyston had the straightaway and 10-mile circular course ready and we took the cars out for testing. I had tried the cars on Gaydon Airfield near Warwick, but the length of the runway there made speeds of over 160 mph impossible. DMH tried the streamliner and was quite happy with it. Some changes were made to the cockpit of the 24-hour car to suit the drivers who had not seen it before.

Next day, 19th August, we assembled in the early morning just as dawn was breaking at the south end of the straightaway. Ten gallons of the fuel mixture were put into the tank of the streamliner and the Graviner chloro bromo methane fire-extinguishing system was coupled up. (It is now known that this

Dawn, 1954. George Eyston leads the way across the unscraped salt to the prepared straightaway. Pushing the streamliner, Roger Menadue, GCH, Jimmy Harrison (of SU), and Roy Jackson-Moore.

DMH lifts the canopy of the 1954 streamliner after completing runs at 192.6 mph. (Robert Mottar)

was a toxic chemical.) The car started easily and I ran it around to warm up the engine and transmission. DMH put on his crash hat, got in and we fitted on the bubbled top canopy. DMH accelerated slowly in the lower gears and disappeared to the north. We all leapt into various cars and raced up the edge of the straight to the north base near the floating island. Lyle Hysert, the American Dunlop tyre expert, checked the tyres while DMH reported the pressures and the temperatures from the gauges that he had seen during the run. All was satisfactory and DMH departed on the return run. We hurried south – it seemed to take an age to cover the 14 miles to where DMH awaited us. He reported that the engine had gone out of tune on this run. We checked and changed plugs but could not get the engine to run evenly on 4 cylinders. A quick compression check revealed that the pressure was low in no. 2 cylinder. Despite this trouble on the second run, the AAA officials gave us the times and the 5-kilometre record was ours at 179.63 mph. So we returned to Wendover with the car.

We quickly removed the cylinder head to investigate the trouble. Number two piston showed signs of burning and pitting on the top and the inlet valve was coated in aluminium. There were signs of the cylinder head joint leaking. We were fortunate that Syd Enever and Alec Hounslow of MG were there, with their vast experience of this sort of trouble, and between us we decided what action to take. The pistons and rods were to be removed and the cylinder bores honed out to remove any trace of aluminium. The burnt piston would be replaced and all the pistons would be filed to increase clearance. All the

Record Breaking

head studs would be removed and the block and head lapped together with valve grinding paste until perfect mating resulted. Additional SU fuel pumps would be added as a safeguard against any shortage of fuel pressure. The richest available SU needle would be fitted to the carburettor and harder spark plugs. As only two people could effectively work on the car at one time, we laid down a rota. Lapping the head was hard work in the daytime temperature and the drivers took turns at this. Clearing away every trace of lapping compound was a difficult task, but after some 29 hours of continuous effort the engine was rebuilt. Before the head went on the eagle-eyed AAA technical representative, Reeves Dutton, measured the bore and stroke. The bores had been enlarged by 0.002 inches to remove all marks.

The next day was a rest day for the weary crew. MG were out breaking records with their car. They had their trouble with centrifugal force on the runs around the circle, causing the oil to flow to the outside, away from the crown wheel and pinion. They fitted extra seals and baffles to effect a cure.

We gave the car a brief run to settle it in and set the tappets. On 22nd August we were at the start point at 5 am. DMH was to make several runs at increasing speed to ensure that the records were broken. The first run was just after 6 am when the temperature was 55° F and the wind 0-6 mph. DMH made a total of six runs, three in each direction. All were completed by 9 am, by which time the wind had dropped and the temperature had risen to 63° F. The last run south was the fastest – 0.193125 minutes for the kilometre, a speed of 193.05 mph. He had broken a number of International and National records at very respectable speeds.

At 9.30 am DMH drove the endurance car on the straightaway, recording 142.50 and 143.95 mph to give an average of 143.22 mph for the kilometer. This was just to determine that this car was ready. The original delays with

The 1954 endurance car passes the pits. In the background, the mountains to the west of the salt flats.

DMH, driving the 1954 streamliner on the straightaway, overtakes the photographer's plane at 192 mph. The black oil line at the edge of the scraped surface provided a guide for the driver.

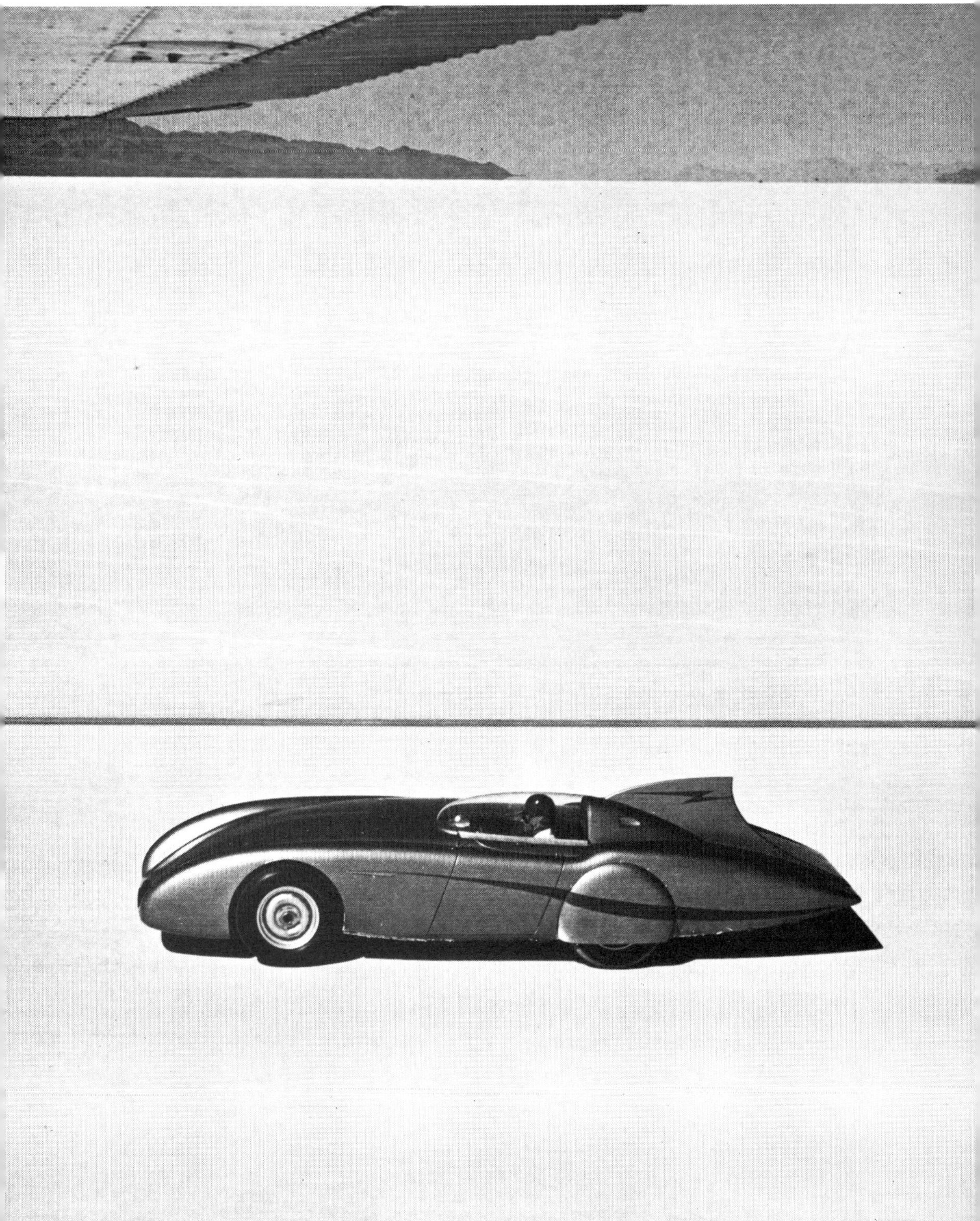

the streamliner meant that time was not on our side and we had to hurry. Next day the 24-hour run started at 7.48 am with DMH at the wheel. 1 hour 29 minutes later, the 200-mile record fell at 133.74 mph. George Eyston then took 3 hours at the wheel, followed by Carroll Shelby, Mort Goodall and Roy Jackson-Moore. At midday the temperature rose to 90°F. After 12 hours we changed the tyres. Mort Goodall enlivened the proceedings by leaving his braking too late for the pit stop, ending up with a slow speed spin.

Night came and the temperature dropped to the 70s. We spent the time talking, drinking tea and eating. The car circulated regularly, passing the pit garage every $4\frac{1}{2}$ minutes. The AAA observers were stationed at intervals around the circle to ensure that the drivers did not take short cuts. For the pit crew, life was pretty easy. Two were always on duty ready for an unscheduled stop but no one left the pit area for the whole of the 24 hours.

I was in charge of the crew, consisting of Roger Menadue from Warwick, Jack Ryan, Eric Miller and Ken Harris from Austin America, George Perry of Lucas, Jimmy Harrison of SU Carburettor Co., Lyle Hysert of Dunlop and Ralph Le Hew of Champion. Reeves Dutton and the other AAA representatives watched every move and told us tales of past record attempts and the Indianapolis races.

The car completed the 24 hours without faltering, with an overall average speed of 132.29 mph.

Following the completion of the 24-hour run, the streamliner, fitted with

Roy Jackson-Moor entering the 'garage' for a pit stop in the 1954 endurance car. The condition of the scraped salt in the foreground is in marked contrast to the ridged salt shown on other photographs,

GCH takes a spell of timing the 1954 endurance run. We kept our own time to control pit stops. Smiths loaned us the board together with their super-accurate chronograph clocks.

distance tyres with more tread rubber than those used at the straightaway, was readied. Carroll Shelby was to drive it around the circular track after the 1-hour and 200-mile records. The tyres were rated safe by Dunlop for continuous speeds up to 160 mph. Carroll, a tall Texan, was a tight fit in the cockpit and had to drive without the bubble top. The run started at 9.58 am with the temperature in the 80s. The car with its whining supercharger and raucous exhaust was a stirring sight as it sped around the track. The fastest lap was 161.01 mph and the average for the hour from a standing start, 156.97 mph.

The 1954 runs were really the best of the three record-breaking expeditions we made, setting some records that were to stand for many years. The 4-cylinder Austin at the peak of its development was a lovable thing, rugged, reliable and very easy to work on. Little did we realise what troubles the new 6-cylinder that followed were to cause us. Tired but happy, the MG and Healey crews once again celebrated their success at the Stateline Hotel, 500 yards up the road from Wendover. Unfortunately, the fate of the two record cars was not a glamorous one. Despite intense hosing down inside and out and treatment with special oil sprays, the salt, driven by the speed into every nook and cranny, caused extensive corrosion which eventually consigned them to the scrapyard.

Modified Austin Healey 100
Summary of Record Results: Bonneville Salt Flats, Utah, USA

22nd, 23rd and 24th August 1954:
Drivers: Donald Healey, Carroll Shelby, Capt. George Eyston, H. Morris Goodall and R. Jackson-Moore.
National Class 'D'

Flying Start:		*Standing Start:*	
	mph		mph
1 km	192.74	
*5 km	182.26	
*5 mile	183.73	
*10 km	183.84	
*10 mile	181.08	25 km	145.61
25 km	157.23	25 mile	149.85
25 mile	157.37	*50 km	151.32
50 km	157.44	*50 mile	153.88
50 mile	157.77	*100 km	154.63
100 km	157.87	*100 mile	155.95
100 mile	157.68	*200 km	156.22
200 km	157.94	200 mile	133.74
		500 km	133.95
		500 mile	132.62
1,000 km	132.99	*1,000 km	132.81
1,000 mile	132.70	**1,000 mile	132.59

Record Breaking

Flying Start:		Standing Start:	
2,000 km	132.80	*2,000 km	132.72
2,000 mile	132.44	*2,000 mile	132.38
3,000 km	132.25	*3,000 km	132.18
3,000 mile	132.21	*3,000 mile	132.16
4,000 km	132.06	*4,000 km	132.02
5,000 km	132.30	*5,000 km	132.27
1 hour	157.92	*1 hour	156.97
6 hours	133.21	*6 hours	133.06
12 hours	132.54	*12 hours	132.47
24 hours	132.33	*24 hours	132.29

*also broke record for International Class 'D'.

Fuel:	Shell	Tyres:	Dunlop
Electrical system:	Lucas	Oil:	Castrol
Carburettors:	SU	Clutch:	Borg & Beck
Brakes:	Dunlop	Wheels:	Dunlop
Engine:	Austin Healey 4-cylinder 2,660-cc capacity		

The records at speeds of over 145 mph were taken by the supercharged streamliner. Those under this speed were taken by the unsupercharged normal-bodied car.

In 1956 we planned some more record attempts to give the 100 Six some publicity and to advertise its arrival. George Eyston, ably assisted by George Williams of Castrol, laid the plans and organised an outing to the Salt Flats once again. DMH would attempt to break 200 mph on the straightaway, using the streamliner fitted with a blown 6-cylinder engine. Distance records of up to 6 hours would also be attempted with the unblown car.

Dr John Weaving of Austin's research department took the opportunity to test the car in the wind tunnel. He made some alterations to reduce drag, reducing the frontal area and removing the fin. A truly streamlined vehicle should be directionally stable and not require a fin. These radical changes gave a slight but vital reduction of drag but ruined the lines of the car. Bill Leyland again undertook the engine development. He had some hair-raising moments with various breakages in the test house before making the engine produce 292 bhp at just over 5,000 rpm.

Gerry Coker designed a body with a lengthened nose and tail based on the 100 centre section for the distance attempts. The radiator air intake was styled in the shape of the 100 Six with its wavy horizontal bar feature. Jensen constructed this body and a further three for racing in aluminium alloy. All cars were finished in the traditional Healey ice blue.

Eddie Maher, chief of Morris Motors' engine research and development department at Courthouse Green in Coventry, prepared the long-distance engines. The extent to which these engines differed from production 100 Six units was deliberately understated in various releases. The engines had a compression ratio of 10.2 to 1, were fitted with triple Weber 40 DCO3 carburettors and produced 164 bhp at 5,500 rpm, running on a mixture of $\frac{1}{3}$ methanol, $\frac{1}{3}$ benzole and $\frac{1}{3}$ premium petrol. On premium fuel only 156 bhp was given at 5,500 rpm. The engine number was XSP234-3.

The cars were run at the Motor Industry Research Association proving ground at Lindley. The Austin back axle designed for 90 bhp in the 100 was quite happy dealing with 292 hp at maximum speed, but it would have failed very quickly if full power had been applied in the lower gears. The technique was to accelerate relatively gently on small throttle openings until fourth gear was engaged when the full power was gradually applied. The acceleration was still pretty impressive although at least a 4-mile run-up to maximum

The 100 Six streamliner, with which DMH was to exceed 200 mph at Bonneville, after being unloaded from the Queen Elizabeth *at New York, July 1956.*

was needed. The tests merely confirmed the functioning of the units and directional stability of the vehicles. Engineers can develop engines on the test bed for ever but the only thing that matters in the end is performance on the road or track. There was only one place where final proof of these efforts could be obtained and that was Bonneville.

When we arrived in Bonneville, we discovered that the cars had sustained some body damage in transit. This we rectified and the cars were ready to run on 9th August. The complicated warming-up procedure was carried out as the sky lightened. The Champion NA12 plugs were fitted and DMH took off on his first run up the straightaway. He accelerated steadily for 3 miles up to 4,800 rpm in fifth gear; then, when he was just over 200 mph, there was a loud explosion and flames shot vertically upwards from the exhaust. DMH quickly brought the car to rest. We discovered that the blower drive had failed and that was the end of the car's running for the day. Next the distance car was warmed up and driven over the straightaway. The car was very disappointing, suffering very bad vapour lock with difficult starting. The engine had an incipient misfire at speed. The inlet manifolds were filed to increase the clearance from the hot exhaust pipes. Fuel line lagging was increased and extra cold air piped to the carburettor area. Fuel flow was checked – at nearly 30 gallons per hour it was definitely enough. The distributor cap was changed as there was evidence of a possible crack.

On 14th August the distance record attempt started. After 60 miles the engine started missing again and a compression check revealed that there was a great lack of compression on number one cylinder. So it was back to Wendover Service Station for removal of the cylinder head. Number one inlet valve was badly carboned and not seating and there was also evidence of imminent gasket failure. Due to casting errors the water passages from the block to the head did not agree. The fitted gasket could not be properly gripped and failure was bound to occur. The valve was replaced and all the valves ground in with fine paste. The cylinder head was replaced with a new gasket liberally coated with Wellworthy's jointing compound. We knew that the life of the gasket would not be a very long one and decided to start the run early in the cool of the day and limit the speed of the car.

On 16th August at 05.55 hours, Carroll Shelby set off. We planned to control the speed of the car by signals so that it just broke the existing records. After 3 hours 27 minutes Shelby was called in. The car was refuelled and Roy Jackson-Moore set off. So far the existing records had been exceeded by the necessary margin. After some two hours, Roy stopped with overheating and misfiring. The car was filled up with water and Wonderweld and Roy set off with instructions to take it easy and watch our signals. At this time and distance the existing records were at a speed of 144.23 mph. Roy carried on maintaining the average at over 145 mph. Some 20 minutes after beating the six-hour record, and 80 miles short of the 1,000-mile record, the gasket gave

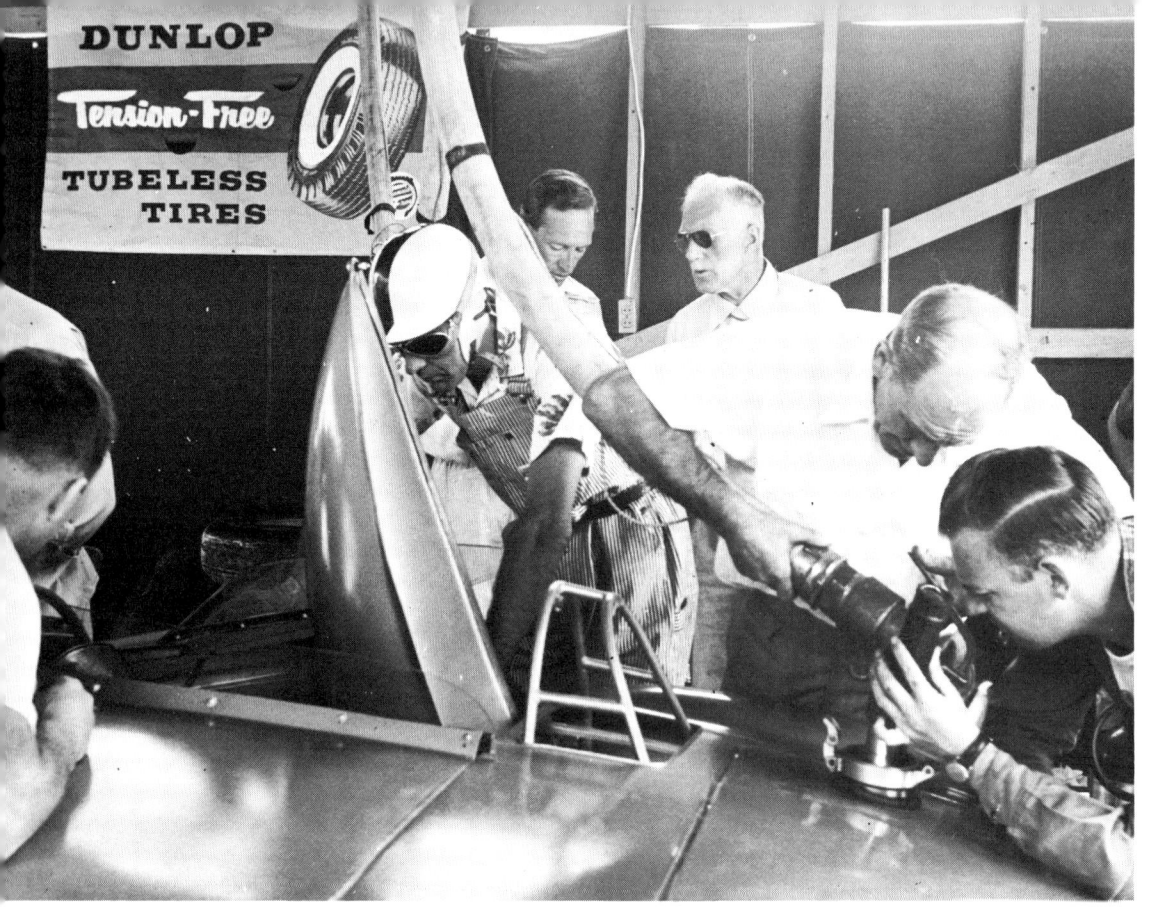

Refuelling stop for the 1956 100 Six endurance car. Carroll Shelby is about to climb in, while Jack Bough of Lucas watches the fuel lever with a torch. (Daniel Rubin)

up the struggle and Roy brought the sick car to the pits. We had broken all the records we were attempting with the exception of the 1,000 miles. We were happy but disappointed as we knew that but for the gasket sealing troubles, records could have been established at a much higher speed. The overall fuel consumption worked out at 12.52 mpg and confirms the light throttle work of the drivers.

We then turned to the streamlined car. The power unit was stripped to reveal a sorry state of affairs. The blower drive chain had broken wrecking the crankshaft sprocket. Three of the six pistons had picked up and scored badly. Using the local service station's equipment, we honed all six cylinder bores until all trace of damage was removed. Each of the six pistons was filed by hand to remove markings and increase the clearance. A phone call to John Weaving as he arrived at work produced a spare set of chains and sprockets within 24 hours. All international phone calls were handled by a helpful lady at the local railroad station. In one room she manned the telegraph, issue of tickets and cooked the food for travellers. The speed, efficiency

Roy Jackson-Moore leaves the 'garage' after a pit stop in the 1956 endurance 6-cylinder

A happy crew, after the 1956 endurance car had completed six hours. Left to right: an unknown, Bill Pringle, George Williams, George Eyston, Carroll Shelby, Phil Harris, Roger Menadue, Roy Jackson-Moore, Eric Vale and GCH. (Daniel Rubin)

Cockpit of the 1956 streamliner showing the rectangular wheel with fireswitch, and oil temperature, oil pressure, boost pressure, rev counter and water temperature gauges. The fuel pressure gauge is just discernable through the wheel. (Robert Mottar)

and courtesy of such telephone and air systems never ceases to amaze the visitor from Europe.

DMH at the wheel of the 1956 streamlined car, at over 200 mph on the straightaway.

We rebuilt the power unit exactly to Bill Leyland's detailed instructions and the car was towed to the straightaway once more.

DMH made two runs in opposite directions. Before the measured mile had been covered on the return, the familiar bang was heard. This time DMH coasted the car for as long as possible. Now we had to wait for the timekeepers to complete their calculations. The timing mechanism was

From left to right: Roy Jackson-Moore, DMH, George Eyston and Carroll Shelby, just after DMH had been officially timed at 203.06 mph in the 1956 streamlined car. Note windsock indicating the direction of the wind.

controlled by light beams, producing an automatic print-out of the time as the car passed each of the various timing points. The first run produced a speed of 203.76 mph over the distance while the return run was at a lower speed. However, the speed over a measured distance in each direction exceeded 200 mph and so the certificate was issued by the officials. DMH was made a member of the select number of people to have exceeded 200 mph on land who form the 200 Miles Per Hour Club. At that time the land speed record was held by John Cobb in the Railton-Mobil Special at 394.2 mph. This car had two Napier Lion engines, each of 24 litres capacity producing a total of 2,600 bhp. George Eyston had previously held the record with his Thunderbolt at 357.5 mph.

Before my return to New York for a press party, I went to Portland Maine to meet Margot. We were delayed due to Hurricane Hazel – something that neither of us had ever experienced. We had had a marvellous week-end with her cousins, eating superb Maine lobster handpicked from enormous tanks. On Monday morning we went up to their log cabin for a picnic and at about

Record Breaking

lunch-time the wind got up. Margot's cousin, Marion, decided we had better batten down the hatches and return to Portland. Her six-year-old son Greg was told to bring in the canoe from the lake: what had been a peaceful extent of water had now become a raging monster. We had great difficulty in getting the canoe out of the water and tied down securely. I was finding it very difficult to stand up and expected Greg to be blown away at any moment. Trees and telephone poles were coming down all around us. Margot suggested we took an axe back with us in case we had to clear the road to get through. Fortunately we did, as I had to wield it on two occasions to clear a way for the car. The destruction and chaos on arriving in the suburbs of Portland was unbelievable. Ice cream was being given away as was all the frozen food. All power lines were cut off. A day late we eventually made it to New York. All along the coast we could see extensive damage. 40-foot cruisers had been blown out of the sea right over the railway line, about a mile inland. When we arrived at our hotel in New York, DMH was on the phone giving us details of the press party due to start in an hour. The heat in New York in early September was horrible. Unless one was in air-conditioned buildings, it was like sitting in a Turkish bath.

The remoteness of the Salt Flats and the efforts of the publicity boys obscure the difficulties experienced in record breaking. Some people imagine it to be a simple matter but in fact it can be very arduous and tiring. However, we now had the results necessary for publicity and the back-up for the new 100 Six. Eddie Maher of Morris Engines was able to deal with the fault in the new 6-port cylinder head before the car went into production.

The 1956 London Motor Show stand featuring the 100 Six record breaker with streamlined bodywork.

Austin Healey 100 Six
Summary of Record Results: Bonneville Salt Flats, Utah, USA

16th August 1956: 10.0006-mile circular course
Drivers: Carroll Shelby and Roy Jackson-Moore
National Class 'D'

Flying Start:

	mph
200 mile	153.53
250 mile	153.52
300 km	153.54
300 mile	153.58
400 km	153.52
400 mile	153.48
500 km	153.58
500 mile	153.48
1,000 km	151.27
3 hours	153.48
6 hours	146.07

Standing Start:

	mph
200 mile	152.58
250 mile	152.74
300 km	152.51
300 mile	152.92
400 km	152.73
400 mile	153.02
500 km	152.95
500 mile	153.14
1,000 km	150.98
3 hours	153.98
6 hours	145.96

International Class 'D'

200 mile	152.58	3 hours	153.98
500 km	152.95	6 hours	145.96
1,000 km	150.98		

21st August 1956: 13-mile straightaway course
Driver: Donald Healey: supercharged 100 Six
For Certificate of Performance
Average speed: 203.11 mph

All results certified by Sports Commission of United States Auto Club.

The record breakers used in 1953, 1954 and 1956 were based on standard 100 chassis frames, centre body sections, suspension and axles. Special ratio crown wheels and pinions were used.

Once the decision to attack records had been made, models for wind-tunnel testing were constructed. A one-eighth scale model was used for the standard car and a larger size model was built of the streamlined car. The streamlined model consisted of the standard 100 centre line of the front wheels and rearward from the rear wheels. The cockpit was covered with a blister cover for the driver and a tail fin for stability. Aerodynamicists have always questioned the value of tail fins on a streamlined vehicle but they do have a psychological value. They also make the car visible at a greater distance.

The 1954 tests were carried out by Sir W. G. Armstrong Whitworth Aircraft Limited in their low-speed wind tunnel at Coventry. Of 5 feet by 4 feet cross section, this uses a tunnel speed of approximately 80 feet per second. Previously, Armstrong Whitworth had completed tests on the 2.4-litre saloon and our 1951 Nash Healey Le Mans coupé. At the same time, George Eyston lent us his model of his Speed Of the Wind record breaker. The actual performance of the full size vehicles relating to these models was well known and the correlation of test and actual figures provided a firm basis for prediction of results.

One problem is the determination of drag caused by the cooling system. Apertures and ducting are added to models to try to reproduce these effects. The models were constructed in modelling clay which made it very easy to change the shape and frontal area and study the different effects. The formula for drag in pounds is: drag = KSV^2, where K is the drag factor, S the cross-sectional area in square feet and V velocity in mph. In addition to drag measurements, lift forces and pressure distribution are recorded. These figures are important in determining the car's stability and positioning air intake and outlet points. Armstrong Whitworth were able to provide a very complete set of results and recommendations that could be used for the actual car design. The results indicated that beyond a certain point of modification, reduction in drag would be very small and that without changing the appearance drastically, very little benefit would be obtained.

Scale model of the 1954 streamlined record breaker, being tested in Armstrong Whitworth's wind tunnel at Whitley, Coventry for airflow.

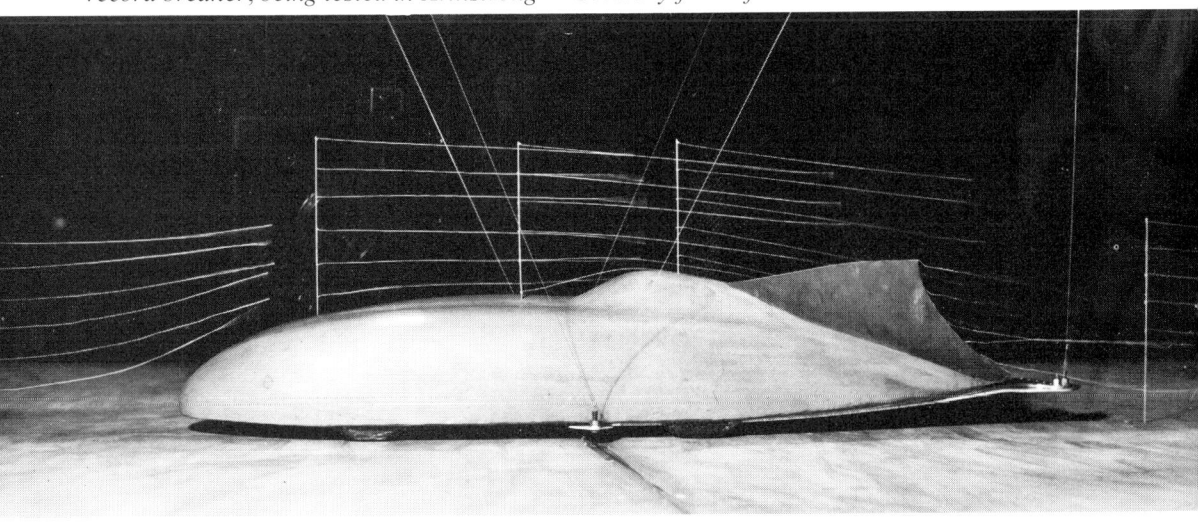

The 1956 endurance car in Austin's full size wind tunnel, complete with bubble fairing to try to reduce drag.

The remarkable accuracy of the results and predictions can be gauged from the following figures:

Model	AWA prediction	True speed obtained
2.4-litre saloon	102	103 (1947)
Austin Healey 100	144	143 (1953)
Nash Healey	133	132 (1951)
Speed of the Wind	180	184
Streamlined car	192	192.67 (1954)

The cars were constructed and then dispatched to Longbridge for testing in Austin's full-size wind tunnel. The wind tunnel facility was not used much except for special investigation purposes. The maximum wind speed possible was comparatively low but the results obtainable were exceedingly accurate. Like Armstrong Whitworth, Doc Weaving's staff had accumulated a great deal of data from previous tests that enabled them to predict the actual results with great accuracy. They had compiled test results on a great number of cars over the years. One test revealed that a certain car could have had a greatly

(Opposite):
This power curve gives the results of Austin's development work on the 'S' type engine. It also shows the reduction in output available at the high altitude of the Bonneville Salt Flats.

Record Breaking

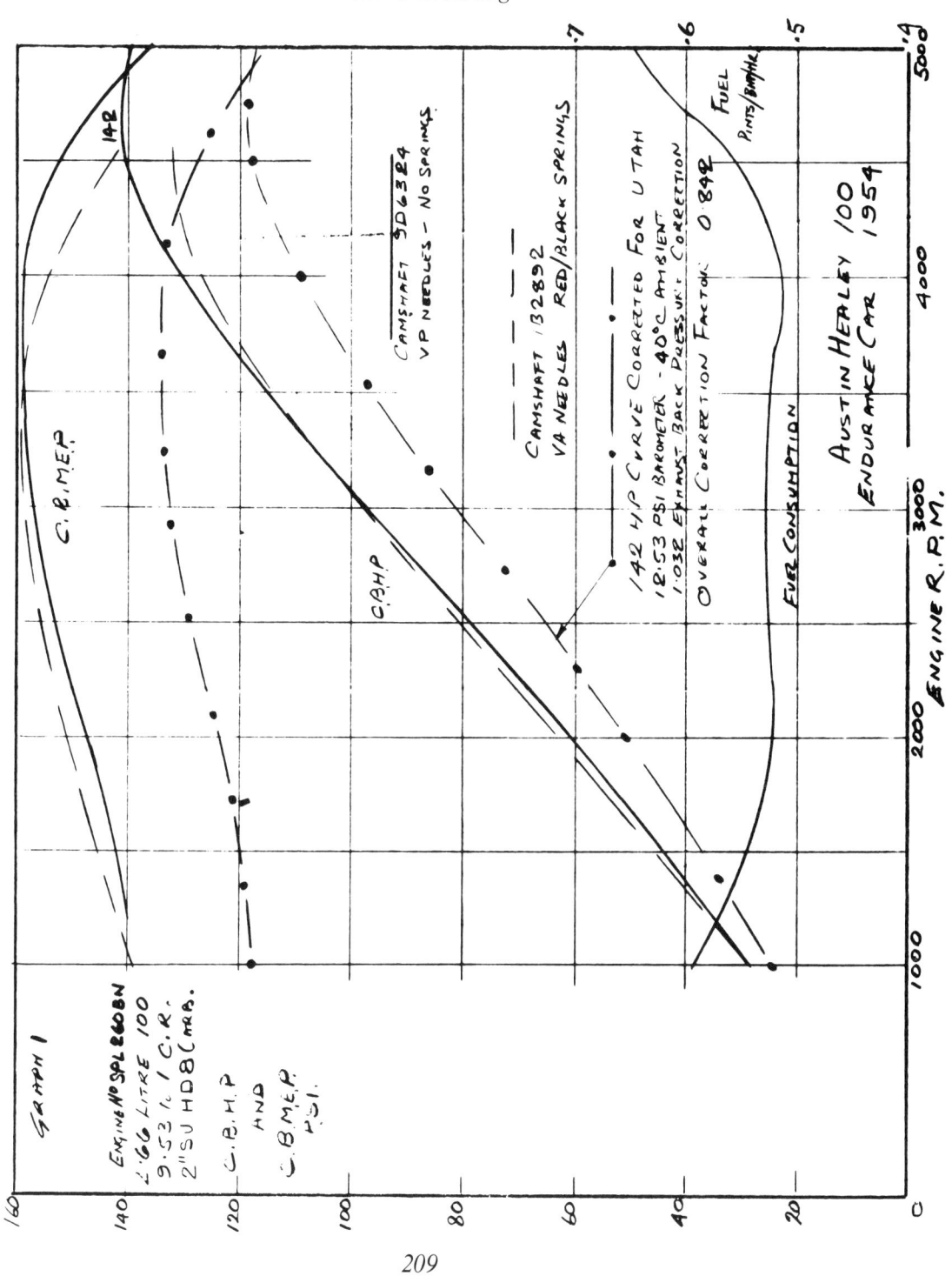

Austin Healey: The Story of the Big Healeys

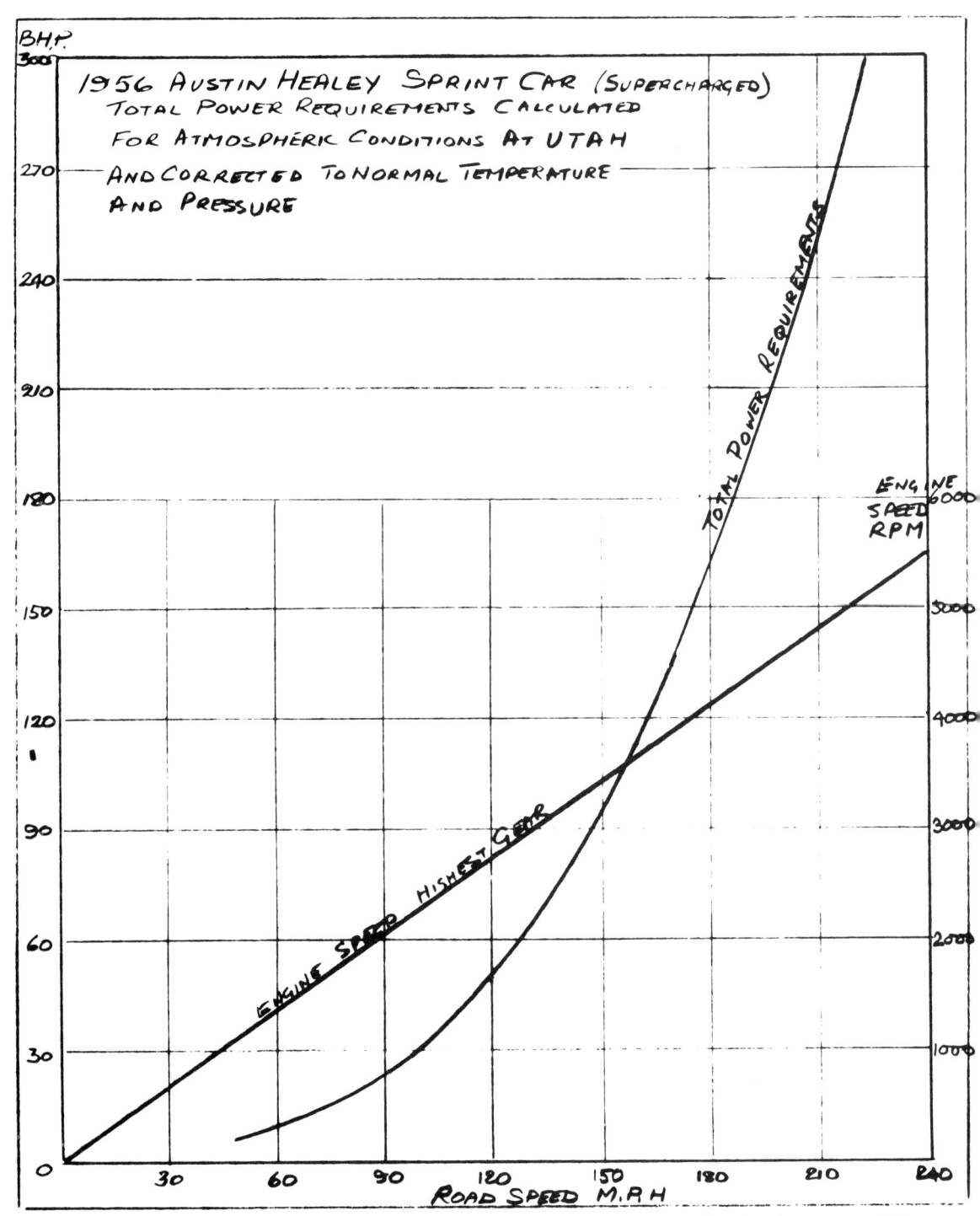

For 1956 Austin modified the streamliner to reduce drag. As shown on this graph, the improvement was small but it did enable DMH to break the magic 200 mph figure.

Record Breaking

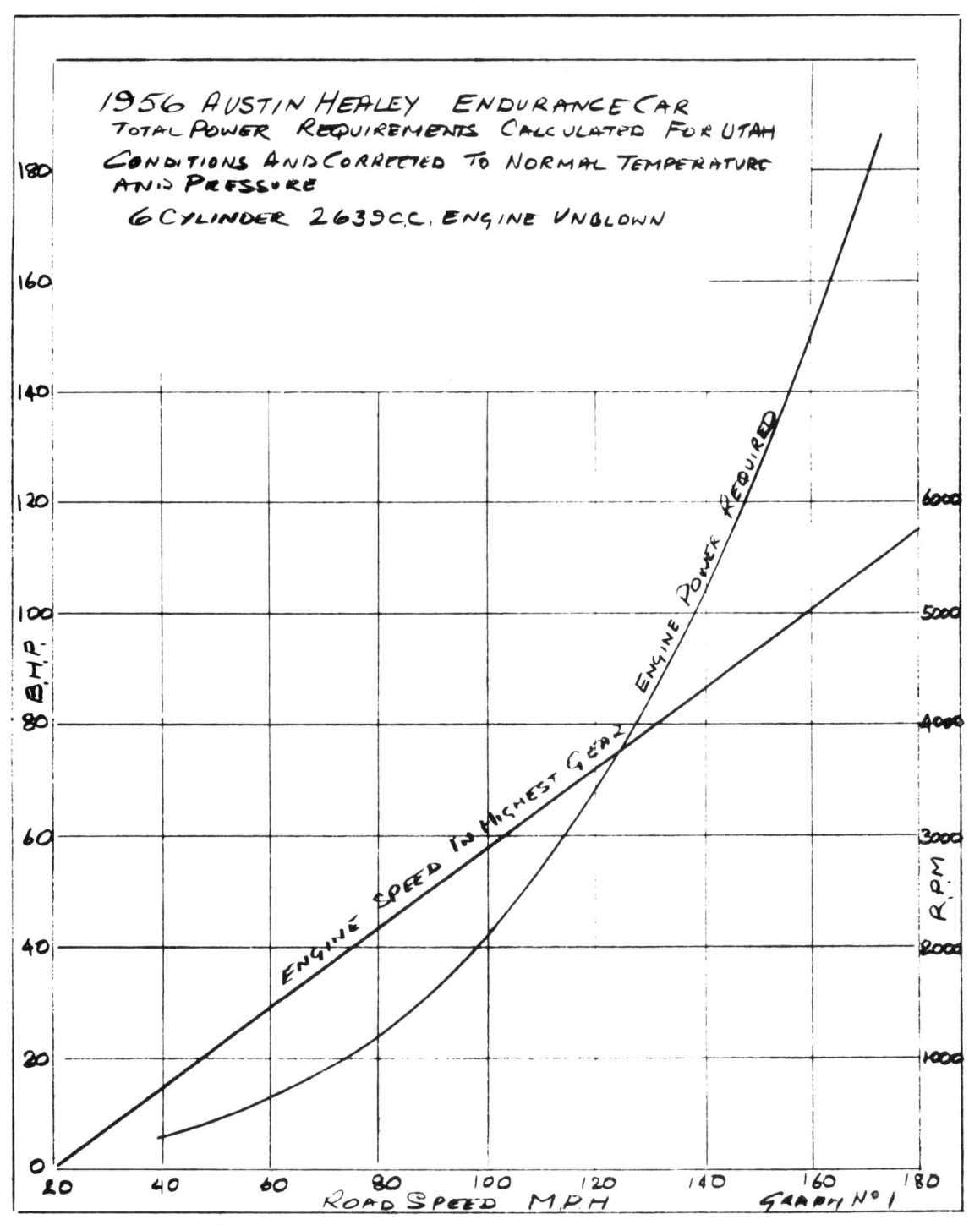

1956 AUSTIN HEALEY ENDURANCE CAR
TOTAL POWER REQUIREMENTS CALCULATED FOR UTAH CONDITIONS AND CORRECTED TO NORMAL TEMPERATURE AND PRESSURE
6 CYLINDER 2639 C.C. ENGINE UNBLOWN

GRAPH N° 1

The 1956 unblown endurance car also benefited from improved drag reduction.

Dunlop wheel and record tyre on the 100 Six, showing the build-up of salt on the wheel arch after a 6-hour run. (Robert Mottar)

increased maximum speed if it was driven in reverse.

Austin tested the 1954 car as received from us and developed the engines for this attempt. The testbed power indicated that the streamlined car would do 192 mph and the unblown endurance car 147 mph. The 1954 unblown engines gave 141 bhp at 4,700 rpm against the 1953 engines' 131 bhp.

For 1956, Austin carried out extensive modifications to ensure that the 200 mph mark would be exceeded. The supercharged 6-cylinder gave 292 bhp at 5,090 rpm and should have propelled the car at 217 mph with full radiator intake to 221.5 with $\frac{2}{3}$ of the area blanked off. As has been described, engine trouble was to prevent this speed being realised.

Graham Page put a lot of effort into producing the necessary information. In the past 20 odd years, great advances have been made in aerodynamic knowledge as applied to motor cars, and much of what we did would now appear to be wrong. Yet, 30 years before, the car would have been fast enough to hold the world's land speed record.

One feature we incorporated was a fire extinguishing system using Graviner equipment. A gravity switch would set this off on shock or alternatively the driver could activate the system by means of a large switch in the centre of the wheel. Fire is an ever-present hazard and burns are one of the nastiest forms of injury. The extinguishant used then and for many years afterwards was chloro bromo methane. It has since been discovered that this can be poisonous and nowadays improved chemicals are used. It was just as well that our drivers, and later MG drivers, never had occasion to press the button.

Dunlop built special tyres for record breaking, using light casings with thin treads to resist the high centrifugal forces involved. Pressures were around 55 lb per square inch. Dunlop have a vast experience of record breaking over very many years and we never experienced a tyre failure on their equipment. Dunlop also built the pressed aluminium wheels which were light and immensely strong.

The Clubs

The many Austin Healey clubs that now exist throughout the world originate from the old Healey Drivers Club. This was formed in 1955, primarily by Peter Cavanagh – a well known radio personality, Brian Healey, John Langrishe and Mort Goodall. It was operated in a very free and easy manner, a high proportion of its members being owners of the older 2.4-litre Healeys.

When BMC moved production of the 100 Six to Abingdon in 1957, John Thornley, a great club enthusiast, suggested that the club be reorganised on the lines of the MG Car Club. Abingdon agreed to provide a home for the club, secretarial facilities and equal space with the MG Club in *Safety Fast*. This excellent little magazine, edited by Stuart Seager, provided interesting and informative reading for sports car owners, although possibly the fact that it was a house magazine, and the consequent restrictions on editorial freedom, reduced its viability. Its cover gave pride of place to MG and Austin Healey cars alternately, and it enjoyed a world-wide circulation. (Like the Healey cars themselves, issues of *Safety Fast* have now become collectors' items, for sadly it was to disappear under the Stokes regime.)

In 1961 the Austin Healey Club Ltd was formed, as proprietor of the various local clubs that had grown up around the world, over which it exercised a very loose control. Its aim was to keep the clubs on the right lines and prevent them from behaving in such a way as to bring discredit to the name. The main activity in this latter respect was confined to pacifying the warring factors – the old 2.4-litre men, the 100 S and 3000 men, and the Sprite

The Clubs

A small selection of t-shirts worn by enthusiastic club members: 'Happiness is frog-eyed', 'Happiness is a Big Healey', and 'Happiness is driving a Big Healey'. The line-up in the foreground is: 'Bird- pullinlipmovineyecatchinlegkillin- backbreakinrenovatinrustfillinbank- ruptinforever pushin . . . Frog-eye'. The numbers and variety are increasing all the time!

owners. These three groups of enthusiasts – and particularly the Sprite owners – tended to squabble. There was quite a lot of resistance to this change – mainly from that small sector which always resists change. John Thornley was suspected of empire building (and he probably was, as he had quite a struggle to build up Abingdon).

The Club was fortunate in securing Peter Browning as its general secretary. With great patience and tact, Peter was able to subdue the warring factions and start forming the scattered sections into a unified club. He spent untold evenings arranging meetings, film shows, quizzes and get-togethers. Works drivers were frequent and amusing visitors to these meetings, giving members an inside view of competition. Panels were a great feature of the 60s, and Peter and Alan Zafer organised a number of these.

The Healey Drivers Club had used the Silverstone badge, with the addition of the words 'Drivers Club', as its badge. The Austin Healey Club badge was

Austin Healey: The Story of the Big Healeys

based on this design. A long bridge was superimposed on the castle, to symbolise the association of Healey at Warwick with Austin at Longbridge. This badge change also produced a certain amount of grumbling from a number of diehards.

Membership during the days when the cars were in production consisted of owners of cars for which spares and service were readily available. Club racing was a major activity. A blown engine or a damaged wing were not a major disaster and technical information could be obtained from the factory without too much difficulty. One activity in which club members were most efficient and essential was signalling at Le Mans. Derek Wooton of Tech Del, makers of the very strong minilite alloy wheels, and 'Digger' Digby organised this on many occasions. With a pitifully small contribution from the company to their expenses, the signallers would make their own way to Le Mans, setting up camp near Mulsanne and living off the land for the 24 hours of the race. Despite the exceedingly primitive French telephone system from the pits, these men never gave an incorrect signal to the drivers.

When Peter Browning moved to take control of BMC's competition department, following the departure of Stuart Turner, Les Needham took over as general secretary. Les was a dedicated enthusiast and first-class

The Sprite team at Le Mans, 1966. Left to right: drivers Hedges and Hopkirk, GCH, D. Morley, C. Hendrie, J. Cashmore, T. Wellman, Mrs Wellman, 'Dan', and drivers Baker and Rhodes.

An Austin Healey 3000 leads the field in an American club race.

timekeeper. He ran the clubs until both *Safety Fast* and the Austin Healey Club Ltd disappeared under the new British Leyland reorganisation. The Healey Drivers Club Ltd was incorporated in April 1969 to carry on these functions. Brian Healey took over the duties of general secretary and carried on without the backing that BMC had provided. However, the organisation of the clubs through one central organisation created a vast amount of paperwork and consumed a lot of money. We realised that this was not the way to continue and so the various local clubs were given greater autonomy in a form of devolution. The somewhat rigid club organisation has now disappeared and the separate clubs continue under their own volition.

Today the clubs provide an opportunity for owners to meet and work out solutions to problems that have developed since the end of production. Now that factory services have ceased, a major problem is the supply of spares and information. Most clubs include some enthusiasts who have acquired great technical knowledge of the cars and have worked out ways of getting around the lack of spares. In addition, groups are better able to arrange the remanufacture of spares at an economic cost. Whilst it is possible to own and run a Healey independently, life becomes much easier as a club member – and more fun as well. In a sense, owning a Healey creates a need to join a club, while the existence of the clubs inspires many people to own a Healey! Club members and the owners of the older cars will find that the monthly publication *Thoroughbred and Classic Cars* provides a great deal of useful and interesting information. Now in its fourth year, it has become essential reading for the enthusiast.

'Healey Hotspurs'– the Midland Centre football team in 1968.

In Great Britain, the largest grouping today is that of the Midland Centre, which has a current membership of around 1,400 with new members joining at the rate of 20 per month. The organisation of this club is typical of what has evolved in the larger centres around the world. The chairman is Keith Boyer, an Australian (his compatriots seem to motivate much that is good in the old country). Secretary Robin Church keeps in touch with members throughout the world. Don Humphries, the owner of the only two 3000 coupés to be built, is the treasurer and keeps the financial affairs in good fettle. Carolyn Walters, the social secretary, organises many of the social events and get-togethers. Roger Godfrey is the competition secretary, responsible for arranging competitive events, sprints and combined events with other one-make clubs. Phil Wilkes edits the club magazine, a small publication filled with interesting articles and useful information on the cars. There are three parts secretaries: Bernard Wills specialises in 3000 and 100 Six models; Keith Boyer finds time to deal with the 4-cylinder 100 between rebuilding the ones he owns; and Derek Ross, an old Healey and Austin man, concentrates on the Sprite. Between the three of them, they help their club members to find parts at reasonable prices. A general committee handles more formal matters. Freed from the restraints previously imposed under the BMC banner, the club has been able to adapt readily to changing circumstances and become much more vital and effective.

National Healey Day is the great occasion in England. The 1975 Day took place at Donington, where Tom Wheatcroft has assembled his unique collection of racing cars and resuscitated the famous Donington Racing Circuit. The day's activities included a Concourse d'Elegance with plenty of classes, and saw a gathering of nearly 300 Healeys and Sprites. The 1977 Day took place on 31st July at Dodington Park, near Bath. The event

Some of the 315-plus Healeys assembled at National Healey Day, 1977, lined up for viewing by 1,500 enthusiasts.

was organised by the National Club and an organising committee drawn from several club centres within the UK. Along with Ted Worswick and John Chatham, I was roped in to judge the annual Concours d'Elegance, which was divided into five classes:

1. Sprites of all marques
2. Jensen Healeys, Warwick-built Austin Healeys and old 2.4-litre Healeys
3. 100, 100 M and 100 S
4. 100 Six, 3000 MkI and early MkII
5. Late 3000 MkII and MkIII convertibles

John judged the cars' overall appearance and condition, Ted did the cockpit

The leading Midlands sports car specialist, Roy Standley, found this late low-mileage 3000 MkIII. Now owned by Derek Ross of Leyland, it was voted the winner of the Concours d'Elegance at the 1977 National Healey Day.

and I covered the engine compartment and boot. When all the marks had been totalled up, the top car from each class was called forward to line up for our assessment of the best car of the meeting. This was no easy task, but by a unanimous verdict we voted Derek Ross's gleaming white 3000 MkIII the outright winner, narrowly beating Roger Moss's early 3000 and Keith Boyer's 100 M. A fun gymkhana was held next, with some spirited and amusing competition, followed by a cavalcade of all entrants. John Chatham drove Ted Worswick and me around the ring at the head of a tremendous line of cars. No less than 315 Healeys were present, of nearly every type excluding the elusive 100 S, viewed by 1500 spectators. Other activities of the day included a tombola and raffle, various trade stalls, and the club bring and buy stall, where new and used spare parts were available.

This was the greatest Healey gathering I have yet attended and it was an exhilerating experience. My father came up for the day from Cornwall, together with Brian and four more members of the family: together with my wife and two daughters, this brought the total Healey contingent up to ten! The sun blazed down throughout the proceedings and club organisers John Smith, Robin Church and Carolyn Walters must have been delighted at the success that followed their painstaking efforts over so many weeks.

Other club activities in Britain, on a smaller scale, include the traditional 'noggin and natter', treasure hunts and film shows. I recently rescued some of the family and publicity films, which will provide some interesting viewing in the winter months.

Over 130 Big Healeys assembled at Eureka in 1976 for DMH's visit to the US clubs. (Kevin Faughnan)

DMH being guided through the Healey line-up by Doris Cross, at Eureka, 1976. (Kevin Faughnan)

The largest club grouping in the USA is the Pacific Center in California. A Pacific Center had existed prior to the formal organisation introduced under the BMC umbrella, but when BMC withdrew its club support it disappeared, like many other overseas clubs. It was reformed in 1970, thanks to a lot of hard work put in by Hank Leach, who became president. By 1972 enthusiastic organisation had resulted in a membership of 450. By 1977 this has risen to 1,300 and is still growing at a healthy rate. In 1976 the American clubs arranged a US tour for DMH. Over 100 Big Healeys turned up at the East Coast Meet which was held at Cherry Hill, New Jersey. The second big meet was held at Eureka, California, and was organised by the Pacific Center. Here, no less than 130 Big Healeys were in attendance. As might be expected, the condition of the American Healeys was of an extremely high order.

In January 1977 the Australian clubs organised a visit by DMH. The Australian climate is kind to motor cars, and the Australians are expert at keeping them in good condition. DMH saw what is probably the greatest collection of 100 S cars still in existence. He returned via Hawaii, the home of another very active Healey club. He finished off the tour by indulging in a return flight on Concorde – he has always liked to sample the latest mode of transport.

No formal listing of the various club centres exists as they tended to become more independent after BMC withdrew their support. The following list is as up to date as possible, but new centres continue to emerge and I apologise for any I have missed. Club members Robin Church and Keith Boyer provided a great deal of information to help bring the club listings up to date.

Australia
Austin Healey Owners Club of New South Wales, GPO Box 2628, Sydney 2001. President: Alan 'Sebring' Jones.
Southern Australian Austin Healey Owners Club, 24 Monalta Drive, Belair, South Australia 5052. President: John Read.
Austin Healey Owners Club of Victoria, Roger Rayson, 18 Brendales Avenue, Blackburn, Victoria 3130.
Austin Healey Owners Club of Queensland, 17 Morehead Avenue, Norman Park, Queensland 4170. President: Carl Stecher.
Austin Healey Sprite Drivers Club, PO Box 248, Box Hill, Victoria 3128. President: Alex Robinson.

Austria
Franz Aigner, A-1200 Wien, Plankenmaisstrasse 20, Osterreich.

Canada
Calgary Austin Healey Club, MPO Box 2293, Calgary, Alberta T2P 2M6. President: Ken Barrow.
Austin Healey Owners Association of British Columbia, PO Box 80274, South Burnaby, British Columbia, V5H 3X5. President: John Swann.

Denmark
Austin Healey Club of Denmark, Morgans Rosenkilde, Rormosevej 20, 2400 NV, Copenhagen, Denmark.

Germany
Peter Kuprianoff, Leopoldstrasse 24A, 7500 Karlsruhe, W. Germany.

Great Britain
Midland Centre. Secretary: Robin Church, 39 Northampton Road, Roade, Northants.
Eastern Centre. Secretary: David Hicks, 102 Fairfax Drive, Westcliff-on-Sea, Essex.
New Forest Centre. Secretary: Mrs Pat Martin, 104 Winchester Road, Shirley, Southampton, Hants.
Southern Counties. Secretary: Mike Allman, 28 Strathearn Avenue, Whitton, Middx.
South Western Centre. Secretary: Carol Marks, 171 Coldharbour Road, Bristol.

The Clubs

Northern Centre. Secretary: Tim Bird, 10 Chatburn Avenue, Clitheroe, Lancs.

Thames Valley Centre. Secretary: Tom Oakman, 14 Burnt Oak, Wokingham, Berks.

Holland
Austin Healey Owners Club Nederlands, J. P. Broers, Van Kinsborgenlaan 35, Baarn, Holland.

New Zealand
Austin Healey Car Club of New Zealand Inc, PO Box 25–016, St. Heliers, Auckland 5, New Zealand. President: Mark Donaldson.

Southern Africa
Austin Healey Club of Southern Africa, Ron Field, PO Box 68399, Bryanston, Transvaal, S. Africa.

Sweden
Austin Healey Club of Sweden, Keneth Andren, Loviselundsvagen 34, 162–35 Vallingby, Sweden.

Switzerland
Austin Healey Club Schweiz, Felix Gugola, Veberlandstrasse 199A, 8600 Dubendorf, Switzerland.

United States of America
Austin Healey Club, Pacific Centre, 3623 West View Drive, San Jose, California 95122. President: Lou Buch.

Austin Healey Club of America, 705 Dimmeydale, Deerfield, Illinois 60015. President: Walter Blanck.

Austin Healey Club of South California, PO Box 4082, Riverside, California 92514. President: Jim Mayfield.

Austin Healey Club of Oregon, 3102 SE 7th Portland, Oregon 97202.

Tidewater Association of Classic Healeys, c/o B & B Foreign Auto Parts, 852 Virginia Beach, Virginia.

Austin Healey Club of Hawaii, 1508 A1 Keeaumoru Street, Honolulu 5, Hawaii. President: Rodney Hudik.

Later Days

It was a sad day for Abingdon, Warwick and the sporting motorist when the last and best of the Big Healeys left the MG production line at the close of 1967. BMC had been under constant pressure from the media and the city and in 1967 Donald Stokes, with political backing, was able to effect a merger with Leyland to produce the British Leyland Motor Corporation. The combination of the new company's rationalisation programme, the end of the old 6-cylinder 'C' series engine, and new American safety and emission regulations was just too much for the 16-year-old design to survive.

Unfortunately, many of the best people left the group soon after the merger. In the resultant reorganisation those who had been most closely allied with BMC seemed to suffer most. Stokes had been very affable on the brief occasions we had had contact with him, prior to the merger, from which we gained the opinion that he would like us in his camp. However, in many years of working with Morris and Austin, and later with BMC, we had developed a great respect for the organisation. To us, the Leyland side did not compare with BMC, and we considered their products to be deficient in engineering. So, prior to the merger, we firmly stayed in the BMC camp and rejected any possibility of a change of allegiance. After the merger, we were gradually eased out of the picture. MG were also cut down in stature. Production of the Big Healey ceased at the end of the year, when a total of some 74,000 models had been built. The successful 'C' series engine was replaced in the BMC engine range by a new engine of identical bore and stroke but

"TAKE THE HEALEY OUT OF PRODUCTION"

This cartoon by Jon was published in the Daily Mail *on 18th January 1968, coinciding with the end of the Big Healey. A superb example of the cartoonist's art, it symbolises the end of an era in motoring history.*

mediocre performance. It was dropped, together with the MG C and Austin 3-litre cars, after a very short production run. Our competition activities were curtailed and ultimately that skilled and devoted band that made up the competitions department was dispersed.

The Austin Healey Sprite continued in production for some years but it was obvious that some way had to be found to avoid paying us for every Austin Healey and MG Midget produced. We were notified that the Austin Healey Sprite would be dropped from production and with it any payments of consultant's fees. British Leyland continues to produce the Midget based on our design today, without DMH receiving any benefit. Though we had been correctly informed of his move in advance, much earlier we realised that there was no way for us to work within the new grouping and so we looked around for another avenue.

We decided to produce a sports car based on the very good Vauxhall units. Before we had got very far with the project, Kjell Qvale approached DMH to come in on the project. After much investigation Kjell obtained control of Jensen and the car was produced as the Jensen Healey. The car underwent a number of changes with which we were not in favour.

Production was late starting and the early cars produced in 1972 were badly finished and troublesome. Faults in the painting system gave rise to considerable problems with rusting. The early Lotus-supplied engines gave troubles which were not sorted out anything like quickly enough. Camshafts used to seize and the toothed timing belt would slip, resulting in damaged valves. The gasket between the camshaft housing and cylinder head would blow out, allowing the engine oil to escape. The needle valves in the Dellorto carburettors were not really effective, allowing the carburettors to flood and fill the engine with petrol. Early cars also suffered badly from water leaks.

The Jensen service department, under Ian Royal and David Millard, worked wonders dealing with the problems which for a variety of reasons continued to occur. In spite of these troubles, the car was popular and sold well. The most disappointed owners were those who had changed from a car that was the most reliable sports car ever, the 3000.

By 1974 the majority of the faults were eliminated and the quality improved. Jensen laid down a programme of new models, the GT, the 'F' and the 'G'. The 'F' was to have been a replacement for the ageing Jensen Interceptor, which DMH and I considered to be a tremendous task. The 'G' or Gull Wing was to have been a small 4-seat saloon of advanced appearance. Syd Enever worked on this project for some time after he retired from MG but it never reached the stage of running. The GT was an adaption of the Jensen Healey with fixed closed top, on the MGB GT formula. The trim and fittings of the GT were of a high standard and the higher price charged would have made a bigger contribution to the company's profits than that of the open car.

Jensen suffered from the oil crisis which reduced demand for the big

Later Days

Interceptor. Production of the open Jensen Healey was cut and replaced by the GT. Unfortunately for Jensen, there was a long gap between the two cars, due to production problems with the new GT, which caused a severe strain on their finances. Together with the oil crisis, and the expenditure on the 'F' and 'G' models, this eventually caused the directors to ask the bank to appoint a Receiver. British Leyland and Chrysler were having difficulties at the same time but fortunately government help was forthcoming for them.

An attempt was made to get Jensen going again with renewed production of the Jensen Healey but this never succeeded. With the end of Jensen, a highly skilled workforce of dedicated engineers and craftsmen was scattered.

The team that created the Austin Healey under DMH consisted of:

Myself:	Chief engineer
Barry Bilbie:	Chief chassis designer
Gerry Coker:	Chief body designer
Roger Menadue:	Chief experimental engineer.

Gerry went to join the American motor industry and Les Ireland took over his duties. Jim Cashmore took over from Roger Menadue. When the Big Healey production ceased we were gradually eased or pushed out of the picture by the British Leyland organisation, until all contact, officially, ended with the cessation of Sprite production. Geoff Price ran the service organisation which like most factory service units was not really profitable. The factory concept of service was that you kept owners happy and contented and much of the costs were born by other parts of the company. The goodwill produced by such operations has no value on a balance sheet. Service today is a real money spinner with very high labour and material mark-ups. Brian ran the sales organisation with great enthusiasm whilst it concentrated on our own products. However, the strain began to tell on his health and wisely he moved to Cornwall to take up a more healthy occupation as a market gardener. In no time he was restored to rude health, apparently shedding years in the process. His efforts more recently have been stymied by nasty people called planners.

I had never been enthusiastic about the retail side of the business, looking on it as a parasitic growth. Various ways of divesting ourselves of the retail side were investigated and in the end Healey Automobile Consultants Ltd and Healey Cars Ltd were seperated out and kept by the family, while the Donald Healey Motor Co Ltd was sold to the Hamblin Group. Of the people concerned with the Austin Healey, only three now remain with the Donald Healey Motor Co Ltd: Geoff Price—service manager, and Mike Guest and Clive Hendrie—two excellent mechanics. Geoff Price continues to be a very active and enthusiastic member of the Austin Healey Club.

The failures of engines and machinery that occurred during record attempts and competitions may come as a surprise to many readers, who have only read press reports or seen publicity films concerning the events described. To put these occurrences in their proper perspective it must be understood that the time and resources available were very limited. Time schedules were set that would be impossible today, and the probability of failure was not considered. Deadlines were met with work continuing to the very last minute. Due to the time involved in shipping the vehicles, it was not unusual for the crew to carry parts that had been developed later and to fit these before the start of the event. One instance I recall was at Sebring, when the crew flew to the circuit with a set of improved pistons to fit to the MG cars before the start!

Men worked very long hours until the job was completed. A lot of good work was done during the night when one was completely free from interruptions, sustained by pungent mugs of tea and sandwiches. The fact that success resulted so often is due to the 'night oil' burnt by Bill Leyland, Doc Weaving, Eric Barham and Don Hawley of Austin, Eddie Maher of Morris Engines and Roger Menadue and Barry Bilbie of Warwick. Much of the work was in addition to their normal duties.

If only a small part of the resources used on the MG C and Fireball XL5 had been channelled to the Big Healey, it could still be earning vast quantities of foreign exchange for the UK and providing pleasure to a lot of people. It need not have died. All the real sports cars with the exception of the Morgan have disappeared. Gone are the AC Cobra, E Type Jaguar, TR6 and Austin Healey. But the interest in Big Healeys is as great as ever as is evident by the activities of the clubs throughout the world. Really, Timo Makinen, the world-famous Finnish driver who loved the Big Healey, summed it up when he told me after a Targa Florio race: 'Geoff, you have bloody good car and bloody good wife!'

Having reminisced over the past, one must look to the present and the future. At present, Healey Cars and Healey Automobile Consultants Ltd, the two companies controlled by the Healey family, are working on a number of projects. One of these is not in the least connected with motor cars, being a very effective wind-powered generator designed to supply 24 volts DC. This work has been going on for some time and interest in it is increasing, as the search for practical alternative power sources becomes ever more urgent. Although we are continuing with design work on motor cars, safety and pollution legislation make this an extremely difficult field. There is a tremendous demand for a new Healey and we are actively trying to work out ways of meeting it – this is the work that really excites us.

Later Days

*End of the line: the last 3000 leaves the
MG plant at Abingdon.*

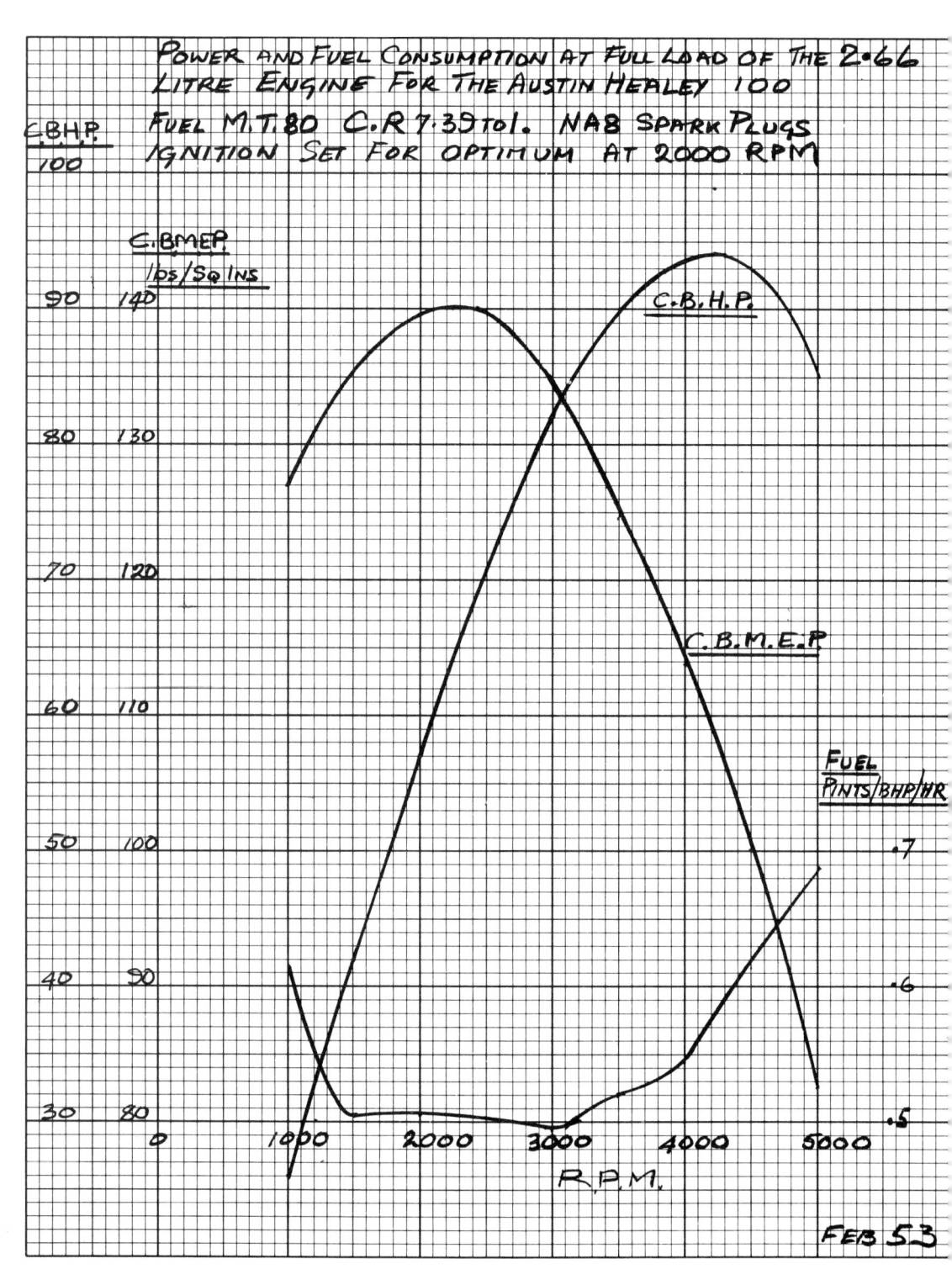

Graph 1: Power and fuel consumption at full load of the 2.66-litre engine used in the Austin Healey 100.

Appendices

The Engines

The 4-cylinder Austin Healey 100 engine has a curious history. During the war, Austin were requested to produce a replacement engine for the Jeep. Under Len Lord's direction, Bill Appleby did this by using 4 cylinders of the 6-cylinder army truck engine. A set of the 6-cylinder pattern equipment was cut up and modified and the castings produced overnight. Most of the work took place during periods when the assembly line was at rest, so that normal production could continue. This engine became the 16-hp Austin engine.

Austin then changed their type designation system, from the RAC hp rating system to one based on bhp. From the 16-hp engine, the 2.2-litre A70 was developed, and it in turn was then bored out to produce the 2.6-litre A90 Atlantic unit. The A90 had a claimed output of 88 bhp – Austin were more than honest in their power claims.

The A90 engine was adopted for the Austin Healey by replacing the Vokes torpedo-shaped air cleaner with two Burgess pancake filters. (The very efficient Vokes unit had to go, as it would not fit under the bonnet.) A series of bench tests was then carried out, using MT80–80 octane fuel. Harry Weslake had developed his heart-shaped combustion chamber so that the engine would run on the low octane 'Pool' petrol of that era, and the excellent fuel consumption at full and part load of the Austin Healey 100 are in part due to Harry's work. The engine had a compression ratio of 7.39 to 1, and was very economical in the 1,500 to 3,500 or normal cruising speed range. See Graph 1.

The need for great power for racing was met by developing the engine later known as the 100 S. Harry Weslake designed a head with four separate inlet ports, known as the 4-port or cross-flow head. Modifications to the top deck of the cylinder block were necessary to accommodate the different head stud location. Graph 2 shows the performance curves of the 100 S engine, number 261BN, used for the 1955 Le Mans race. With the larger SU HD8 carburettors and a compression ratio of 9.48 to 1, this gave 139 bhp at 4,750 rpm.

When the Austin Healey 100 was in production, Triumph introduced their TR2 sports car, powered by a more up-to-date engine, designed by Ted Grinham. This car gave good performance with economic fuel consumption and was clearly a sales threat. In fact, Austin Healeys and Triumphs were to battle it out for many years on tracks and in rallies. We took a hard look at the possibility of uprating the smaller bore Austin A70 engine as a replacement for the A90 unit. A high compression version of the A70, using Austin Healey 100 manifolds and carburettors was produced and tested. On the relatively high compression ratio of 8.7 to 1, it gave 94 bhp at 4,700 rpm. Due to its smaller swept volume, its output at lower speeds was inferior to the A90. Road tests of a 100 fitted with this engine gave performance similar to the A90 unit, but it was more fussy and not liked.

The 100 S engine was considered to involve too many changes and tooling alterations and to have too high a unit cost to warrant it going into full production. The 100 therefore continued with the A90-based engine until it was replaced by the 100 Six. The 100 Six engine was based on the 6-cylinder C series, designed by Morris Motors for the BMC group. The C series was designed for saloon cars and was not initally a high performance unit. The first engines in this series gave 92 bhp at 4,500 rpm, on a 7.2 to 1 compression ratio (see graph 4). The cylinder head had 4 separate inlet ports fed from a gallery cast in the head. This gallery, in contact with cooling water, should have given good economy but in fact output and fuel consumption were very disappointing in the early units (see graph 4). As described in the text, some pretty acrimonious discussions took place over the impending use of this engine in the Austin Healey. Eddie Maher of Morris produced a version with a higher compression ratio of 8.1 to 1, giving 106 bhp at 4,500 rpm. This was the basis for the 100 Six BN4 engine.

Harry Weslake at Rye was consistently producing greater power outputs which one group tried to disprove. They checked his equipment, test procedure and results without finding any discrepancy. They concluded that the air at Rye must be a contributing factor, bottled samples and had it analysed. Sea air is known to be beneficial to the performance of human beings but no parallel benefit for engines was discernable. The variations in power output of the early 6-cylinder engines were very high and the reasons difficult to determine. The investment in tooling limits what changes can be made to

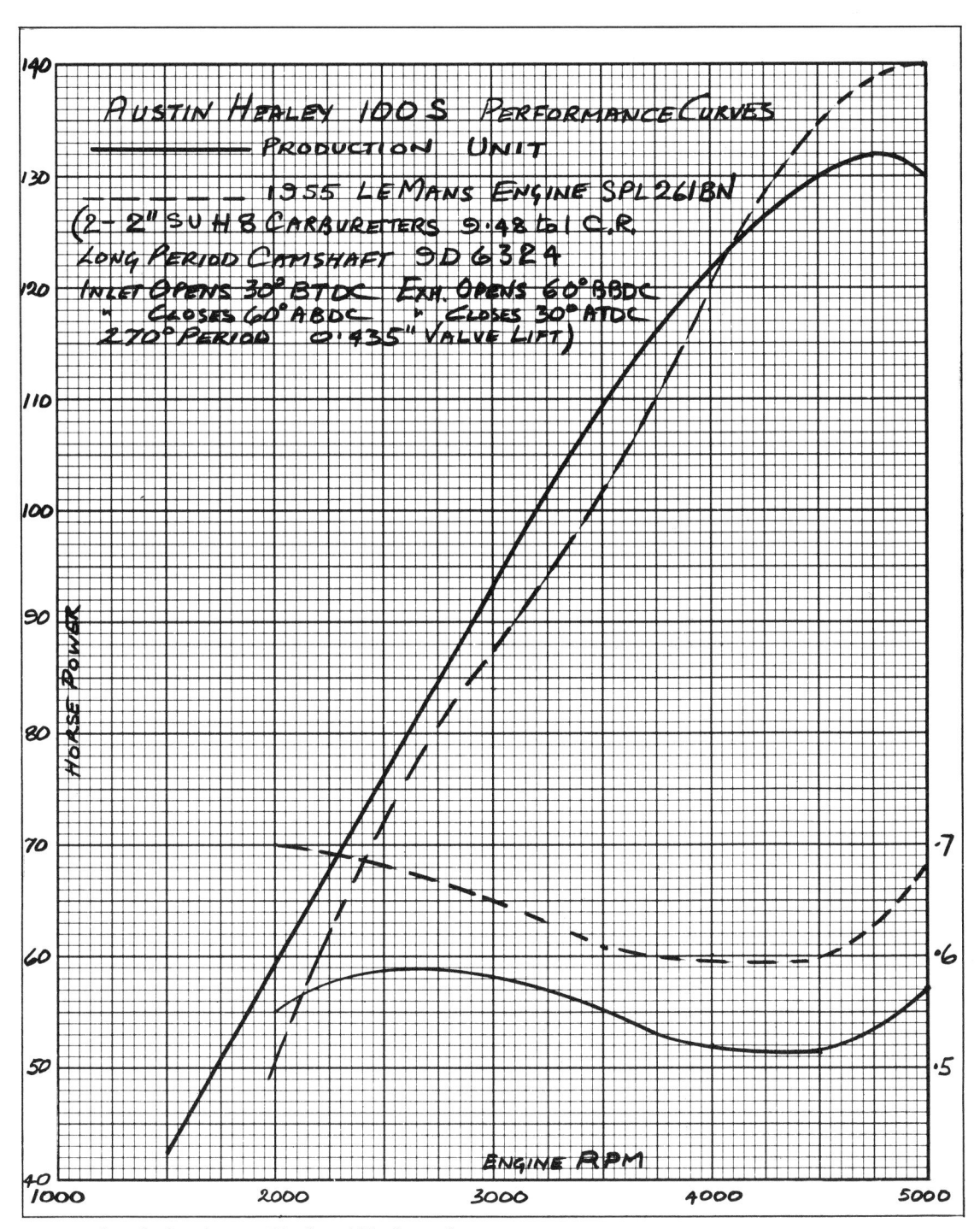

Graph 2: Austin Healey 100 S performance curves.

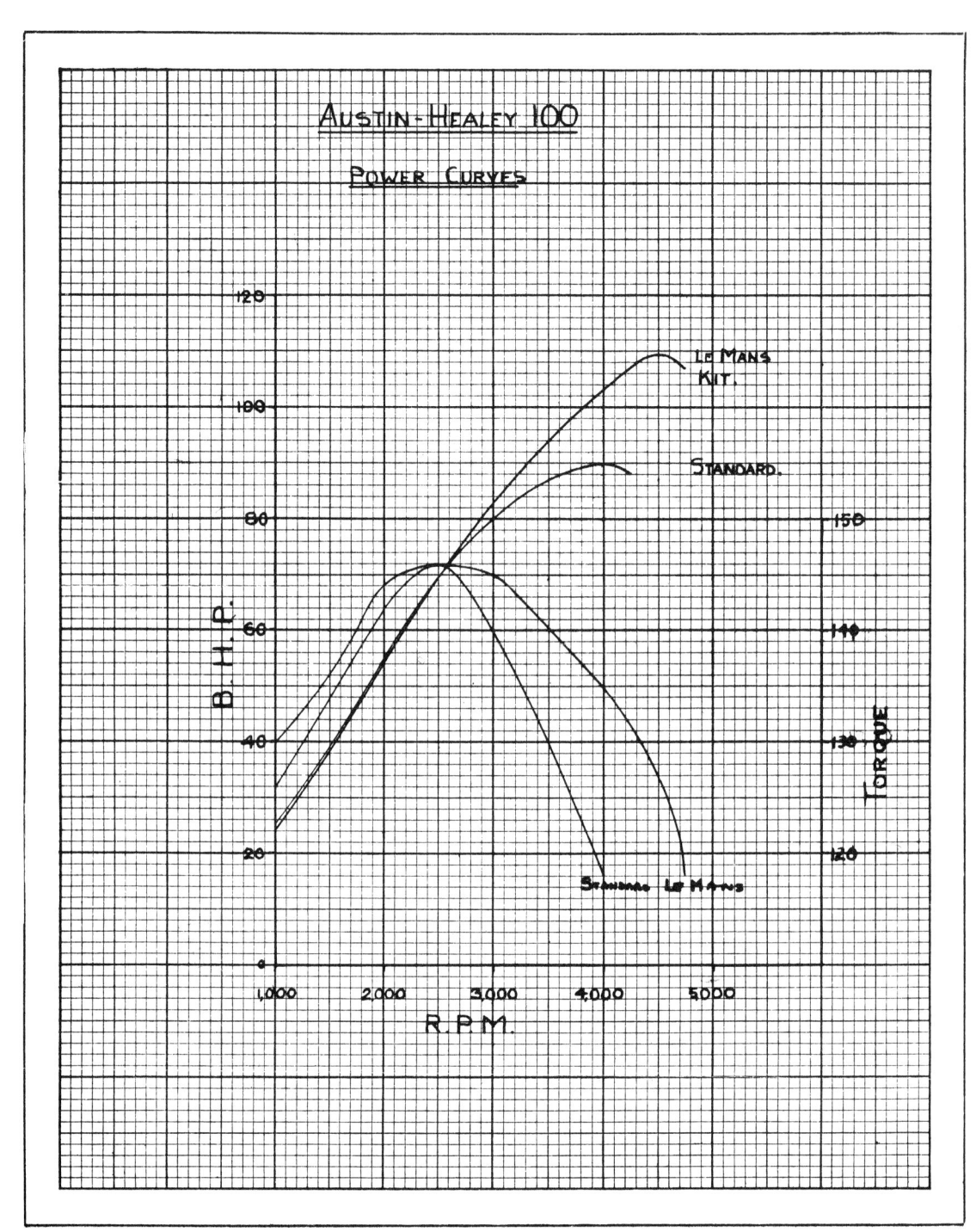

Graph 3: Austin Healey 100 power curves.

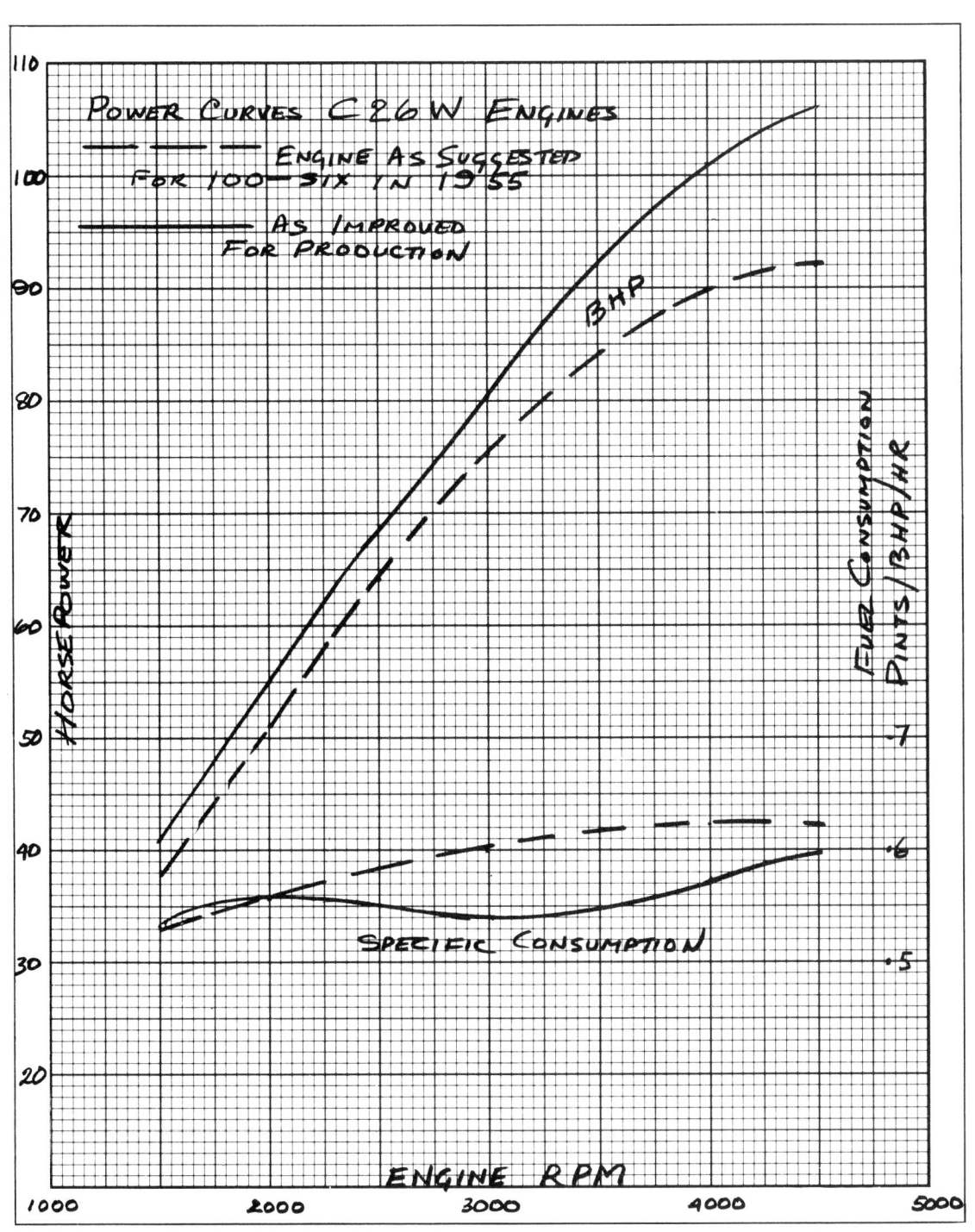

Graph 4: Power curves for C26W engines.

production units and the production men finally control what is produced.

Eddie Maher realised the limitation of the C engine's gallery head design and at Morris Engines produced a modified head with a separate inlet manifold. 6 separate inlet ports were improved in shape and the inlet valve seats were changed to improve breathing. Although this development took place at an early stage, it was not possible to incorporate it in production until the advent of the BN6 series in 1957. This head resulted in a drop in compression ratio from 8.4 to 7.9 to 1. Flat-top pistons, with the top near the top of the cylinder block, gave a ratio of 8.6 to 1 and an increase in power to 111 at 4,800 rpm. The head was first made available as an extra for increased performance. After considerable test bench and road development it became a standard fitment on all BN6 models. It was a major advance and was to continue in production until the end of the Austin Healey 3000. Its output of 117 bhp at 4,850 rpm was, however, still a long way short of the 100 S engine's 130 bhp (see graph 5).

Eddie Maher also prepared the endurance engine for the 1956 record attempts. This used the 6-port head and gave a maximum of 169 bhp at 5,500 rpm. The curve of this engine (see graph 6) shows its output on the various grades of fuel. Amoco fuel was used for the record attempts, and this gave slightly more power than the premium grade then available in the UK.

The next step was to increase the cylinder bore, from 3.125 inches (79.4 mm) to 3.282 inches (83.36 mm), giving a capacity of 2,912 cc (177.7 cu in). In this form, 124 bhp at 4,600 rpm was obtained for the first of the 3000 series.

Graph 7 of 12.11.59. shows the performance of one of the first competition 3000 engines, as used at Nassau. This was equipped with the early set-up of three Weber carburettors with 38 mm chokes. (Considerable controversy existed over the power output of the MkII 3000 in its 3- and 2- carburettor forms: in fact, the 3-carburettor engine had only a slightly greater output.) Later editions of this engine were improved by lengthening the manifolds and staying the carburettors to reduce fuel frothing. The Austin type ball joints, which had a tendency to come apart, were replaced with the very reliable Coventry movement joint. The Nassau engine proved to be completely dependable and from this development of the competition 3000 engines really got under way.

Graph 8 shows the different outputs obtained from the production and competition engines of the 3000 MkIII. The high-lift long-period camshaft suffered from rapid wear of the cam lobes and cam follower faces. This wear took place mainly at low speed, being particularly severe immediately after starting the engine. The cams and followers gave satisfactory life under competition conditions of hard use and would last for several events. Castrol 'R' 40, a castor-based oil, was particularly good in minimising this wear but it was not really satisfactory for normal motoring. It was very viscuous when

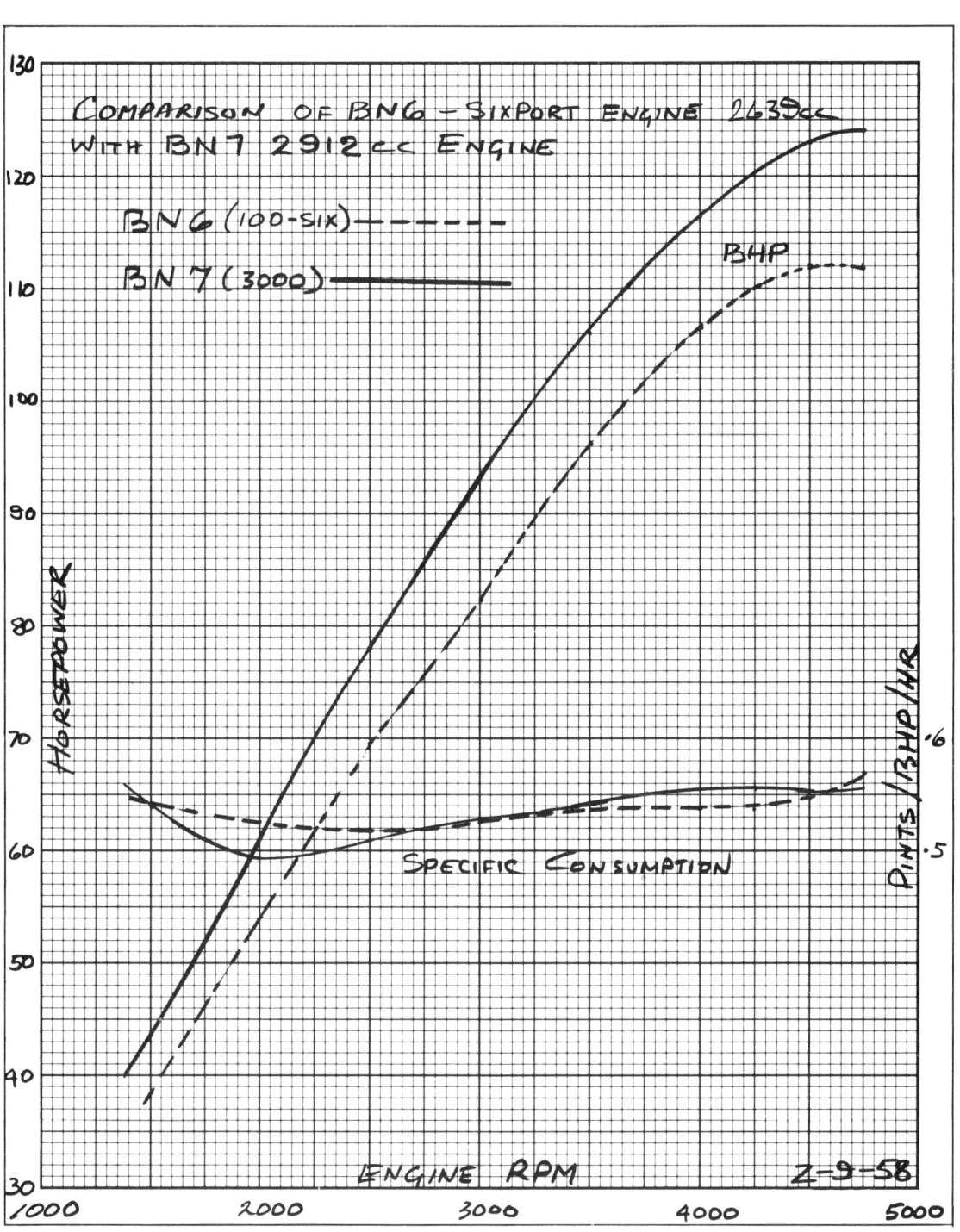

Graph 5: Comparison of 6-port engine of 2,639-cc with BN7 engine of 2,912-cc.

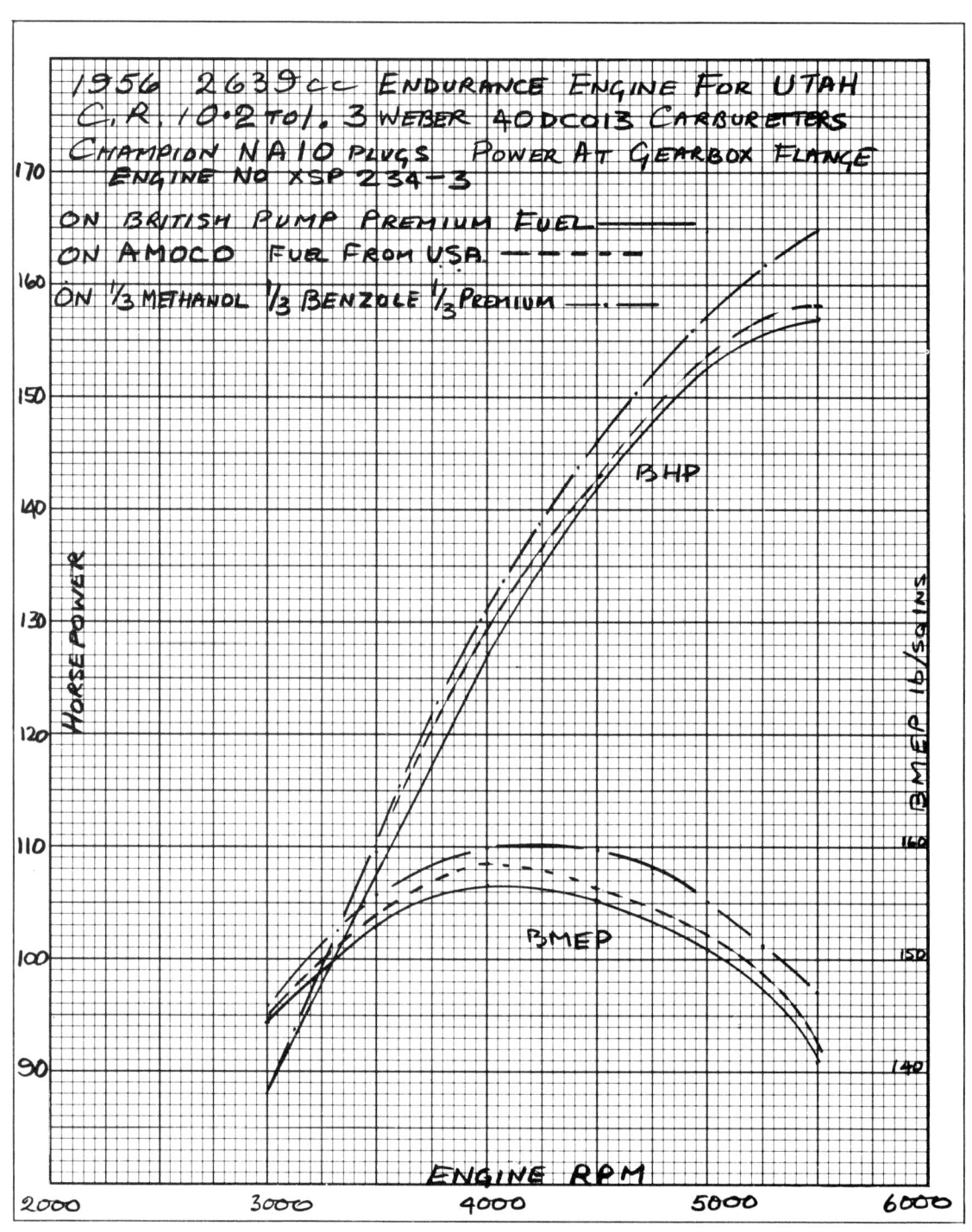

Graph 6: Power curves of 2,639-cc endurance engine at Utah, 1956.

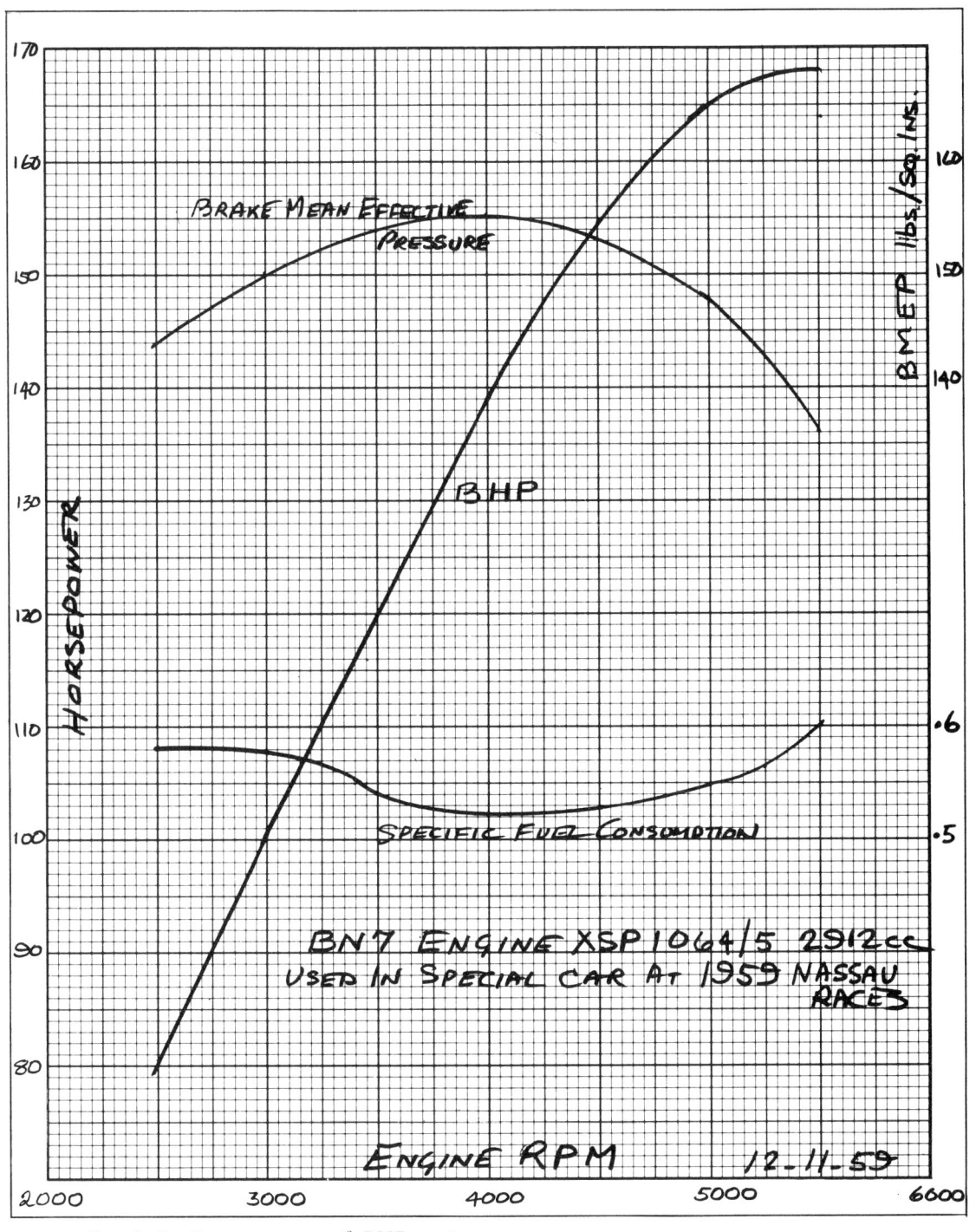

Graph 7: Power curves of BN7 engine XSP 1064/5 of 2,912-cc, used in special car at 1959 Nassau Races.

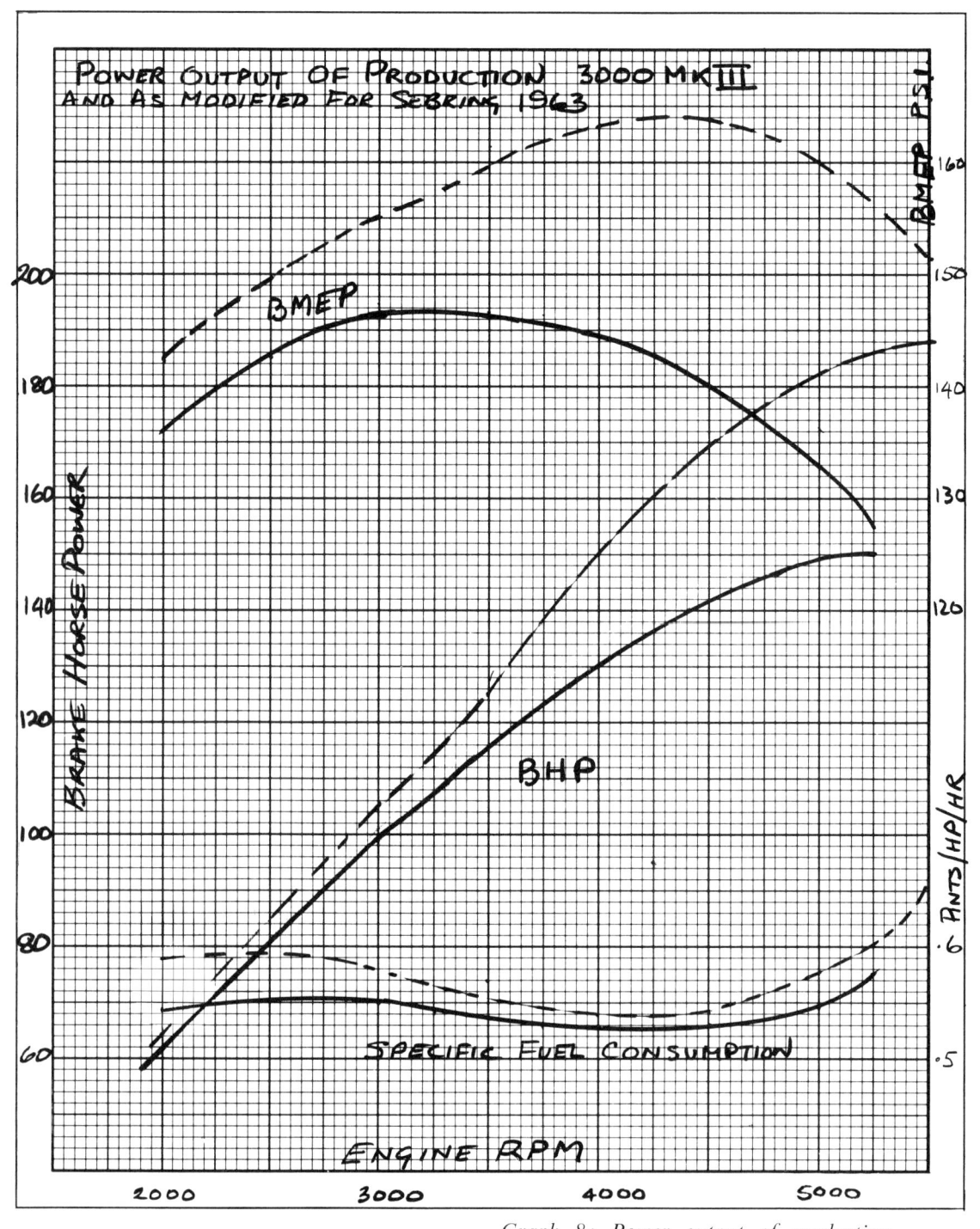

Graph 8: Power output of production 3000MkIII and as modified for Sebring 1963.

The Engines

cold and could give rise to difficult starting. It also needed changing more frequently than normal mineral oils.

Eddie Maher at Morris Engines was able to compile a basic specification for the competition MkIII engine, listing the parts needed, so that engines could be built up to give consistently accurate results. When bored out to 0.040 inches oversize and with the special pistons resulting in a capacity of 2,982-cc, a maximum power output of nearly 200 bhp could be obtained at 5,750 rpm. In fact, the best engines built to this specification probably exceeded the magic 200 bhp figure. Since maximum power and maximum recommended engine speed were so close together, the engine would give maximum power very briefly and the slight differences under these conditions were not very important. Compression ratios were in the region of 11 to 1 and the engines were very happy on the best commercially available petrols of the super grade. Graph 9 shows the output of the 1965 Sebring Race engine and is typical of the final form of competition 3000 engines.

The true output of the 3000 competition engines is subect to much conjecture. The highest recorded power is that of the supercharged 2,639-cc unit for record breaking, which achieved 292 bhp at 5,200 rpm. From America we had one claim of 237.6 bhp at 6,550 rpm with the following valve timing:

March 1960: Eddie Maher's first edition of the 3000 competition engine, showing the 45DCOE carburettors, aluminium alloy head and cast iron exhaust manifolds. This engine gave 174 bhp at 5,500 rpm, and a maximum bmep of 157 lb/sq in at 2,700 rpm.

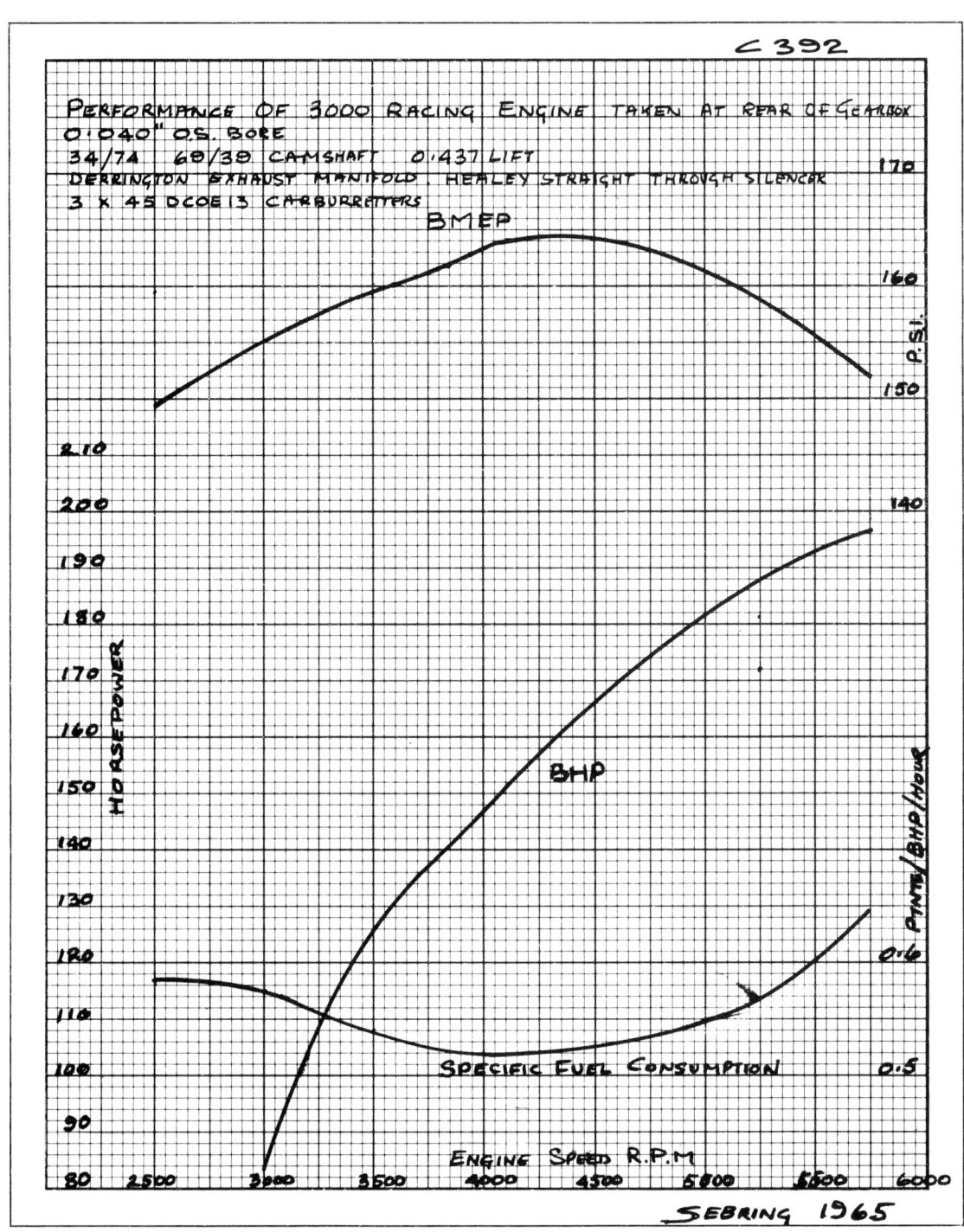

Graph 9: Performance of 3000 racing engine used at Sebring, 1965, taken at rear of gearbox.

The Engines

inlet opens 41° btdc, inlet closes 75° abdc, exhaust opens 75° bbdc, exhaust closes 41° atdc and a compression ratio of 12.56 to 1. Joe Huffaker claimed 215 bhp at 6,000 rpm and 204 at 6,500 rpm on two 2-inch SU HD8s using domed pistons and his no. 16 cam. The cars Joe prepared were always very fast and successful. The regulations in the USA and the length of their normal sports car races did result in a different approach to tuning. Morris Engines' Eddie Maher, who was responsible for nearly all the work on the 6-cylinder engines, produced the engines for long-distance events. He never claimed over 200 bhp but he measured power at the back of the gearbox with the exhaust system as used on the car. The use of a special test bed system and measuring power at the flywheel would have shown higher figures. The installed figure is what matters when getting performance from a car.

The main virtues of the 3000 engine was its ability to hold its tune over prolonged periods and to deliver good power at low speeds. The light alloy heads did not really increase the power output but the reduction in front-end weight improved road holding and reduced steering effort. Even at the end of a very long event there would be little change in output.

The later competition gearboxes used straight cut or spur gears. Spur gears are noisy compared to the helical gears used in modern gearboxes, but they are stronger and less subject to tooth breakage. The close ratio racing boxes used 22 teeth on the input shaft in constant mesh with 23 teeth on the laygear. The remaining pairs of gears were:

First	13 to 30	gearbox ratio	2.43 to 1
Second	17 to 28	gearbox ratio	1.722 to 1
Third	21 to 24	gearbox ratio	1.194 to 1

The rally box used different ratios of 21 and 24 teeth on the input with:

First	13 to 30	gearbox ratio	2.637 to 1
Second	17 to 28	gearbox ratio	1.882 to 1
Third	20 to 25	gearbox ratio	1.429 to 1

The 0.82 Laycock overdrive used with this gearbox gave an additional three ratios that filled the wider gaps:

Second	overdrive	1.543 to 1
Third	overdrive	1.171 to 1
Top	overdrive	0.82 to 1

The rally car had a ratio available to suit the great variety of conditions met in its competition life. These two sets of ratios are typical but there were variations for specific conditions. The close ratios of the racing boxes greatly reduced syncromesh loading and speeded gear changing.

Spare parts for the competition engines are now very scarce, and carefully husbanded by their fortunate owners.

Record of 100 S Sales

Invoiced to:	Customer	Chas.	Number Eng.	Body	Date Despatched
		AHS	1B		
Austin New York, USA	Briggs Cunningham	3501	222701	44	10.2.55.
	Bob Fergus	3502	222702	36	10.2.55.
Austin Canada	J. Fergusson	3503	222704	31	8.2.55.
Austin New York	Jackie Cooper	3504	222705	32	7.2.55.
	Fred Allen	3505	222703	34	7.2.55.
	Dr. Fenner	3506	222706	35	7.2.55.
	V. Sardi	3507	222708	37	9.2.55.
Gough Industries, Los Angeles, USA	—	3508	222709	38	18.2.55.
S & W Motors, Northampton, UK	David Shale	3509	222710C	39	25.2.55.
British Motor Car Distrib., San Francisco, USA	—	3510	222711	40	18.2.55.
Austin New Zealand	—	3601	222707C	79	14.10.55.
AFIVA, Paris, France	F. De Vries	3602	222712C	41	8.4.55.
Austin New York, USA	—	3603	222713	42	8.3.55.
Etablissement Erwin Lutz, Switzerland	—	3604	222714C	43	15.3.55.
British Motor Car Distrib., San Francisco, USA	—	3605	222715C	46	22.3.55.
Sogida, Brussels, Belgium	M. Franssen	3606	222716C	47	15.3.55.
British Motor Car Distrib., San Francisco, USA	—	3607	222717C	48	23.3.55.
	—	3608	222718C	49	23.3.55.
	—	3609	222719C	50	22.3.55.
	—	3610	222721C	51	23.3.55.
York Motors Pty Ltd., Sydney, Australia	David Smith	3701	222720C	54	4.4.55.

Record of 100 S Sales

John Dalton, UK	—	3702	222722C	45	30.3.55.
Chas Clark & Son Ltd, Wolverhampton, UK	Ron Flockhart	3703	222723C	52	24.3.55.
Mintex, UK	L. Clegg	3704	222724C	53	7.4.55.
AB Hans Osterman, Sweden	Arne Lindberg	3705	222726	55	4.5.55.
Gough Industries Los Angeles, USA	—	3706	222725	56	21.4.55.
	—	3707	222731	57	21.4.55.
	—	3708	222727	58	21.4.55.
	—	3709	222728	59	22.4.55.
	—	3710	222729	60	22.4.55.
	—	3801	222730	61	22.4.55.
Royston Distributors Inc., USA	—	3802	222732	62	15.4.55.
	—	3803	222734	63	15.4.55.
Ship & Shore Motors, W. Palm Beach, USA	Ed Bussey	3804	222736	64	19.11.55.
Austin Canada	—	3805	222733	65	22.4.55.
Rourafric & Far Eastern, Madagascar	M. Poisson	3806	222735	66	19.4.55.
J. J. Concalves Sucrs., Lisbon, Portugal	—	3807	222737	67	25.5.55.
Austin New York USA	—	3808	222738	68	6.6.55.
J. McBain & Co Ltd, UK	J. Somervail	3809	222739	69	3.6.55.
East Cairo, Egypt	Raymond Flower	3810	222740	70	10.6.55.
AFIVA, France	Da Silva Ramos	3901	222741	71	2.7.55.
Ronil, East Africa	—	3902	222742	72	30.6.55.
New York, USA	—	3903	222744	73	9.6.55.
Drayson Motors, UK	H. Riddell	3904	222745	74	8.6.55.
Austin, Sydney, Australia	Larke Hoskins	3905	222743	75	20.7.55.
Austin, Melbourne, Australia	—	3906	222748	76	22.7.55.
	—	3907	222749	77	12.8.55.
Austin, New Zealand	Seabrook Fowlds	3908	222750	80	29.8.55.

Austin, Melbourne, Australia	—	3909	222746	81	20.7.55.
Ab Hans Osterman, Sweden	—	3910	222747	78	1.7.55.

Works Cars

Registration Number	*Chassis*	*Engine*	*Body*
NOJ 391	SPL224B	SPL260BN	5 & 24
NOJ 393	SPL226B	SPL261BN	25
OON 440	SPL257BN		22
OON 439	SPL256BN		33
OON 441	SPL258BN		23
Endurance record car	SPL227B	SPL228B	8
Sprint record car (streamliner)	SPL259BN	SPL259BN	27

Production Figures for the Big Healeys

It is difficult to determine accurately the true number of cars completed, as records have become somewhat muddled as a result of the various group and factory changes. From a variety of sources, the following would appear to be the most accurate production figures:

100	BN1	10,688	Jan. 1953 to 1955
	BN2	3,924	1955 to 1956
100 M	BN2	1,159	1955 to 1956
100 S	AHS	55	Feb. 1955 to Nov. 1955
100 Six	BN4	10,826	Aug. 1956 to Mar. 1959
	BN5	1	
	BN6	4,150	Mar. 1959
3000 MkI	BT7	10,825	1959 to 1961
	BN7	2,825	1959 to 1961
MkII	BT7	5,095	1961 to 1962
	BN7	355	1961 to 1962
	BJ7	6,113	1962 to 1964
MkIII	BJ8	1,390	1964
(phase two)	BJ8	16,322	1964 to Dec. 1967
Total		73,728	

The last known production 3000 to leave Abingdon as a complete car was number HBJ8 43026. In addition, a number of cars have since been built 'quite legally' out of parts.

Specifications of the Big Healeys

Model	100		100 M	100 S	100 Six		3000	MkII	MkII	MkIII
Type no.	BN1	BN2	BN2	AHS	BN4 (4 port)	BN4/BN6 (6 port)	BN7/BT7	BN7/BT7	BJ7	BJ8
1st chassis no.	133134	228047		3501	50769	501	101	13751	17551	25315
Production dates	53–55	55–56	55–56	2/55–11/55	56–57	57–59	59–61	61–62	62–64	64–67
Weight (lb)	2148	2168	2170	1960	2334	2354	2358	2375	2375	2390
Max bhp	94 at 4200		110 at 4500	132 at 4700	101 at 4600	117 at 4750	124 at 4600	132 at 4750	134 at 4750	150 at 5250
Torque (lb/ft)	150 at 2000		150 at 2200	168 at 2500	142 at 2400	150 at 3000	162 at 2700	167 at 3000	167 at 2700	173 at 3000
bmep (lb/sq in)	139		139	157	141	139	141	142	142	147
Compression ratio	7.5 to 1		8.1 to 1	8.3 to 1	8.3 to 1	8.7 to 1	9.03 to 1	9.03 to 1	9.03 to 1	9.1 to 1
Acceleration (secs)										
0–30	3.3		3.3	3.2	4.2	3.6	3.5	3.5	3.2	3.1
0–50	7.6		7.4	7.2	9.2	8.2	8.0	7.8	7.2	6.4
0–60	10.3		10.0	9.8	12.9	11.6	11.4	10.8	10.3	9.5
0–70	13.4		13.2	12.5	17.5	14.8	14.3	13.8	12.9	12.5
0–80	18.0		16.8	15.4	22.6	20.1	18.9	17.6	16.7	15.5
0–90	25.6		22.6	19.0	32.3	25.8	24.8	23.4	21.3	19.2
0–100	32.8		30.4	24.4		37.0	32.8	31.5	29.4	24.4
Standing $\frac{1}{4}$-mile	17.5		17.2	16.8	18.9	18.1	17.9	17.4	17.3	17.0

Max speed	111	118	126	104	111	114	113	116	125
Engine prefix	1B	1B	1B	C26	26D	29D	29E	29F	29K
Cubic capacity (cc)	2660	2660	2660	2639	2639	2912	2912	2912	2912
Bore (mm)	87.3	87.3	87.3	79.4	79.4	83.34	83.34	83.34	83.34
Stroke (mm)	111.1	111.1	111.1	88.9	88.9	88.9	88.9	88.9	88.9
Inlet valve dia	1.725	1.725	1.813	1.69	1.75	1.75	1.75	1.75	1.75
Inlet opens °btdc	5	10	10	5	5	5	5	5	16
Inlet closes °abdc	45	50	50	45	45	45	45	45	56
Exhaust valve dia	1.415	1.415	1.625	1.42	1.56	1.56	1.56	1.56	1.56
Exhaust opens °bbdc	40	45	45	40	40	40	51	51	51
Exhaust closes °atdc	10	15	15	10	10	10	21	21	21
Valve lift	0.390	0.435	0.435	0.314	0.314	0.314	0.368	0.368	0.368
Carburettors	2 × SU-H4 1½-inch	2 × SU-H6 1¾-inch	2 × SU-H6 1¾-inch	2 × SU-H4 1½-inch	2 × SU-HD6 1¾-inch	2 × SU-HD6 1¾-inch	3 × SU-HS4 1½-inch	2 × SU-H6 1¾-inch	2 × SU-HD8 2-inch
Carburettor needle	QW	OA7	KW1	AJ	CV	CV	DJ	BC	UH
Spark plug	N9Y	N9Y	N9Y	N9Y	N9Y	N9Y	N9Y	N9Y	N9Y
Initial static ignition setting °btdc	5	8	5	6	6	5	12	5	10
Recommended tyres	Dunlop Road Speed 5.90 × 15, or Dunlop SP 165-15 or 185-15								

Index

Aaltonen, Rauno, 153, 157, 158, 160, 164, 169, 170
Abarth, 98; Simca, 166
ABC, 12
Abecassis, George, 47
AC Cobra, 165, 168, 170, 228
Acropolis Rally 1961, 150
Aldington, 'Aldy', 26
Alfa Romeo, 12, 49
Allan, Wally, 17
Allard, Sydney, 27
Allen, Fred, 70
Alpine Rally: 1947, 25; 1948, 25; 1949, 25; 1958, 148; 1959, 149–50; 1960, 150; 1961, 150; 1962, 152; 1965, 157
Alvis, 39
American Automobile Assoc, 23, 176, 177, 190, 191, 194
Amoco, 55, 236
Appleby, Bill, 98, 231
Appleyard, Ian, 25
Armstrong suspension, 44, 78, 119
Armstrong Siddeley, 14, 24, 26, 145, 185
Armstrong Whitworth Aircraft Ltd, Sir W. G., 207, 208
Aston, Peter, 49, 54
Aston Martin, 27, 47, 49, 149, 188
Aston Martin Lagonda, 35
Austin: sales and policy decisions of, 31, 60, 64, 85–6, 120, 145–6, 173; A90 units in Healey Hundred, 31, 34, 35, 43, 231–2; 1,500-cc engine, 34; and Austin Healey 100, 42, 43, 44, 55; and 100 Special Test, 46, 50, 59, 61, 63; and 100 S, 64, 73; and 100 M, 78, 79; and 100 Six, 83–6, 94; and 3000, 108; and Sprite, 114, 115–16; and Fireball XL5, 143–5; and ADO 24, 145–6; and engine development for record breakers, 173–4, 178, 185–8, 197, 208, 212; numbering system of, 128–9
Austin America, 67, 90, 176, 184, 189, 194
Austin of Canada, 92, 97, 98
Austin cars: 1800, 143; Cambridge, 145; Mini, 153, 154, 157; Mini Cooper, 166; Princess, 143–4, 145; taxi, 46
Austin Healey 100, 41–63; early development see Healey Hundred; body, 42, 44, 81; brakes, 43, 44, 55, 60; competition, 42; coupés, 60, 130; engine, 81, 231, 232; exports, 43, 44–5, 182; production, 42–3, 47, 55–7, 60, 247; record breaker, 173, 176, 178, 180, 184; specials, 130, 132–4; specification, 248–9; steering, 44
Austin Healey 100 Special Test Cars: body, 46; brakes, 51, 54–5, 59, 61, 178; carburettors, 46, 55, 178; competition, 47–54, 59, 61–3; clutch, 48–9; engine, 46, 50, 59, 60–1, 62–3, 174, 178; gearbox, 46, 59; record breaker, 174–6, 178, 180–1; road test, 47; tyres, 55, 61, 178
Austin Healey 100 S, 64–76; body, 64, 67; brakes, 66, 69–70; carburettors, 67, 72, 76, 185, 191, 232; chassis, 64; competition, 68–76, 80; engine, 60–1, 64–6, 73, 75–6, 184, 185, 212, 232; exports, 67, 76, 244–6; production, 64, 67, 128, 244–6, 247; record breaker, 184, 185–7, 212; specification, 248–9
Austin Healey 100 M, 76–81; body, 78, 81; carburettors, 76; competition, 80; engine, 76–8, 79, 81; production, 78–9, 128, 247; specification, 248–9; suspension, 78, 79

250

Index

Austin Healey 100 Six, 82–94; body, 82, 86; brakes, 84, 91; carburettors, 89, 91, 236; chassis, 82, 86; competition, 86–91, 91–2, 148–9; engine, 82, 84, 86, 89, 91, 92–3, 149, 198, 205, 212, 232–6; gearbox, 82, 92, 152–3; production, 85–6, 94, 247; record breaker, 197–206, 212, 236; specification, 248–9; suspension, 83, 86; tyres, 158; wheels, 148

Austin Healey 3000, 95–113; body, 96, 105, 106; brakes, 98, 100, 106, 111, 162, 168; carburettors, 97, 100, 102, 105–6, 107, 160, 243; chassis, 98, 103–4; competition, 97–9, 149–72; engine, 95, 96–7, 149, 160–2, 224, 236–43; exports, 113; gearbox, 98–9, 106, 243; hard top for, 106–7; production, 95–6, 101, 103, 113, 146, 224, 247; specials, 132–3; specification, 248–9; suspension, 103, 111; tyres, 163, 168, 172; wheels, 111; MkII, 101; MkII Convertible, 103–7; MkIII, 107–11; MkIII Stage Two, 111–12

Austin Healey ADO 24, 145–6
Austin Healey Fireball XL5, 143–5, 228
Austin Healey/MG (commonised), 141–3, 228
Austin Healey Sprite, 114–127; body, 114, 116, 121; brakes, 114, 158; carburettors, 115; chassis, 114; competition, 122, 135, 157–60, 166–7, 170; engine, 114–15, 116, 120, 122, 124; production, 116–20, 127, 226; road test, 115; specials, 120, 122–5, 134–5; suspension, 115, 119; MkII, 120, 121

Austrian Alpine Trial 1964, 153
Autocar, 148
Automobile Club of Italy, 21
Autosport, 39

Baker, Clive, 137–9, 157, 160, 164, 166–70, 172
Ballisat, Keith, 55
Banks, Warwick, 169, 170–1
Barham, Eric, 228
Bastow, D., 14
Belgian Automobile Club, 40
Benett, John Gordon, 180
Benford Ltd, 17, 23
Bentley, John, 90–1
Bentley, 14, 73
Bentley, W. O., 14
Bentley Drivers Club, 14
Bequart, Marcel, 50, 54
Bilbie, Barry, 35, 43, 114, 227, 228
Billingsley, Oliver, 23
Binda, Count, 47
Blunsden, Dereck, 159
Bolster, John, 39, 41

Bond, John, 41
Bonetto, Felice, 49
Borg & Beck, 54, 69, 160, 172
Bowden, Ben, 13, 15, 18
Boyd, Max, 41
Boyer, Keith, 80, 218, 220, 222
Boyle, Edward, 26
Brabham, Jack, 140
Brandish, Harry, 20
Braunschweig, Robert, 47
Breeden, Wilmot, 46
Bren-Carrier engine, 23
Brennan, Merl, 169
Bristol, 26
British Hot Rod Assoc, 23
British Leyland Motor Corp, 10, 17, 76, 121, 127, 160, 217, 221, 226, 227
British Motor Corp (BMC), 17, 60, 66, 82, 84, 86, 90, 92, 98, 180, 116, 133, 141–3, 214, 224; Competition Dept, 89, 97, 107, 127, 137, 143, 147–72 *passim*, 216; Service Dept, 100; *see also* Austin, Morris, MG
BMC Canada, 168, 170
BMC USA, 52, 170
British Racing Motors (BRM), 59
British Petroleum, 55
British Piston Ring Co, 77
Brocklehurst, Roy, 96
Brooke Stevens Excalibur, 62
Brookes, Ray, 149
Brown, David, 35; gearbox, 59, 61, 188
Browning, Peter, 137, 138, 160, 164, 169, 215, 216
Buckingham, Bill, 35
Bucknum, Ronnie, 164, 166, 168
Bueb, Ivor, 90
Burgess, Gerry, 149
Burzi, Dick, 133
Bussey, Ed, 69, 92

Cabantous, Yves Giraud, 50
Cadillac Allard, 27
Cahier, Bernard, 157
Cape factory, Warwick: design and assembly of: Healey 2.4-litre, 23; Austin Healey 100, 44, 57; 100 Special Test, 46, 57; 100 S, 64, 67, 75–6; 100 M, 78–9; 3000, 103–4, 106; Sprite, 114, 120; record breakers, 185, 197
Cape Engineering, 99
Cardew, Basil, 40, 41
Carlisle, Christabel, 164, 166
Carlsson, Eric, 152
Cashmore, Jim, 227
Castagneto, Renzo, 47
Castrol, 55, 94, 157, 158, 160, 173, 182, 197, 236
Cavanagh, Peter, 214

251

Challen, Keith, 41
Chambers, Marcus, 14, 72, 73, 89, 91, 97, 148, 150–2
Champion plugs, 40, 55, 95, 194, 199
Chaparral, 165, 168, 170
Chapman, Colin, 90
Charles, Geoffrey, 41
Chatham, John, 172, 219, 220
Chisholm, Mr, 13
Chrysler, 185, 227
Church, Robin, 218, 220, 222
Clark, Grant, 168
Clarke, Bill, 95
Clegg, Lionel, 54
Cobb, John, 204
Coker, Gerry, 35, 38, 43, 60, 64, 114, 120, 185, 197, 227
Cole, Tom, 27, 49
Colgate, John, 164, 166, 167, 168
Collins, Peter, 47, 90, 131
Commission Sportive Internationale, 155
Cooper, Geoff, 31, 43, 44, 114
Cooper, Jackie, 70–2, 180
Corvette Stingray, 165, 168, 170
Cousins, Cecil, 96
Coventry Climax engines, 1,100-cc, 120; V8, 135–6, 137; company, 136, 137
Coventry Hood & Sidescreen Co, 38
Coventry Timber Bending Co, 100
Croft-Pearson, Sam, 149
Cross, Tony, 54, 168
Cunard liners, 44–5, 174
Cunningham, 54
Cuomo, Ray, 90–1, 92
Cutler, Mervyn, 14, 24, 145

Daetwyler, Willy, 47
Daily Express, 41
Daily Telegraph, 27
Daimler, 20
Davis, Sammy, 13, 73
Delaselles, George, 60
Dellorto carburettors, 226
Densham, John, 14
De Portago, Marquis, 90, 131
Derrington, Vic, 11
Digby, 'Digger', 137, 216
Dixon, David, 172
Dodington Park, 218–19
Donald Healey Motor Co Ltd, 15, 24, 42, 227
Donington Racing Circuit, 218
Dowty Boulton Paul Ltd, 43, 86
Duckworth, Keith, 160
Duncan, Ian, 39
Dunlop brakes, 69, 73–4; on 100 Special Test, 59, 61; on 100 S, 66; on record breakers, 178

Dunlop tyres: on Healey 2.4-litre, 19, 24; on 100 Special Test, 55, 61; on 3000, 163, 168; on record breakers, 181–2, 190, 194, 213
Dunlop wheels, on Healey Hundred, 41; on record breakers, 178
'Dunlop Mac', 55, 61
Dunn, Mr, 38
Dutton, Reeves, 191, 194

Easter, Paul, 157
Eden, Anthony, Lord Avon, 18
Edwards, Courtney, 41
Ehrmann, Gus, 92
Elliot Ltd, 18
Enever, Roger, 137, 138, 140
Enever, Syd, 89, 96, 98, 104, 107, 116, 119–21, 134, 143, 145–6, 148, 190, 226
Engineering Products Ltd, 44
England, Lofty, 27, 73, 75
Esso, 55, 185
Eykin, Malcolm, 10
Eyston, Capt George, 173–8, 180, 184–5, 189, 194, 197, 204, 207

Fangio, Manuel, 49, 74–5, 76, 90–1
Farina, Pinin, 29, 30, 35, 144
Fawcett Publications, 104
Fenner, Roy, 54
Ferrari, 24, 44, 49, 69, 72, 76, 90, 149, 158, 166, 168
Ferrari X224, 130–2
Fink, J., 20
Fitch, John, 47, 54
Flaherty, Jack, 164, 166
Ford: GT 40, 170; Model A, 180; V8, 23, 160
Foster, Bernard, 124, 125
Freer, Frederick, 78
Fere, P., 90
Frost, Derek, 95, 122
Fuller, 180

Gallimore, Dick, 60
Garnier, Peter, 148, 149
Gatsonides, Maurice, 50–1, 54
Geitner, Maj Gil, 90–1, 92, 98
General Motors, 140, 180
Geneva Motor Show, 1953, 47
Geneva Rally, 1965, 157
German Rally, 1959, 150
Girling brakes on Healey 2.4-litre, 24; on Healey Hundred, 35; on 100 Special Test, 51, 54, 59; rejected on 100 S, 66; on 3000, 98, 100, 111, 132, 162, 168
Glover, Stan, 55
Godfrey, Roger, 218
Goffin, Jack, 95, 122
Goodall, Mort Morris, 27, 61, 180, 194, 214

Index

Gott, John, 148, 149, 150, 172
Grant, Gregor, 39, 41
Green, Doug, 124
Gregory, Ken, 90
Gregory, Maston, 90
Griffiths, Pat, 47
Griffiths, Peter, 23
Grinham, Ted, 165, 232
Griswold, General, 52
Guest, Mike, 227

Hadley, Bert, 47, 48, 50, 54
Hall, Anne, 149
Hall, Nobby (Luigi), 160, 164
Hamblin Group, 227
Hambro Automotive Co, 90, 92
Hamilton, Duncan, 27, 54
Hands, Laurie, 55
Hansgen, Walt, 90
Harriman, George, 20, 85, 108, 115–16, 121, 141–2
Harris, John, 134, 137, 139, 140, 158, 171
Harris, Ken, 194
Harris, Phil, 176
Harrison, Jimmy, 40, 55, 194
Harrison, Robert, 140
Hassan, Wally, 136, 137, 139
Hastings, Harold, 41
Hawkins, Paul, 157, 158, 169, 171
Hawley, Don, 228
Hawthorn, Mike, 69, 72, 74–5, 90
Hay, Jack, 149
Hayter, Don, 96
Healey, Brian (Bic), 12, 14, 57, 128, 136, 139, 214, 217, 220, 227
Healey, Donald (DMH): early career, 11–14; and Healey 2.4-litre, 15–17, 20, 23; and Nash Healey, 26; and Healey Hundred, 31–41; and Austin Healey 100, 41–2, 45, 60, 182; and 100 Six, 83; and 3000, 108; and Sprite, 114–21, 226; and Ferrari X224, 130; and commonised AH/MG, 141, 143; and Fireball XL5, 144; and ADO 24, 145; and Jensen Healey, 226; and record breaking, 172, 178, 180, 184–5, 189–91, 197, 199, 203–5; and competition, 24–6, 27–8, 47, 61, 153; and clubs, 220, 221; and British Leyland merger, 224–6
Healey, Emmie, 11, 12
Healey, Geoffrey (GCH): childhood and early career, 12–14, 20, 21–2; and Healey 2.4-litre, 23; and Nash Healey, 29; and Healey Hundred, 31–5, 39–41; and Austin Healey 100, 47, 54–5; marriage of, 58; and 100 S, 66; and 100 M, 77; and 100 Six, 89, 94, 148; and 3000, 172; and Sprite, 115, 121, 124–5; and commonised AH/MG, 143; and Fireball XL5, 144; and ADO 24, 145; and Jensen Healey, 226; and record breaking, 174, 181, 189, 194, 204–5; and competition, 23–6, 27–8, 47, 49, 51–4, 69, 72, 74–5, 91, 92, 157–9, 166; and homologation, 91, 171; and clubs, 219–20; and British Leyland merger, 224–6
Healey, JF (Fred), 11–12, 14
Healey, John, 12, 14
Healey, Ivy, 13, 14
Healey, Margot, 9, 47, 158, 204–5, 228
Healey 2.4-litre, 15–26; carburettors, 17; chassis, 15, 17; competition, 24–6, 27–8; engine, 15–17; exports, 23; gearbox, 25; production, 17–20, 23, 31; roadster body, 18; road test, 21; saloon body, 18; Silverstone body, 26; suspension, 15, 19; tyres, 19, 24
Healey Automobile Consultants Ltd, 227, 228
Healey Cars Ltd, 15, 227, 228
Healey Drivers Club, 214, 215
Healey Drivers Club Ltd, 217
Healey Hundred, 31–41, 130; body, 34, 35–6; brakes, 35; carburettors, 40; chassis, 34–5; engine, 31, 34, 35, 39; road test, 39, 40; wheels, 41; *see also* Austin Healey 100
Healey SR, 135–40
Hedges, Andrew, 137, 140, 157, 169
Hendrie, Clive, 227
Heynes, Bill, 73, 140
Hill, Jimmy, 55
Hill, Phil, 69, 72
Hobson, HM, Ltd, 13
Holdaway, Capt Keith, 22
Hooper, Malcolm, 180
Hopkirk, Paddy, 153, 157, 158, 164, 166, 168, 169
Horner, Fred, 90, 174
Hounslow, Alec, 96, 190
Huffaker, Joe, 243
Humber, 13, 15; Scout, 13
Humphries, Don, 133, 218
Huntoon, George, 62, 76
Hutt, Ralph, 23
Hysert, Lyle, 181, 190, 194

International Motor Sports Show, New York 1953, 45
Invicta, 7, 12, 61, 153
Ireland, Les, 106, 116, 120, 227
Iskenderian, 180
Issigonis, Alec, 44

Jacobs, Dick, 75
Jackson, Reg, 96
Jackson-Moore, Roy, 71–2, 76, 90–1, 180, 194, 199–200

Jaguar, 27; D Type, 69–72, 73–5, 90; E Type, 172, 228; 3.8-litre, 166, 168; XK120, 31, 47, 48, 51, 54; and ADO 24, 146
James, Dick, 23
Japanese cars, 44, 76, 92
Jeffrey, Dick, 168
Jennings, Christopher, 20
Jensen: body production of: Austin Healey 100, 42–3, 44; 100 Special Test, 46; 100 S, 67; 100 M, 78; 100 Six, 86; 3000, 104, 106, 133, 141, 154; ADO 24, 146; record breakers, 197–8
Jensen cars: F, 226, 227; G. Gullwing, 226, 227; GT, 226, 227; Interceptor, 226, 227; *see also* Jensen Healey
Jensen, Dick, 86
Jensen Healey, 212, 226–7
John Thompson Motor Pressings, 35, 64, 86, 114
Johnson, Leslie, 27–9, 47, 48, 54
Jones, Rupert, 150

Kahn, Zadoc, 75
Kemp, Michael, 41
Kenny, Tom, 26
Kinchloe, Col Bill, 92
Klementaski, Louis, 49
Kunz, Dr, 92

Ladd, Harry, 44
Lancia, 49, 61–2
Langrishe, John, 214
Law, Don, 55
Laycock & Lucas, 39, 152, 178
Leach, Hank, 221
Learoyd, Rod, 52, 166
Lee, Lennard, 136
Le Hew, Ralph, 194
Le Mans, 216, 122; 1950, 26–7; 1952, 28; 1953, 49–54, 72, 76; 1954, 59, 72; 1955, 72–5, 232; 1968, 135–9; 1969, 139; 1970, 140
Le May, Gen Curtis, 52–3
Leston, Les, 73
Levegh, Pierre, 74–5
Leverett, Vic, 20
Leyland, Bill, 186, 197, 203, 228
Liège-Rome-Liège Rally: 1958, 149; 1959, 150; 1960, 150; 1963, 153
Light, Ken, 35, 54
Lockett, Johnny, 47, 48, 50, 54
Lockheed, 12, 54
London to Land's End Trial, 12
Lord, Len, 31, 41–2, 145, 231
Lotus, 90, 166; engine, 226
Lucas equipment, 20, 24, 30, 49, 51, 55, 86, 97, 131, 136, 170, 174, 194

Lurani, Johnny, 24, 25, 26, 47, 48, 157
Lyon, Ben, 23
Lyons, Bill, 31

Mac, Roger, 169
McCahill, Tom, 104
McCluggage, Denise, 164, 166
McKenzie, W. A., 27, 29, 41
Macklin, Lance, 12, 61–2, 64, 68–76
Macklin, Sir Noel, 12, 61
McQueen, Steve, 167
McManus, Jim, 133
Maggi, Count Aymo, 25, 47
Maher, Eddie, 16, 24, 72, 91, 95, 122, 198, 205, 228, 232, 236, 241, 243
Makinen, Timo, 153, 157, 158, 169, 228
Mann, Nigel, 27
Marzotto, Giannino, 49
Maserati, 72, 90, 91
Mason, George, 26
Matra, 140
Menadue, Roger, 20, 24, 26–7, 35, 38, 39, 67, 74, 169, 174, 181, 194, 227, 228
Mennem, Peter, 41
Mercedes, 50, 73–5, 149
Mercer, Flt Lt Bertie, 47, 48
Merrells, Jack, 86
MG: production of: 100 Six, 86, 91, 94, 95–6, 149; 3000, 96, 103–4, 221, 149; Sprite, 95, 116, 119, 127
MG cars: A, 97, 131, 149; B, 141, 142, 143, 159, 164, 168, 169, 170, 226; C, 141–3, 226, 228; C-GT, 133; Midget, 10, 121, 122, 127, 133, 134, 157, 158, 169, 226; record attempts, 191, 195, 213; at Le Mans, 72, 75
Miles, Ken, 90
Millard, David, 226
Millard, Peter, 92
Mille Miglia: 1948, 24–5; 1949, 25–6; 1950, 26; 1951, 27; 1952, 27–9, 47; 1953, 47–9; 1954, 59; 1957, 86
Miller, Eric, 194
Mintex equipment, 23, 27, 35, 49, 51, 54, 59
Mitchell, Nancy, 148, 149
Mitchell, Terry, 96
Mobil, 55
Monte Carlo Rally, 131; 1929, 12; 1931, 12, 61; 1935, 13; 1949, 25; 1957, 86; 1958, 148; 1963, 153
Montgomery, F. M., 12
Montlhéry, 173
Moor, Fred, 92
Moore, John, 54
Moore, Read, 30
Moore, Sam, 148, 149
Morgan, 165, 228
Morley, Don, 150, 152, 155, 164, 166, 168

254

Index

Morley, Erle, 150, 152, 155
Morrell, Frank, 169
Morris: engine production for: Austin Healey 100, 60; 100 S, 64; 100 Six, 82, 84, 86, 89, 91, 205, 232–6; 3000, 95, 103, 241–3; Sprite, 122; record breaker, 198, 236
Morris Minor, 133
Moss, Pat, 148, 149, 150, 152, 153
Moss, Roger, 220
Moss, Stirling, 47, 48, 54, 60, 62, 68–72, 90, 97
Motor, 20, 21
Motor Cycling Club, 12
Motor Industry Research Assoc, 14, 198
Motor Show, London: 1952, 39, 41, 130; 1953, 58, 184; 1956, 115
Murdoch, Geoff, 55

Napier Lion engine, 204
Nassan races, 131–2, 236
Nash Healey, 26–30; body, 26, 29; brakes, 27, 51; carburettors, 26; chassis, 26, 34; competition, 26–9; 47–54; engine, 26, 27; production, 30, 31; road test, 26
Nash Motors, 26, 29, 30, 38, 65
Nash Kelvinator International, 30
Nash Metropolitan, 30
National Hot Rod Assoc, 180
Neale, Eric, 44
Needham, Les, 137, 216–17
Neubauer, Alfred, 73
Noble, Dudley, 41
Nottingham Sports Car Club, 24
Nuffield, Lord, 59
Nuvolari, Tazio, 24

Olthoff, Bob, 164, 166, 168
O'Neill, Jim, 96
Osca, 61–2

Packer, Geoff, 54
Page, Graham, 212
Parker, Nigel, 54
Parker, Philip Fotheringham, 130
Parkinson, Jim, 164, 166
Parnell, Gordon, 12, 13
Parnell, Reg, 47, 49
Paulson, Bill, 41
Pearce, Lewis, 13
Pease, Al, 169
Perry, George, 55, 174, 178, 194
Phillips, Jack, 144, 146
Picard, Brad, 169
Pirelli tyres, 24
Poole, Alec, 137, 138
Porsche, 90, 139, 159, 166, 168
Price, Geoff, 20, 25, 57, 79, 227

Qvale, Kjell, 166, 226

Railton-Mobil Special, 204
Rawson, Lionel, 185
Reece, Brian, 95
Reid, Jock, 47, 48, 61–2
Renault, 90
Rene Bonnet, 166, 170
Repco Brabham engine, 140
Richardson, Stan, 44
Riley: company, 15; engine in Healey 2.4-litre, 15–17, 31, 34; gearbox in Healey 2.4-litre, 25
Riley, Peter, 98, 150, 152
Rix, J., 116
Road & Track, 23
Robinson, E. Forbes, 76, 90
Rolls-Royce, 144; 4-litre engine, 143–4, 145, 146
Rolt, Tony, 27, 47, 54
Rootes, Timothy, 23
Rose, Geoffrey, 84–5
Ross, Derek, 218, 220
Rover, 24, 66
Royal, Ian, 226
Royal Automobile Club, 17, 49, 129, 171
RAC Rally, 12; 1959, 150; 1961, 152; 1962, 153; 1964, 157; 1965, 157; 1967, 160–4
Royal Electrical & Mechanical Engineers, 14, 20
Royston, Fred, 92
Ryan, Jack, 194

Sabra, 166
Safety Fast, 214, 217
Salvadori, Roy, 132
Sampietro, A.C. (Sammy), 13, 15
Saxton, John, 23, 27
Sayers, Malcolm, 73
Scott Brown, Archie, 76
Seager, Stuart, 214
Sears, Jack, 98, 148, 149, 150
Sebring Grand Prix of Endurance: 1954, 59, 61–3, 64; 1955, 68–72; 1956, 75–6; 1957, 89–91; 1958, 91–2; 1960, 97–8; 1962, 167; 1963, 164–8; 1964, 168; 1965, 169–71
Sestrière Rally 1957, 86, 148
Shadoff Chrysler, 180
Sharp, Mick, 51, 54
Shelby, Carroll, 69, 72, 168, 194, 195, 199
Shell, 55
Shepherd, Bill, 148, 149, 150
Ship & Shore Motors, 69, 76, 92
Shorrock supercharger, 186
Silverstone, 131, 132
Simpson, Ray, 55
Smiths equipment, 86, 145

255

Smith, Cyril, 86–9
Smith, John, 220
Smith, Maurice, 41
Smith, Peter, 148
Smith, Reg, 69
Snipe engine, 13
Sopwith Aviation, Co, 11
Spa-Sofia-Liège Rally 1964, 153
Spear, Bill, 180
Spears, Harry, 136, 137
Speed of the Wind, 207, 208
Sportsmobile bodies, 185
Sprang, Mr, 114
Spratt, Doug Wilson, 133
Stiles, Phil, 76, 90, 92
Stokes, Lord, 224
SU carburettors in: Nash Healey, 26; Healey Hundred, 40; 100 Special Test, 46, 55; 100 S, 67, 73; 100 M, 76; 100 Six, 91; 3000, 97, 100, 102, 107–8, 132; Sprite, 115; record breakers, 178, 186, 188, 191, 194
Symons, Humfrey, 13

Talbot, 74
Targa Florio, 124, 158, 160, 228; 1948, 25, 157; 1965, 157–9
Tassara, Filippo, 47
Texaco, 55
Thornhill, Peter, 26, 27
Thornley, John, 95, 127, 141, 214, 215
Thoroughbred and Classic Cars, 217
Thorpe, Doug, 133
Thunderbird, 204
Tickfords, 35, 42
Tooley, Chris, 148, 149, 150
Trintignant, Maurice, 131
Triumph: cars, 12, 165, 168; company, 12–13, 17, 20; Dolomite, 12, 13; 4-cylinder engine, 165; Gloria, 12; Seven, 12; TR series, 115, 228, 232
Trounson, Donald, 24
Tulip Rally: 1958, 148; 1959, 149; 1961, 150; 1965, 157, 158
Turle, Brian, 55
Turner, Gerry, 116
Turner, Philip, 41
Turner, Stuart, 150–2, 154, 157, 159, 160, 166, 169, 171, 216
TVR, 166
200 Miles Per Hour Club, 204

Ulmann, Alec, 69
USA: Healey 2.4-litre in, 23; 100 in, 43; clubs in, 221; importance as export market, 31, 52–3, 94, 95, 101, 113, 164–5; record breaking in, 173–213; sports car racing in, 241–3; *see also under* Nash Healey, Sebring
US Forces, 42, 57
Utah State Highway Dept, 176

Vaccarella, Nino, 155
Vage, Trevor, 125
Vauxhall, 14, 226
Veyron, Pierre, 50
Volvo, 166
Von Hanstein, Huske, 90

Wade, G. R., 20
Walters, Carolyn, 218, 220
Walters, Phil, 54, 69, 72
Ward Co, Thos, 13
Watson, Bill, 14
Watsonian Sidecars Ltd, 107
Watt, James, 20
Weaving, Dr John, 185, 188, 197, 200, 208, 228
Weber carburettors in: 100 S, 76; 100 Six, 89–90; 3000, 160, 236; record breakers, 198
Wellman, Tommy, 169
Weslake, Harry, 60–1, 62, 129, 130, 174, 178, 231–2
Westland Aeroparts, 15, 18, 24
Wheatcroft, Tom, 218
Whitby, Gordon, 176
Wilkes, Peter, 24, 66, 132, 134
Wilkes, Phil, 218
Wilkins, Gordon, 50, 51, 52, 55
Wilkins, Joyce, 51
Willday, Ray, 47
Williams, George, 197
Williamson, John, 148, 149
Wills, Bernard, 218
Wilson, Frank, 92
Wilton-Clark, Gill, 148
Winby, Cecil, 51, 77, 86
Wisdom, Ann, 86, 148, 149, 150, 152
Wisdom, Bill, 150
Wisdom, Tommy, 13, 25–6, 27, 28, 40, 47, 63, 86–9, 116, 148, 149, 150, 157
Wood, George, 55
Wood, Ray, 55, 136
Wooton, Derek, 216
Worswick, Ted, 157, 172, 219, 220
Wyer, John, 188

Zafer, John, 215